Philadelphia Flavor

Philadelphia Flavor

Restaurant Recipes from the City and the Suburbs

Connie Correia Fisher with Joanne Correia

Foreword by The Honorable John F. Street

small potatoes press

for bill

"It's gold, Jerry! Gold!"
And so are you.

ISBN 0-9661200-5-1
Library of Congress Card Number: 00-190809

Cover photo of David Greer by Jennifer Lynn Lewandowski

Although the author, editor, and publisher have made every effort to ensure the accuracy and completeness of information contained in this book, we assume no responsibility for errors, inaccuracies, omissions, or any inconsistency herein.

Small Potatoes Press
1106 Stokes Avenue
Collingswood, NJ 08108
856-869-5207

ATTENTION ORGANIZATIONS, SCHOOLS, AND EDUCATIONAL FACILITIES:

Quantity discounts are available on bulk purchases of this book for educational purposes or fund-raising. Special books or book excerpts can also be created to fit specific needs.

foreword

Congratulations to Connie Correia Fisher and Joanne Correia, a daughter-mother team, who have compiled fantastic recipes from some of Philadelphia's finest chefs. The culmination of their efforts has given birth to this delightful cookbook, *Philadelphia Flavor: Restaurant Recipes from the City and the Suburbs*.

As you look through the pages of *Philadelphia Flavor*, it's as if you are taking a walking tour of over 100 of our City's premium restaurants.

Welcome to *Philadelphia Flavor*!

John F. Street
Mayor
City of Philadelphia

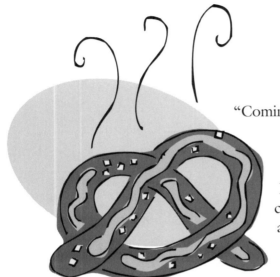

"Coming to Philadelphia to cook and to eat is for me a recurring pleasure. The cooking in its restaurants always entices and I believe that only a very few cities in this country can boast as many competent, and better, chefs and restaurants."

— Eileen Yin-Fei Lo
Author of *The Chinese Way*
and *The Chinese Kitchen*

table of contents

introduction

In a 1999 magazine article, John Mariani, one of the nation's top food writers, called the Philadelphia restaurant scene "amazing." He wrote, "...with so much that's now new and good, it may take you several trips to savor all Philly has to offer." I think the same applies to cookbooks. Several volumes may be needed in order to capture, record, and savor all the wonderful recipes our area chefs have to offer. After all, a city like Philadelphia is always in transition: new restaurants open; chefs bop around; food trends change. Happily, what doesn't change is the talent, commitment, and generosity of Delaware Valley chefs and restaurateurs.

And what generosity! Over 100 chefs contributed recipes to *Philadelphia Flavor*! The large variety of recipes received provides a cook's tour of dishes perfect for family meals, splashy cocktail parties, midday munches, elegant entertaining, and quick-day meals. Each is organized and "mom-tested" so that even novice cooks will have kitchen confidence. The recipes *will* bring you great results but remember: recipes are guidelines, jumping off points for creative cooking. Feel free to experiment; to incorporate seasonal products as much as possible; to improvise and have fun!

But *Philadelphia Flavor* is more than just a collection of recipes. It is a tool for selecting your next Philadelphia-area dining destination, a reference for wine and food pairing, a resource guide for ingredients and kitchen supplies, and, hopefully, a source of inspiration.

I sincerely hope that you will USE this book. My own favorite cookbooks look like well-loved toys: tattered, stained, food encrusted. If I visit your kitchen, I'd love to find *Philadelphia Flavor* sporting food smudges and a broken spine. That would be "amazing."

Best regards,
Connie Correia Fisher

cocktail party

Crab and Artichoke Dip 12

Chimichuri "Salsa of the Millennium" 13

Truffled Chicken Liver Pâté   14

Wild Boar and Scottish Hare Terrine   15

Bruschetta with Creole Italian Tapenade   16

Mixmaster Bruschetta   17

Onion Parmesan Puffs   17

Marinated Beef and Scallion Skewers with Garlic Dipping Sauce 18

Caribbean "Jerk" Chicken Bites   19

Bitter Balls   20

Hoisin Duck Spring Roll   21

Crab Cake Orientale   22

Wasabi Stuffed Shrimp with Asian Ginger Dipping Sauce   24

Hazelnut Crusted Shrimp   25

Cornmeal Fried Oysters with Pickapeppa® Rémoulade   26

Tempura Battered Mussels with Curry Rémoulade   27

Cold Mussels Monterey   28

Chilled Monk's Mussels   29

Crab and Artichoke Dip

Executive Chef Robert Cloud
The Oak Grill at the Marshalton Inn, West Chester, PA

1 pound jumbo lump crabmeat
½ pound cream cheese
1 cup artichoke hearts
½ cup diced roasted red peppers
½ pound Boursin cheese
2 tablespoons Old Bay Seasoning

Combine all ingredients over a double boiler. Mix until hot and combined. Serve hot with crostini or crackers.

Serves 8

Chimichuri
"Salsa of the Millennium"

Chef/Owner Susanna Goihman
Azafran, Philadelphia, PA

1 large onion, coarsely chopped
1 bunch parsley
1 bunch cilantro
2 large cloves garlic
1 tablespoon dry oregano
⅓ cup olive oil
⅓ cup fresh lime juice
Salt and pepper
1 jalapeño pepper, seeds included

Place onion in a food processor and pulse chop until finely chopped but not pureed. Set aside. Combine remaining ingredients in a food processor and pulse chop until fine. Blend onion into mixture and stir to combine. Easy!

Chef's Note

This sauce, although traditionally eaten with steak, can be served with tuna, mahi mahi, or chicken breast. It's also great when used "as is" for dips and marinades.

Truffled Chicken Liver Pâté

Chef/Owner Michèle R. Haines
Spring Mill Café, Conshohocken, PA

½ pound chicken livers
½ pint heavy cream
2 tablespoons Madeira
Pinch of dried basil
Big pinch of dried thyme
Pinch of salt
Pinch of white pepper
Pinch of dried oregano
4 tablespoons truffle shavings

Preheat oven to 375°. Butter an ovenproof terrine. Blend all ingredients, except 1 tablespoon truffle shavings, in a food processor until very smooth. Pour mixture into terrine and decorate with remaining truffle shavings. Cover with buttered wax paper and then with aluminum foil. Place terrine in a water bath and bake for 15 minutes. (Pâté should be soft but not too firm. Do NOT overcook.) Allow to cool; then store in refrigerator. Turn out onto a serving plate and serve with crackers or crostini.

Wine Notes

Recommended Wine: Vin de Pays des Côtes de Gascogne Gros Manseng Cassagnoles 1998 ($10.00)

Description: Here's an uncommon 100% varietal Gros Manseng aged *sur lie* from the heart of the *Sud-Ouest*, where the local cuisine is dominated by rich flavors (goose, duck) and full-bodied wines. This is a highly aromatic, well-structured, and mouth filling wine with lots of acid and good alcohol level and a texture that is almost "gummy."

Sommelier: Luca Mazzotti, Moore Brothers Wine Co.

Wild Boar and Scottish Hare Terrine

Executive Chef Tom Hannum
Hotel Dupont, Wilmington, DE

1 cup sun-dried cherries
½ cup brandy
3 pounds boneless wild boar meat
3 pounds boneless Scottish hare
1 tablespoon chopped fresh sage
1 tablespoon chopped fresh thyme
Salt and pepper
Olive oil
1 cup red wine
Flour
2 eggs, beaten
½ cup pistachio nuts
¼ cup fresh chopped parsley
½ pound bacon, sliced

Toss cherries with brandy and let marinate for 1 hour. Strain and reserve liquid. Pass 2 pounds each of boar and hare meat through a meat grinder. Place in a large bowl and set aside.

Dice remaining meats. Toss sage, thyme, and salt and pepper and add to diced meats. Sauté in olive oil until lightly browned. Remove meats and deglaze with red wine. Reduce liquid by half and reserve. Combine liquid from cherries and red wine reduction. Stir in enough flour to make a thick paste. Stir in eggs. Add this mixture to ground meats along with cherries, diced meats, pistachios, parsley, and salt and pepper. Mix well. Chill for 1 hour.

Preheat oven to 350°. Line a terrine mold with bacon. Pack meat mixture in mold; cover and place in a water bath in oven. Bake for 90 minutes or until internal temperature reaches 160°. Let terrine cool for about 1 hour; then uncover. Weigh down by placing another terrine mold on top of mixture and refrigerate for 4 hours.

Serves 6

Bruschetta
with Creole Italian Tapenade

Executive Chef/Owner Dominic Ventura
Euro Cafe, Philadelphia, PA

3 large red tomatoes, diced
1 medium red onion, diced
2 cloves garlic, crushed
1 teaspoon kosher salt
½ teaspoon Creole or Cajun seasoning
½ teaspoon raw brown sugar
½ teaspoon red pepper flakes
Black pepper
½ cup extra virgin olive oil
1 large loaf flat Italian bread
Fresh garlic cloves
Olive oil

Place tomatoes and onion in a mixing bowl. Mix in crushed garlic and all seasonings. Stir in olive oil. Reserve.

Preheat oven to 400°. Cut bread into ¾-inch slices. Rub slices with fresh garlic. Brush each side with olive oil. Place bread on a sheet pan and bake for about 4 to 6 minutes per side or until each side is golden.

Spoon tapenade evenly on each slice of bread. Enjoy.

Serves 8 to 10

Euro Cafe

Known for:
very romantic restaurant; great for private parties

Years in business: 10

Most requested table:
#10, #15, #31

Menu:
Creole Italian

Chef: Dominic Ventura

Chef's training:
Rutgers University; 20 years in family's various kitchens

Chef's hobbies/ accomplishments:
purchasing real estate rehab rental properties

Chef's favorite foods:
pizza and anything spicy

Chef's favorite cookbook:
New Orleans Seafood Cookbook, Todd English's *Olives Table*

Mixmaster Bruschetta

Executive Chef/Owner Jon Hallowell
Mixmaster Café, Malvern, PA

1 loaf French bread
1 cup extra virgin olive oil
5 large tomatoes, diced to ¼-inch
1 yellow bell pepper, diced
1 red bell pepper, diced
1 red onion, diced
6 cloves fresh garlic, minced
½ cup Parmesan cheese
½ cup balsamic vinegar
3 tablespoons chopped fresh basil
3 tablespoons chopped fresh oregano

Preheat oven to 450°. Cut bread into 8 to 12 half-inch rounds. Brush with oil. Place on a cookie sheet and bake for 8 minutes or until toasted.

Combine tomatoes, peppers, and onion in a mixing bowl. Mix in remaining ingredients. (This is best when prepared 1 to 2 days ahead of time to allow the vegetables to marinate.) Spoon over toasted bread.

Yields 8 to 12 hors d'oeuvres

Onion Parmesan Puffs

Director of Culinary Arts Joseph E. Shilling
The Art Institute of Philadelphia, Philadelphia, PA

1 baguette French bread
1 small onion, finely minced
½ cup mayonnaise
½ cup grated Parmesan cheese

Preheat broiler. Slice bread into ¼-inch rounds. Mix together onion, mayonnaise, and cheese. Spread a generous amount on each bread slice and place on a baking sheet. Broil until hot and bubbly, about 12 to 15 minutes. Serve immediately.

Serves 8 to 10

Marinated Beef and Scallion Skewers with Garlic Dipping Sauce

Chef/Owner Donna Leahy
Inn at Twin Linden, Churchtown, PA

⅓ cup extra virgin olive oil
2 tablespoons soy sauce
2 tablespoons rice wine vinegar
2 tablespoons dark brown sugar
3 tablespoons chopped fresh mint
1 teaspoon finely chopped garlic
1 tablespoon minced ground ginger
1 teaspoon ground mustard
1 teaspoon coarsely ground black pepper
½ teaspoon salt
1 pound Delmonico or strip steak, pounded to ⅛-inch thick
6 scallions
Garlic Dipping Sauce (Recipe appears on page 296.)

Soak 12 bamboo skewers in water for at least 12 hours prior to grilling.

Whisk together first 10 ingredients. Place steak in a shallow, airtight container or zip lock bag. Pour in marinade and cover steak completely. Refrigerate for 1 to 2 hours.

Preheat broiler or prepare coals for charcoal grilling.

Trim off root ends of scallions and discard. Trim off green flared tops and set aside. (The remaining piece will be approximately 4 to 6 inches long.) Remove steak from marinade. Cut steak into six 1½-inch-wide strips, each long enough to cover a trimmed scallion. Wrap each scallion in a strip of steak, overlapping the edges to cover scallion completely. Cut lengthwise into four 1- to 1½-inch sections. Place 2 sections crisscrossed on the end of each skewer.

Grill or broil for about 1 minute per side until just browned and medium rare or until desired doneness. Serve with garlic dipping sauce and garnish with green scallion trimmings.

Serves 6

Caribbean "Jerk" Chicken Bites

Director of Culinary Arts Joseph E. Shilling
The Art Institute of Philadelphia, Philadelphia, PA

1 small onion, chopped
2 serrano peppers
1 chipolte pepper
4 cloves garlic
¼ cup soy sauce
2 tablespoons lime juice
2 tablespoons oil
2 teaspoons allspice
1 teaspoon thyme
1 teaspoon paprika
½ teaspoon cinnamon
1 tablespoon finely chopped fresh ginger
2 pounds chicken breasts, cut into bite-size cubes

Sauté onion until tender. Place onion and all ingredients, except chicken, in a food processor. Blend until smooth. Toss chicken with jerk rub. Grill or bake in a pre-heated 375° oven for 15 to 18 minutes. Skewer with toothpicks or wooden skewers and serve hot. Lime or pineapple yogurt make great dipping sauces.

Chef's Note

This dish is spicy. You can reduce the heat by eliminating the serrano peppers. The Caribbean Jerk rub is great on steak, shrimp, fish, duck, and just about anything you want to spice up, including vegetables.

Bitter Balls

Owner Eric Van Merkensteÿn
Van M's Music Bar and Grille, Philadelphia, PA

¼ pound cooked pork (or any roasted meat)
3 to 4 slices bread
½ cup chopped onion
¼ cup flour
1 teaspoon pepper
1 egg, lightly beaten
Breadcrumbs
Oil

Grind pork, bread, and onion in a food processor. Transfer to a mixing bowl and stir in flour and pepper. (You can add hot spices, if you like.) Shape mixture into balls, about ½-inch in diameter. Dip in egg; then in breadcrumbs. Heat oil in a pot or a deep fryer to about 350°. Fry balls, a few at a time, until brown and crispy. Serve hot.

Serves 4 to 6

Van M's Music Bar and Grille

Known for:
smoke free, live music, good food

Years in business: 1

Most requested table:
near the music

Menu:
American

Chef: Richard Lees

Hoisin Duck Spring Roll

Executive Chef John Anderson
Solaris Grille, Philadelphia, PA

1 teaspoon sesame oil
1 carrot, chopped
1 red pepper, sliced
1 scallion, chopped
1 cup chopped broccoli
Pinch of crushed garlic
1 pound duck confit, picked clean
2 tablespoons hoisin sauce
8 spring roll wrappers
1 egg, lightly beaten
1 carrot, finely chopped
¼ cup finely chopped daikon
1 cup mirin
1 tablespoon rice vinegar
Canola oil

Heat sesame oil in a sauté pan or wok. Add next 5 ingredients and sauté. Add duck confit and hoisin sauce and stir to combine. Remove mixture from heat and cool.

Position wrapper on a work surface with tip pointing vertically (looks like a tall diamond). Place one-quarter filling in center and fold wrapper in half horizontally. Fold left and right sides of wrapper over filling and roll up to top point. Brush with egg to seal. Wrap in a second wrapper so that roll holds together well.

Combine finely chopped carrot, daikon, mirin, and rice vinegar. Reserve.

Heat oil in a small pan or deep fryer. When oil is very hot (about 360°), fry rolls, one at a time, turning occasionally until golden brown. Remove and drain on paper towel. Repeat until all rolls are cooked. Cut in half and serve hot with dipping sauce. (We serve the dipping sauce in a shot glass for a colorful effect.)

Serves 4 to 8

Philly Foodie Fact

Mirin, Japanese rice wine, has a lightly sweet, almost flowery taste. It is available at Chung May Food Market in Philadelphia and in Asian markets throughout the area.

Crab Cake Orientale

Executive Chef James Huang
CinCin, Chestnut Hill, PA

1 pound shrimp, peeled and deveined
4 tablespoons finely chopped scallions, white only
2 egg whites
3 tablespoons gin
1 tablespoon minced ginger
½ teaspoon sugar
⅓ teaspoon kosher salt
Dash of white pepper
1 tablespoon heavy cream
2 teaspoons unsalted butter
¾ pound fresh crabmeat
6 cups cubed white bread, crusts removed (approxi-
    mately 12 slices)
3 quarts corn oil for deep-frying
Tomato Ginger Dipping Sauce (see recipe)

Dry shrimp with paper towel and puree in a food
processor. Transfer to a mixing bowl and stir in scallions,
egg whites, gin, ginger, sugar, salt, and white pepper.
Refrigerate for 30 minutes.

Mix in heavy cream and butter. Fold in crabmeat. Divide
mixture into 48 balls. (They should be about 1 inch in
diameter.) Cover with bread cubes and press to form
small cakes. (Cakes can be prepared in advance and
refrigerated until ready to deep-fry.)

Heat oil in a heavy pan to 325°. Fry cakes for 2 to 3
minutes per side or until golden brown. Remove and
drain on paper towels. Serve with tomato ginger dipping sauce.

Yields 48 cakes

CinCin

Known for:
Chinese cuisine with
French flair

Years in business: 4

Menu:
fusion dishes

Chef: James Huang

Chef's training:
Culinary Institute of
America and various
chefs

**Chef's hobbies/
accomplishments:**
cooking, traveling

Chef's favorite foods:
grilled food

**Chef's favorite
cookbook:**
Barbecue Bible

Tomato Ginger Dipping Sauce

⅓ teaspoon corn oil
¼ cup minced ginger
¼ cup minced shallot
1 cup finely chopped seeded plum tomatoes
1 cup rice wine or white wine
1 cup ketchup
1½ cups sugar
⅓ teaspoon kosher salt

Heat corn oil in a saucepan over medium heat. Add ginger and shallot and sauté for 1 minute. Add tomatoes, wine, ketchup, sugar, and salt. Bring to a boil. Serve hot or cold.

Yields 4 cups

Wasabi Stuffed Shrimp with Asian Ginger Dipping Sauce

Chef/Owner Marianne Cuneo-Powell
A Little Cafe, Voorhees, NJ

2 eggs
¼ cup chopped scallion
¼ cup chopped red onion
2 tablespoons grated ginger
1 teaspoon minced fresh garlic
Oil
¼ cup soy sauce
1 teaspoon sriracha sauce (available at Kam Moon
    Oriental Store in Cherry Hill, NJ)
1 cup sweet chili sauce
Salt and pepper
12 shrimp (U12), peeled, deveined, tails on
4 tablespoons wasabi
12 strips bacon, parcooked

Place eggs, scallion, red onion, ginger, and garlic in a food processor. Pulse until blended. With machine running, slowly add oil until mixture emulsifies and becomes a mayonnaise. Add soy sauce, sriracha sauce, and sweet chili sauce and blend until orange in color. Season to taste with salt and pepper.

Preheat oven to 350°. Stuff shrimp with wasabi. Wrap each with 1 piece bacon. Place on sheet pan and bake for 7 to 10 minutes or until cooked through. Serve hot with dipping sauce.

Serves 12

A Little Cafe

Known for:
rack of lamb

Years in business: 4

Most requested table:
#1

Menu:
trans global new world cuisine

Chef: Marianne Powell

Chef's training:
The Restaurant School in Philadelphia

Chef's hobbies/ accomplishments:
ice skating

Chef's favorite foods:
McDonald's

Chef's favorite cookbook:
Silver Palate

Hazelnut Crusted Shrimp

Executive Chef Joe Stewart
GG's at the DoubleTree, Mount Laurel, NJ

2¼ cups water
1 cup sugar
½ cup Frangelico
2 cups heavy cream
1 pound jumbo shrimp, peeled and deveined, tails on
Salt and pepper
2 eggs
2 cups finely chopped toasted hazelnuts
Peanut oil

Cook sugar and 2 cups water in a heavy pot until sugar starts to caramelize and turns golden brown. (The caramel should read about 310° on a candy thermometer. Be careful.)

Remove caramel from heat. Slowly stir in Frangelico and cream. Return pan to heat and stir with a wooden spoon until smooth. Remove from heat and let cool to room temperature.

Season shrimp with salt and pepper. Whisk together eggs and remaining ¼ cup water to make an egg wash. Dip shrimp in egg wash and roll in chopped nuts.

Pour about 1 inch of oil into a large heavy skillet and heat to 325°. Fry shrimp, 4 to 6 at a time, for about 3 to 4 minutes. (Work in batches so the oil maintains an even temperature.) Drain shrimp on paper towel and serve warm with dipping sauce.

Serves 4

Wine Notes

Recommended Wine: Soave Monte Carniga Cantina del Castello 1998 ($15.00)

Description: This single 40-year-old vineyard "Monte Carniga" (in the heart of the Soave Classico appellation) makes Soave of rich, creamy flavors, well balanced by sharp acidity untainted by oak flavors.

Sommelier: Luca Mazzotti, Moore Brothers Wine Co.

Cornmeal Fried Oysters with Pickapeppa® Rémoulade

Chef/Proprietor Walter Staib
City Tavern, Philadelphia, PA

1½ cups yellow cornmeal
½ cup all-purpose flour
4 eggs, lightly beaten
24 extra-large bluepoint oysters
4 cups vegetable oil
Pickapeppa® Rémoulade (Recipe appears on page 297.)
2 lemons, each cut into 4 to 6 wedges

Place cornmeal, flour, and eggs in separate dishes. Dip each oyster into flour, then egg, and finally cornmeal. Place coated oysters on a baking sheet and refrigerate until ready to fry.

Heat oil over high heat in a deep-fat fryer or a heavy 4-quart saucepan until temperature reaches 350°. (If you drop a small amount of the cornmeal mixture into the oil and it sizzles, it's hot enough.) Carefully drop oysters, one at a time, into oil. Fry a few at a time for 2 minutes until golden. Use a slotted spoon to remove oysters from oil and place to drain on a paper towel-lined baking sheet. Repeat until all oysters are fried.

Arrange oysters on individual serving plates and serve with rémoulade. Garnish with lemon wedges.

Serves 4 to 6

Chef's Note
Oysters can be tricky to open. I recommend buying oysters already shucked from your favorite fishmonger.

Tempura Battered Mussels with Curry Rémoulade

Executive Chef Joe Stewart
GG's at the DoubleTree, Mount Laurel, NJ

4 ounces white wine

4 ounces clam juice

1 teaspoon minced garlic

1 teaspoon chopped shallot

Pinch of red pepper flakes

24 large whitewater or New Zealand mussels

2 teaspoons curry powder

1 cup mayonnaise

1 teaspoon chopped capers

4 ounces chopped tomato

¼ cup chopped parsley

2 cups flour

1 cup cornstarch

1 egg

12 ounces seltzer

½ teaspoon paprika

Salt and pepper

3 cups oil

Combine wine, clam juice, garlic, shallot, and pepper flakes in a pot with a tight fitting lid. Bring to a boil and add mussels. Cover and steam until mussel shells are just opened. Remove with a slotted spoon and cool. (Discard unopened mussels.)

Add curry powder to cooking liquid. Simmer until liquid is reduced to 2 tablespoons. Remove from heat and allow to cool. Whisk together cooled liquid, mayonnasie, capers, tomato, and parsley until just incorporated. Reserve.

Sift flour and cornstarch together. Add egg, seltzer, paprika, and salt and pepper and whisk until smooth. (Add more seltzer if too dry.) Remove cooked mussels from shells. Clean and reserve 24 half shells for garnish. Coat mussels with tempura batter.

Heat oil in a large sauté pan over medium-high heat. Fry mussels until golden, about 3 minutes. Place mussels back in cleaned shells and top with curry rémoulade. Serve on bed of greens with extra sauce on the side.

Serves 4

Cold Mussels Monterey

Executive Chef Luigi Baretto
Ram's Head Inn, Absecon, NJ

½ cup white wine

3 dozen fresh mussels

2 eggs, boiled

4 anchovy fillets

1 medium onion, quartered

½ green pepper

½ red pepper

3 cloves garlic

2 tablespoons chopped fresh parsley

1 teaspoon capers

1 tablespoon red wine vinegar

1 tablespoon lemon juice

½ cup olive oil

Salt and white pepper

Heat wine in a shallow pot over medium heat. When wine beings to boil, add mussels. Cover and boil until shells are completely open. Remove pan from heat. Remove mussels from liquid. Discard empty half shell. Reserve 1 cup cooking liquid.

Grind eggs, anchovies, onion, green and red peppers, garlic, parsley, and capers in a meat grinder or a food processor until fine. Transfer to a mixing bowl. Add vinegar, lemon juice, olive oil, and reserved cooking liquid. Season to taste with salt and white pepper.

Arrange mussels in a serving dish and top each with 1 teaspoon sauce.

Serves 4 to 6

Chilled Monk's Mussels

Chef/Owner Tom Peters
Monk's Café, Philadelphia, PA

1 bag precooked frozen New Zealand Green Lip mussels (2.2-pound bag)
½ cup finely diced red onion
2 cloves garlic, finely diced
1 teaspoon finely diced shallots
1 cup peeled, seeded, and diced plum tomatoes
1 teaspoon black pepper
¼ teaspoon salt
¼ cup Boon Gueuze (Belgian beer)
1 teaspoon finely chopped fresh parsley
2 teaspoons finely chopped fresh chervil
1 teaspoon finely chopped fresh chives
1 teaspoon finely chopped fresh basil
Parsley, optional

Remove mussels from package and thaw overnight in refrigerator.

Lightly sauté onion, garlic, shallots, tomatoes, pepper, salt, and beer for about 1 minute in a hot sauté pan. Do not overcook — mixture should be slightly crunchy. Add chopped herbs. Refrigerate until cool.

Arrange cold thawed mussels on a serving plate. Stir to recombine marinade and spoon over each mussel. Sprinkle with parsley or other herb, if desired. Serve with a crisp, white wine or a Victory HopDevil, Nodding Head IPA, Duvel or any full-flavored pale ale.

Serves 4

Chef's Note

You can't be a Belgian restaurant without serving lots and lots of mussels. Monk's Café serves between two and three tons of mussels each month. That's alot of mussels! We offer half a dozen hot mussel dishes, but this chilled dish is a big hit in the summer months. We use New Zealand Green Lip mussels for this dish, although we have used Maine cultivated mussels on occasion. Many grocers carry both styles. I use the New Zealand grocer pack when I make this dish for guests at home.

appetizers

Oyster Rockefeller 32

Roasted Oysters 32

Clams Oreganato 33

"New Delhi" King Shrimp Scampi 34

Drunken Shrimp 35

Spanish Garlic Shrimp 36

Crab Martini with Oriental Ratatouille and Dijon-Lime Sauce 37

Salmon Corn Cakes 38

Atlantic Salmon Ceviche with Chile and Maple Sour Cream 39

Fresh Tuna Carpaccio with Fingerling Potato Risotto 40

Russian Crêpes with Sour Cream Dill Sauce and Caviar 41

Gateau of Belgian Endive 42

Jeanne d'Arc 43

Peppers Stuffed with Goat Cheese 43

Greenhill Mushrooms 44

Kennett Square Portobello Mushrooms with Jumbo Lump Crab 45

Oyster Rockefeller

Executive Chef Cary Neff
Sansom Street Oyster House, Philadelphia, PA

1 pound fresh spinach, stems removed
8 tablespoons salted butter
½ cup chopped parsley
2 anchovy fillets
1 tablespoon Pernod
1½ teaspoons Worcestershire sauce
½ cup fresh breadcrumbs
3 drops Tabasco sauce
Salt and pepper
24 oysters, shucked with deep shell
1 cup fresh grated Parmesan cheese

Blanch spinach in boiling water for 2 to 3 minutes. Drain and chop. Heat butter in a sauté pan. Add spinach, parsley, and anchovies. Add Pernod, Worcestershire sauce, and breadcrumbs. Transfer mixture to a food processor and puree. Season to taste with Tabasco and salt and pepper.

Preheat oven to 450°. Arrange oysters in shells on a baking tray. Top oysters with spinach mixture. Top spinach with Parmesan cheese. Bake for 5 to 10 minutes until cheese melts and lightly browns.

6 servings

Roasted Oysters

Executive Chef Cary Neff
Sansom Street Oyster House, Philadelphia, PA

4 ounces olive oil
4 ounces white wine
2 tablespoons minced garlic
2 tablespoons minced parsley
24 shucked oysters

Preheat broiler. Mix olive oil, wine, garlic, and parsley together. Top oysters with mixture. Broil for 2 minutes.

Serves 4

Clams Oreganato

Executive Chef/Owner Dominic Ventura
Euro Cafe, Philadelphia, PA

50 littleneck clams, washed
2 cups chicken stock or fish stock or plain water
4 tablespoons butter
¼ cup chopped scallions
1 clove garlic, finely chopped
1 teaspoon chopped fresh parsley
2 teaspoons oregano
2 teaspoons crushed red pepper
Salt and pepper
1 cup white wine

Heat clams and stock in a large sauté pan over medium heat. Cover and steam until clams start to open. Uncover and add butter and remaining ingredients except wine. Heat through. Add wine and simmer for a few minutes before serving.

Serves 4 to 6

Wine Notes

Recommended Wine: Racemo Frascati 1998 ($11.50)

Description: A limited production from the single vineyard "L'Olivella," this is a blend of Malvasia del Lazio (50%), Malvasia di Candia (20%), and equal parts of the native Bellone, Trebbiano Giallo, and Trebbiano Toscano grown on the volcanic soil of Monte Tuscolo. Because of the mineral richness of the soil and the careful selection of the fruit, the product is a fragrant, medium-bodied, aromatic, and well-balanced wine that would suit many fish and meat dishes. It also works beautifully as an aperitif.

Sommelier: Christian Lane, Moore Brothers Wine Co.

"New Delhi" King Shrimp Scampi

Chef/Owner Albert Paris
City Grill, Philadelphia PA

1 mango, diced
2 plum tomatoes, seeded and chopped
1 cup mango chutney (I use Major Grey's.)
Juice of 1 orange
1 tablespoon chopped cilantro
16 jumbo shrimp
2 teaspoons kosher salt
1 teaspoon olive oil
2 yams, grated
1 egg
1 teaspoon curry
1 teaspoon salt
3 scallions, chopped
1 tablespoon vegetable oil

Combine mango, tomatoes, chutney, orange juice, and cilantro in a saucepan over medium heat. Simmer for 10 minutes. Reduce heat and keep warm until ready to use.

Preheat oven to 350°. Toss shrimp with kosher salt and olive oil. Place on a sheet pan and roast for 10 minutes.

Mix together yams, egg, curry, salt, and scallions. Form into 8 cakes. Heat vegetable oil in a skillet. Add cakes and pan fry until golden on each side.

Place 2 on each plate. Surround with 4 shrimp. Drizzle with sauce.

Serves 4

City Grill

Known for:
copper-clad pizza oven, large outdoor cafe

Years in business: 1

Most requested table:
anything near the windows

Menu:
California/Napa Valley mission-style lodge

Chef: Albert Paris

Chef's training:
11 years in San Francisco; 4 years in Napa Valley

Chef's hobbies/ accomplishments:
cooking, Kung Fu, blues harmonica

Chef's favorite foods:
anything with life

Chef's favorite cookbook:
Physiology of Taste

Drunken Shrimp

Chef/Owner Susanna Goihman
Azafran, Philadelphia, PA

12 large shrimp
1 cup good quality dark rum
¼ cup honey
¼ cup soy sauce
¼ cup olive oil
Juice of 1 lime or ½ orange
1 tablespoon mustard
1 tablespoon chopped fresh ginger
2 large cloves garlic, minced
½ teaspoon dried red parsley flakes
Salt and pepper

Peel and devein shrimp. Place in a shallow bowl and set aside. Combine remaining ingredients. Pour marinade over shrimp and refrigerate for 30 minutes.

Remove shrimp from marinade and reserve marinade. Heat skillet over high heat. Pan sear shrimp until cooked through; then remove from pan. Add marinade and cook until reduced to a syrupy glaze. Pour over shrimp. For a great entree, serve shrimp over rice.

Serves 2

Wine Notes

Recommended Wine: Albert Mann Pinot Auxerrois VV 1998 ($12.00)

Description: In the southern Alsace, Albert Mann produces rich and flavorful wines that, frankly, deserve to be better known. Pinot Auxerrois, known as Klevner in Alsace, is a white grape that makes aromatic wine with natural richness and broad appeal. Albert Mann's old vines Pinot Auxerrois is a complex and well-balanced wine with vibrant honey and spice on the palate. While it is drinking very well now, the 1998 vintage would still benefit from a few more years of aging.

Sommelier: Christian Lane, Moore Brothers Wine Co.

Spanish Garlic Shrimp

Executive Chef/Owner Dominic Ventura
Euro Cafe, Philadelphia, PA

24 large shrimp, peeled
Flour
2 teaspoons oil
2 teaspoons butter
2 scallions, chopped
¼ cup chopped celery
1 teaspoon Cajun seasoning
½ teaspoon cayenne pepper
¼ cup Tabasco or red pepper sauce
Salt and pepper

Dredge shrimp in flour. Heat oil and butter in a large sauté pan over medium heat. Add shrimp to pan. Stir in scallions, celery, and all spices. Raise heat and sauté for about 3 to 5 minutes or until shrimp are firm. Turn heat off. Pour Tabasco over shrimp. Cover and let stand for 1 to 2 minutes. Season to taste with salt and pepper.

Serves 4 to 6

Wine Notes

Recommended Wine: Lusco Albarino 1999 ($19.00)

Description: A rich, full, and lush wine with good acidity and freshness to cut through this spicy dish.

Sommelier: John McNulty, Triangle Liquors

Crab Martini with Oriental Ratatouille and Dijon-Lime Sauce

Chef/Proprietor Philippe Chin
Chin Chin, Philadelphia, PA

1 small onion
1 green bell pepper
1 red bell pepper
1 large tomato
1 small zucchini
1 small yellow squash
½ small eggplant
2 tablespoons olive oil
3 cloves garlic, chopped
1 tablespoon chopped cilantro
1 tablespoon oyster sauce
Salt and pepper
8 ounces lump crabmeat
1 tablespoon lime juice
2 tablespoons mayonnaise
1 tablespoon Dijon mustard
1 cup chopped greens
1 green papaya, shredded

Dice all vegetables into ¼-inch pieces.

Heat olive oil in a large sauté pan over high heat. Add onion and peppers and sauté for 3 minutes. Add garlic and remaining vegetables and cook for 5 minutes. Remove from heat and chill.

When chilled, mix in cilantro and oyster sauce. Season with salt and pepper to taste.

In a mixing bowl, toss crabmeat with lime juice, mayonnaise, and mustard. Reserve.

Place chilled ratatouille in 1 large or 4 regular-size martini glasses. Top with crabmeat and garnish with chopped greens and papaya.

Serves 4

Philippe's Bistro

Known for:
authentic French bistro

Years in business:
6 months

Most requested table:
the booths

Menu:
all entrees $17.00

Chef: Philippe Chin

Chef's training:
Paris, France; world's youngest Maitre Cuisinier (Master Chef) of France

Chef's hobbies/ accomplishments:
riding my Harley-Davidson/earned many commendations

Chef's favorite foods:
ethnic

Salmon Corn Cakes

Chef/Proprietor Walter Staib
City Tavern, Philadelphia, PA.

2 ears fresh white corn
6 cups Court Bouillon (Recipe appears on page 302.)
1½ pounds salmon fillets, ¾-inch thick, skinned and boned
1 small yellow onion, finely chopped
1 large red bell pepper, finely chopped
1 large green bell pepper, finely chopped
2 eggs
¼ cup dry fine breadcrumbs
¼ cup lemon juice (about 1 large lemon)
1 tablespoon finely chopped fresh dill
Dash of Worcestershire sauce
Dash of hot pepper sauce
4 tablespoons unsalted butter

Cut kernels from ears of corn. Place in saucepan and cover with salted water. Boil until tender, about 5 to 8 minutes. Drain and let cool.

Bring court bouillon to a boil in a medium saucepan over high heat. Add salmon. Reduce heat to medium and simmer until salmon is cooked and light pink throughout, about 5 to 8 minutes. Remove salmon from liquid and drain. Transfer to a medium mixing bowl. Let cool.

Break salmon into ¼-inch pieces. Add cooked corn, onion, peppers, eggs, breadcrumbs, lemon juice, ½ tablespoon dill, Worcestershire sauce, and hot pepper sauce. Mix well. Using your hands, form salmon mixture into 8 patties. Place patties on a baking sheet and refrigerate for 30 minutes.

Preheat oven to 350°. Melt butter in a large skillet over medium heat. Add patties and cook until brown, about 2 minutes on each side. Return patties to baking sheet and bake for 10 minutes. Serve garnished with remaining dill.

Serves 8 as an appetizer
Serves 4 as an entree

City Tavern

Known for: atmosphere

Years in business: 227

Menu: Colonial American

Chef: Walter Staib

Chef's training: over four decades of culinary experience, having received formal training in fine European hotels and restaurants

Chef's favorite foods: Early American and Asian

Chef's favorite cookbook: *City Tavern Cookbook: Two Hundred Years of Classic Recipes from America's First Gourmet Restaurant*

Atlantic Salmon Ceviche with Chile and Maple Sour Cream

Executive Chef David Leo Banks
Harry's Savoy Grill and Ballroom, Wilmington, DE

1½ ounces pure olive oil

1 tablespoon kosher salt

1 teaspoon crushed red chile pepper

1 teaspoon sugar

1½ pounds North Atlantic salmon, shaved

3 tablespoons EACH finely minced plum tomato and red bell pepper

2 tablespoons finely minced onion

2 tablespoons chopped fresh parsley

2 tablespoons chopped fresh cilantro

8 asparagus spears

1 ripe avocado

2 teaspoons chile powder

2 tablespoons pure maple syrup

1 cup sour cream

4 tablespoons fresh squeezed lime juice

2 tablespoons fresh squeezed lemon juice

Mix together olive oil, kosher salt, crushed chile pepper, and sugar in a stainless steel or glass bowl. Place salmon in bowl, toss with mixture, and cover tightly with plastic wrap. Refrigerate overnight.

One hour before service, gently toss cured salmon mixture with tomato, bell pepper, onion, parsley, and cilantro. Refrigerate.

Blanch and shock asparagus. Cut in half lengthwise. Peel and slice avocado lengthwise into 16 slices. Blend chile powder and maple syrup. Whip into sour cream.

Just before service, toss salmon mixture with lemon and lime juices. Season to taste with additional salt, lemon, and lime. Spoon ceviche into 8 martini glasses (or serving glasses). Do not flatten mixture: leave it fluffy.

Arrange asparagus and avocado slices around sides of glasses. Place a dollop of chile sour cream on top. Serve immediately.

Serves 8

Fresh Tuna Carpaccio with Fingerling Potato Risotto

Executive Chef Jean-Marie Lacroix
Four Seasons Hotel, Philadelphia, PA

4 shallots, finely chopped
4 tomatoes, blanched, seeded, and concasse
Juice of ½ lemon
Salt and pepper
4 tablespoons extra virgin olive oil
1 tablespoon chopped garlic
1 tablespoon Dijon mustard
2 cups chicken stock
4 tablespoons whole butter
12 fingerling potatoes, sliced and blanched
3 tablespoons finely chopped parsley
3 tablespoons grated Parmesan cheese
8 ounces tuna (sushi grade #1), thinly sliced
Plume of chervil

Mix half of chopped shallots with tomatoes, and lemon juice. Season with salt and pepper. Reserve.

Heat olive oil in a medium saucepot over medium-high heat. Add remaining shallots and garlic and cook until tender and translucent. Add mustard and cook for approximately 1 minute. Deglaze with chicken stock and whisk in butter.

Add potatoes and cook until hot. Finish with chopped parsley, grated cheese, salt, and fresh cracked pepper. (The consistency should be creamy, similar to risotto.)

Place potato risotto in a shallow bowl. Season tuna with salt and coat generously with reserved tomato dressing. Gently slide tuna onto risotto. Season with fresh cracked pepper. Garnish with chervil.

Serves 4

Russian Crêpes with Sour Cream Dill Sauce and Caviar

Chef Marie Jarzenski
Warsaw Cafe, Philadelphia, PA

3 tablespoons sour cream

12 ounces cream cheese, softened

¼ teaspoon fresh lemon juice

½ pound smoked trout, coarsely chopped

½ pound salmon fillet, poached or steamed and coarsely chopped

Handful of fresh spinach, chopped

1 medium tomato, coarsely chopped

1 small zucchini, coarsely chopped or 1 small cucumber, peeled, seeded, and
  chopped

1 tablespoon chopped scallions

½ teaspoon minced fresh garlic

2 tablespoons capers

Pinch of dill

Pinch of parsley

Pinch of paprika

Salt and pepper

12 Crêpes (Recipe appears on page 246.)

Sour Cream Dill Sauce (Recipe appears on page 293.)

6 teaspoons caviar (I like Ketovya salmon caviar.)

Blend sour cream, cream cheese, and lemon juice until smooth. Fold in fish, vegetables, garlic, capers, dill, parsley, paprika, and salt and pepper. Reserve.

Preheat oven to 350°. Lay prepared crêpes flat and place 2 heaping tablespoons filling in center of each crêpe. Spread mixture over whole crêpe and fold one side over the other. Place crêpes, seam sides down, on a baking sheet. Bake uncovered for 15 to 20 minutes.

Transfer crêpes to a serving platter. Cover each with 2 tablespoons sour cream dill sauce and ½ teaspoon caviar.

Serves 6

Gateau of Belgian Endive

Executive Chef/Co-owner Jack Gudin
The Black Walnut, Doylestown, PA

4 tablespoons sherry vinegar
8 tablespoons walnut oil
4 tablespoons sour cream
4 ounces Roquefort cheese
Salt and freshly ground pepper
1 seedless English cucumber, peeled
Vegetable oil
4 ounces organic mesclun greens
3 heads Belgian endive
4 radishes, thinly sliced
¼ cup walnuts, toasted

Combine sherry vinegar, walnut oil, sour cream, and Roquefort cheese in a blender or food processor. Pulse until smooth. Season to taste with salt and pepper. Reserve. (Dressing can be made in advance. Simply whisk ingredients together before serving.)

Trim root end from cucumber. Slice lengthwise into 4 thin slices. Rub vegetable oil on inside of two 4-inch biscuit cutters or ring molds. Line inside of each ring with 2 cucumbers slices and overlap so they stay in place.

Toss greens with three–quarters of dressing. Trim root end from endive and separate leaves. Place half of endive in the center of each ring. Top each with tossed greens. Pour remaining dressing over tops of salad. Garnish with sliced radishes and walnuts.

Serves 2

The Black Walnut

Known for:
intimate fine dining

Years in business: 5

Most requested table:
alcove

Menu: new French

Chef: Jack Gudin;
Charles Klein is Chef de
Cuisine

Chef's training:
Gudin — Plaza Hotel;
Klein — Johnson and
Wales University

**Chef's hobbies/
accomplishments:**
fly fishing, gardening,
bicycling

Chef's favorite foods:
anything delicious,
chocolate

**Chef's favorite
cookbook:**
*La Menair aux Quat
Saisons*

Jeanne d'Arc
Peppers Stuffed with Goat Cheese

Chef/Owner Jean Sarne
JeanneNatalia Bistro, Philadelphia, PA

1 pound goat cheese, crumbled
⅓ pound cream cheese
1 tablespoon crushed garlic
1 tablespoon chopped shallots
2 tablespoons herbes de Provence
Salt and pepper
8 whole roasted peppers (Jarred is fine.)
1 cup cooked couscous
1 tablespoon white truffle oil

Preheat oven to 400°. Combine goat cheese, cream cheese, garlic, shallots, and herbs in a food processor and process until smooth. Season to taste with salt and pepper. Stuff peppers with cheese mixture. Place on a baking sheet and bake for 8 to 10 minutes.

Place couscous in center of 4 serving plates. Top with stuffed baked peppers. Drizzle with truffle oil.

Serves 4

JeanneNatalia Bistro

Known for:
brandy cake, soups

Years in business: 1½

Most requested table:
11 and 17

Menu:
French +

Chef: Jean Sarne

Chef's training:
self taught

**Chef's hobbies/
accomplishments:**
all sports/owning my
own restaurant (again)

Chef's favorite foods:
veal, lamb, duck, and
foie gras

**Chef's favorite
cookbook:**
Silver Palate

Greenhill Mushrooms

Executive Chef Daniel Dogan
The Terrace at Greenhill, Wilmington, DE

1 small loaf French bread
2 tablespoons minced garlic
4 ounces Roquefort cheese
2 tablespoons olive oil
5 shiitake mushroom caps, sliced
1 large portobello cap, sliced
3 large white mushrooms, sliced
2 teaspoons minced shallots
2 ounces white wine
4 ounces canned beef broth
Salt and pepper
Fresh herb sprigs

Preheat oven to 350°. Slice bread on a bias into four 1-inch-thick slices. Measure out 1 tablespoon minced garlic and spread an equal amount on top of each bread slice. Toast in oven until golden brown. Remove from oven and cool. Spread Roquefort cheese on each slice and reserve.

Heat oil in a sauté pan over medium heat. Add remaining garlic, mushrooms, and shallots and sauté for 3 minutes. Add white wine and simmer until liquid is reduced by half. Add beef broth and simmer until mixture begins to thicken. Season to taste with salt and pepper.

Place 2 Roquefort croutons on 2 salad plates. Ladle mushroom mixture over each crouton. Garnish with fresh herb sprigs.

Serves 2

Kennett Square Portobello Mushrooms with Jumbo Lump Crab

Executive Chef Paul L. Henderson
Rembrandt's Restaurant and Bar, Philadelphia, PA

4 large portobello mushrooms, washed and stems and ribs removed
1 pound jumbo lump crabmeat
1 red bell pepper, diced
¼ cup breadcrumbs
1½ tablespoons mayonnaise
1 tablespoon Dijon mustard
½ tablespoon finely chopped fresh parsley
Salt and pepper

Preheat oven to 350°. Invert mushroom caps on a baking sheet and roast for 20 minutes. Allow to cool. Keep oven on.

Gently blend remaining ingredients in a large mixing bowl. Fill cooled caps with crabmeat blend. Return mushrooms to oven and bake for 5 to 7 minutes. Serve warm.

Serves 4

Wine Notes

Recommended Wine: Chehalem, Dry Riesling Reserve 1996 ($18.50)

Description: A late harvest (In 1996, it occurred on November 12.) of overripe Riesling grapes from vines grown in the single vineyard Correl Creek has produced this very elegant and well-balanced wine of Alsatian-like intensity and pure Willamette Valley spicy aromatics. Stainless steel vinified with a careful selection of yeasts, this is a concentrated yet elegant, mouthfilling yet easily drinkable style of wine, extremely food-friendly, and capable of long aging.

Sommelier: Greg Moore, Moore Brothers Wine Co.

salads

Sesame Orange Orzo Salad 48

Famous Chopped Salad with Smoked Tomato Vinaigrette 49

Mediterranean Cole Slaw 50

Whole Grain Mustard Potato Salad 51

Eggplant Salad 52

Caren's Shrimp Salad 53

KoDu Salad with Roasted Pepper Raspberry Vinaigrette 54

The Restaurant School Brie Salad with Champagne Vinaigrette 55

Spinach Salad with Roasted-Vegetable Vinaigrette 56

Warm Applewood Spinach Salad 58

Portobello Mushroom Salad 59

Seared Filet Mignon over Watercress 60

Grilled Lamb Salad with Mint Habañero Vinaigrette 61

Pancetta Seared Squab Salad with Golden Beets
and Warm Walnut Pesto Vinaigrette 62

Pan-seared Duck Breast with Caramelized Pears, Mâche, and Goat Cheese 63

Fried Crawfish Salad with Tomato-Leek Vinaigrette 64

Fried Oyster Tostada Salad with Toasted Pumpkin Vinaigrette 66

Sesame Orange Orzo Salad

Executive Chef/Co-owner Anne-Marie Lasher
Fork, Philadelphia, PA

1 cup dried currants
½ cup sherry
1 pound orzo pasta
3 scallions, thinly sliced
2 medium carrots, grated
3 oranges, chopped zest and juice
⅛ cup chopped mint
⅛ cup chopped cilantro
¼ cup sesame oil
1 tablespoon honey
1 tablespoon lime juice
1 teaspoon salt or to taste

Soak currants in sherry for 15 minutes. Meanwhile, cook pasta according to manufacturer's directions and cool.

Combine all ingredients in a large mixing bowl and toss. Taste and adjust seasoning, if needed.

The salad is best served the day it is made, but it will keep for 1 or 2 days refrigerated. However, the pasta will start to get soft as it absorbs the liquid ingredients.

Yields about 3 quarts

Chef's Note

My favorite way to serve this salad is as an hors d'oeuvre with endive spears as the scooping device. The bitterness and crispiness of the endive contrast perfectly with the slightly sweet taste and soft texture of the salad. It would also pair well with grilled shrimp or chicken as a side salad. It can easily be made in about 30 minutes. Chopped toasted peanuts, cashews, or almonds might make a nice texture contrast too.

Famous Chopped Salad

Chef/Owner Albert Paris
City Grill, Philadelphia, PA

½ sweet potato
½ cup vegetable oil
½ avocado, diced
½ red onion, diced
½ head romaine, shaved
2 hard boiled eggs
2 ounces Stilton English cheese, crumbled
4 tablespoons chopped bacon
1 plum tomato, diced
6 tablespoons Smoked Tomato Vinaigrette (see recipe)

Peel and shred sweet potato. Heat oil in deep fryer or in saucepan to 350°. Deep fry potato shreds for about 1½ minutes or until crispy. Drain on paper towel.

Combine remaining ingredients in a bowl. Divide between plates. Top with sweet potato frizzles.

Serves 2 to 4

Smoked Tomato Vinaigrette

3 large tomatoes, peeled, seeded, smoked, and diced
3 cloves garlic, minced
5 tablespoons tomato juice
4 tablespoons Dijon mustard
5 cups blended oil
9 ounces chili sauce
1 cup mayonnaise

Combine tomatoes, garlic, tomato juice, and mustard in a bowl and mix well. Slowly stir in oil. Stir in chili sauce. Fold mayonnaise into mixture. Chill before serving.

Mediterranean Cole Slaw

Executive Chef/Owner Jon Hallowell
Mixmaster Café, Malvern, PA

1 head cabbage
1 large carrot
1 red onion
2 teaspoons dry basil
2 teaspoons dry oregano
½ cup honey
½ cup extra virgin olive oil
¼ cup red wine vinegar
4 cloves garlic, minced
Salt and pepper

Shred cabbage, carrot, and onion to desired consistency and place in a large bowl. Combine remaining ingredients, add to bowl, and toss well. Season with salt and pepper to taste.

Serves 8

Chef's Note

Because it has no mayonnaise, this recipe is a healthy alternative to traditional cole slaw. It keeps well for picnics and outdoor summer fun and is a nice side dish for sandwiches.

Whole Grain Mustard Potato Salad

Owner Ann-Michelle Albertson
Parties in the Kitchen, Wynnewood, PA

3 pounds small red bliss potatoes
⅓ cup finely diced red onion or scallions
⅔ cup whole grain mustard
¼ cup rice or white wine vinegar
½ teaspoon finely minced garlic
1½ teaspoons sugar
2 tablespoons oil
1 teaspoon kosher salt
1 teaspoon pepper

Boil potatoes until tender. (Do not overcook.) Immediately rinse in cold water. When cool, slice potatoes, keeping skins intact. Transfer to a serving dish. Add onion.

Combine mustard, vinegar, garlic, sugar, oil, salt, and pepper in a blender. Pour mixture over potatoes and onion and gently toss. Refrigerate until serving. (This salad is also delicious when warmed in the microwave.)

Yields 2 ½ quarts

Parties in the Kitchen

Known for:
working with kids, birthday parties

Years in business: 26

Menu: foods that kids like to bake and eat

Chef:
Ann-Michelle Albertson

Chef's training:
La Varenne, Johnson & Wales University, Peter Kump's

Chef's hobbies/ accomplishments:
rollerblading, mountain biking, hiking

Chef's favorite foods:
pizza, anything Italian

Chef's favorite cookbook:
CookWise, Joy of Cooking, Gourmet, New York Times food section

Eggplant Salad

Chef/Manager Nina Kouchacji
Marrakesh, Philadelphia, PA

2 ripe tomatoes, peeled and chopped
1 green pepper, chopped
1 large eggplant, cut into medium-size cubes
1 tablespoon tomato paste
⅓ cup hot water
2 tablespoons ground onion
½ tablespoon ground garlic
1 tablespoon ground parsley
2 tablespoons extra virgin olive oil
2 teaspoons salt
1 teaspoon black pepper
1 teaspoon cumin

Combine tomatoes, green pepper, and eggplant in a pot. Dissolve tomato paste in hot water and add to pot. Add remaining ingredients. Cover and cook over low heat for 45 minutes, gently mixing every 15 minutes. Dish is done when eggplant is soft and can be cut easily with a spoon.

Serves 4

Chef's Note

This dish can be eaten hot or cold and is delicious scooped up with Moroccan bread. Italian bread or French baguettes are good substitutions if Moroccan bread is not available.

Caren's Shrimp Salad

Owner Howard Nutinsky
Corned Beef Academy, Philadelphia, PA

2 quarts water
1 lemon, cut in half
1 to 2 bay leaves
1 teaspoon paprika
2 pounds large shrimp
2 to 3 stalks celery, chopped
1 teaspoon course ground pepper
1 teaspoon Old Bay Seasoning
¾ teaspoon celery seed
1 cup Russian dressing
Salt

Combine water, lemon, bay leaves, and paprika in a pot and bring to a boil. Add shrimp and cook until shrimp turn pink and start to "curl." Remove shrimp and wash in cold water to stop cooking. Peel, devein, and chop shrimp into large pieces. Mix chopped shrimp with celery, pepper, Old Bay Seasoning, and celery seed. Add Russian dressing and mix well. Taste and correct seasoning with salt and pepper, if needed. Serve in sandwiches or on chopped greens as a salad. Garnish with additonal lemon.

Serves 4 to 6

KoDu Salad

Chef/Owner Brian W. Duffy
Kristopher's, Philadelphia, PA

1 cup cashews
¼ cup sugar
1 cup stemmed shiitake mushrooms
Olive oil
Salt and pepper
1 pound mixed field greens
Roasted Pepper Raspberry Vinaigrette (see recipe)
¼ cup Roquefort cheese, crumbled
3 red apples, cored and thinly sliced

Toast cashews in a medium sauté pan over medium-high heat. Add sugar and cook until sugar is fully melted and cashews are caramelized. (Don't let cashews burn.) Transfer to a sheet pan and let cool to room temperature.

Heat a grill pan over medium-high heat. Lightly season mushrooms with a splash of olive oil and salt and pepper. Place mushrooms in pan and grill.

Toss greens with vinaigrette. Arrange greens on salad plates. Top with mushrooms, Roquefort cheese, and caramelized cashews. Fan apples around plates.

Serves 6

Roasted Pepper Raspberry Vinaigrette

1 pint fresh raspberries
¼ cup roasted peppers
1 tablespoon chopped shallots
1 teaspoon chopped garlic
⅛ cup raspberry vinegar
1 teaspoon dry tarragon
Salt and pepper
¾ cup olive oil

Combine all ingredients, except oil, in a food processor and pulse until smooth. Add oil in a slow, steady stream to create an emulsion.

Kristopher's

Known for: great presentation, eclectic food, open kitchen

Years in business: 1

Most requested table: the ones in front of the kitchen

Menu: American eclectic

Chef: Brian W. Duffy

Chef's training: The Restaurant School; my mom and dad

Chef's hobbies/ accomplishments: rugby, day traveling/ recently voted #1 restaurant in North East Philly

Chef's favorite foods: game and breakfast

Chef's favorite cookbook: *Local Flavor, Eat Like a Wild Man, Larousse*

The Restaurant School Brie Salad

Chef/Instructor Philip G. Pinkney
The Restaurant School, Philadelphia, PA

¾ pound Montasio cheese, grated
1½ heads Boston lettuce
½ head radicchio
1 bunch arugula
Pinch of minced fresh thyme
Champagne Vinaigrette (see recipe)
1 pint yellow tear drop tomatoes, halved

Divide grated cheese into 12 equal portions. Heat a nonstick pan over medium heat. Spread one portion of cheese evenly in pan. Gently cook until a golden crust forms. Turn over and repeat cooking process. Cool on paper towel. Continue process with remaining cheese.

Tear all greens into bite-size pieces. Place greens and thyme in a bowl. Toss with dressing to taste. Dot with tomato halves and cheese crisps.

Serves 6

Champagne Vinaigrette

⅓ cup champagne wine vinegar
1 cup olive oil
3 ounces Brie cheese
1 tablespoon minced shallot
1½ teaspoons Dijon mustard
1¼ teaspoons sugar
1 teaspoon salt
¼ teaspoon freshly grated black pepper
2 tablespoons water
1 tablespoon snipped chives

Whisk together all ingredients until well combined. Reserve.

Spinach Salad with Roasted-Vegetable Vinaigrette

Executive Chef/Co-owner Anne-Marie Lasher
Fork, Philadelphia, PA

2 bunches spinach, washed and destemmed
1 yellow pepper, julienned or cut into ¾-inch chunks
½ red onion, julienned
¼ pound kalamata olives, pitted or not, depending on your preference
Roasted-Vegetable Vinaigrette (see recipe)
Croutons

Toss all ingredients together and arrange on luncheon plates.

Serves 6

Chef's Note

This recipe was created for a tossed salad contest. The focus of the contest was on vegetables, so I thought that it would be interesting to use them in the vinaigrette, as well as in the actual salad. Well, I didn't win the contest, but the salad is a favorite with our staff, and the recipe has been sought after by many customers. The Roasted-Vegetable Vinaigrette makes use of the glorious garden vegetables abundant in the summer. You can add cheese to the salad — perhaps a goat cheese or a feta — if you like. The vinaigrette will keep for several days in the refrigerator and can also be used as a dip for crudité or pita or a sauce for grilled chicken. At Fork, we make croutons from day-old bread tossed with olive oil, rosemary, salt, and pepper and then cooked in a low oven until crisp.

Roasted-Vegetable Vinaigrette

1 medium zucchini
1 red pepper
½ green pepper
½ small eggplant
1 medium white onion
5 plum tomatoes
2 tablespoons minced garlic
¼ cup olive oil
2 tablespoons chopped basil
1 cup tomato juice
1 tablespoon tomato paste
½ cup red wine vinegar
1½ cups olive oil
Salt and pepper

Preheat oven to 400°. Cut all vegetables to 1-inch size. Toss with garlic and olive oil and arrange in a single layer in a roasting pan. Roast for about 15 minutes until vegetables start to brown on edges. Let cool.

Purée vegetables in a blender or food processor. Transfer purée to a large bowl. Add basil, tomato juice, tomato paste, and vinegar. Whisking constantly, add olive oil slowly to form emulsification. Season with salt and pepper.

Yields 3 cups

Warm Applewood Spinach Salad

Executive Chef Mustapha Rouissiya
Rococo, Philadelphia, PA

1 pound bacon
½ cup olive oil
1 red onion, diced small
1 cup red wine vinegar
½ cup Dijon mustard
½ cup toasted and roughly chopped pine nuts
¼ cup sugar
¼ cup honey
1 teaspoon pepper
1 cup vegetable oil
2½ pounds spinach, stemmed
Grated Parmesan cheese

Cook bacon until crispy. Drain, dice, and reserve.

Heat olive oil in a medium pot over medium heat. Add onions and sweat for about 5 minutes or until soft and translucent. Add vinegar, mustard, pinenuts, sugar, honey, and pepper. Heat thoroughly. Stir in vegetable oil.

Toss spinach with bacon and warm dressing, using as much or as little dressing as desired. Garnish with cheese. (Save remaining dressing — it lasts a very long time in the refrigerator. Just reheat to use.)

Serves 4

Wine Notes

Recommended Wine: Verdicchio dei Castelli di Jesi Classico San Nicolò Brunori 1998 ($13.00)

Description: Having produced excellent Verdiccio for three generations, the Brunori family has achieved a perfect balance of tradition in the vineyard (no chemicals, hand-harvesting, respect of the sandy soils) and innovation in the cellar (soft-pressing and micro filtering). The result is a wine of structure and fleshinesss with beautiful aromatics and a lovely nutty finish.

Sommelier: Kevin McCann, Moore Brothers Wine Co.

Portobello Mushroom Salad

Executive Chef Joe Stewart
GG's at the DoubleTree, Mount Laurel, NJ

6 large portobello mushrooms
Balsamic Vinaigrette (see recipe)
1 pound arugula, rinsed and dried
3 plum tomatoes, diced
½ pound fresh Romano cheese, shaved

Brush dirt from tops of mushrooms and cut off stems. Marinate mushrooms in half of balsamic vinaigrette for 4 hours.

Heat grill or grill pan to medium heat. Shake off excess vinaigrette from mushrooms and grill until tender, about 5 minutes per side.

Divide arugula between salad plates. Slice mushrooms on a bias and place on arugula. Top with tomatoes, Romano cheese, and remaining balsamic vinaigrette.

Serves 6

Balsamic Vinaigrette

1 tablespoon chopped garlic
1 tablespoon chopped shallot
2 tablespoons EACH chopped fresh thyme, oregano,
    and rosemary
1 tablespoon Dijon mustard
1 cup aged balsamic vinegar
3 cups good quality olive oil
Pinch EACH of salt and pepper

Place all ingredients, except oil and salt and pepper, in a bowl. Whisk to combine. Slowly add oil, whisking until vinaigrette emulsifies. Whisk in salt and pepper.

GG's at the DoubleTree

Known for:
fresh seafood, Asian tuna, hazelnut shrimp, live piano music Tuesday - Saturday

Years in business: 9

Most requested table:
any of our window seats

Menu: creative American

Chef: Joseph Stewart

Chef's training:
Philadelphia's Restaurant School

Chef's hobbies/ accomplishments:
spending time with son

Chef's favorite foods:
foie gras, smoked salmon, scallops, any type of game

Chef's favorite cookbook:
*Fish and Shellfish,
Larousse Gastronomique*

Seared Filet Mignon over Watercress

Executive Chef Hoc Van Tran
Le Colonial, Philadelphia, PA

½ pound filet mignon, cut into ½-inch cubes
2 teaspoons honey
2 teaspoons soy sauce
⅔ teaspoon chopped garlic
4 slices white onion
Black pepper
2 tablespoons minced red onion
4 teaspoons red wine vinegar
2 teaspoons sugar
Pinch of salt
1 bunch watercress
8 slices tomato
¼ cup vegetable oil

Place filet cubes in a shallow bowl. Combine honey, soy sauce, garlic, onion, and pinch of black pepper and pour over cubes. Refrigerate for 1 to 2 hours.

Mix together minced red onion, red wine vinegar, sugar, pinch of pepper, and pinch of salt. Toss with watercress. Divide watercress between 2 salad plates. Arrange tomato slices around edges of plates.

Heat vegetable oil in a wok over high heat. Add beef and marinade. Stir frequently until medium rare. Remove from wok and place on watercress.

Serves 2

Wine Notes

Recommended Wine: Fleurie Colonge 1998 ($14.50)

Description: *La reine du Beaujolais*, Fleurie is one of the ten villages of the region of Beaujolais that is allowed to single cru *appellation*. The best of its wine display an irresistible aromatic range that encompasses red fruit scents and flavors, floral perfumes and mild spices, with a palate of ripe flavors and velvety tannins. Fleurie Colonge by André Colonge is a marvelous and blossoming rendition of this wine.

Sommelier: Greg Moore, Moore Brothers Wine Co.

Grilled Lamb Salad with Mint Habañero Vinaigrette

Chef Paul Trowbridge
Vega Grill, Philadelphia, PA

6 ounces lamb tenders
2 portobello mushrooms
2 ounces EACH tatsoi, arugula, and red mustard greens
2 ounces Mint Habañero Vinaigrette (see recipe)
4 tablespoons coarsely ground Spicy Walnuts (Recipe appears on page 282.)
Salt and pepper

Preheat grill or grill pan over medium-high heat. Place lamb and mushrooms on grill and cook to desired doneness. (Lamb is best when medium rare.) Slice lamb and mushrooms and reserve.

Combine tatsoi, arugula, and red mustard greens and toss with vinaigrette. Divide greens between 2 plates. Top with grilled lamb and mushrooms and sprinkle with walnuts and salt and pepper to taste.

Serves 2

Mint Habañero Vinaigrette

1 bunch mint
½ cup rice wine vinegar
1 habañero pepper, minced
¾ cup vegetable oil
Salt and pepper

Combine mint, rice wine vinegar, and habañero in a blender. With motor running, slowly add oil. Season to taste with salt and pepper.

Vega Grill

Known for:
named "Best Fish Dish in Philly, 1999" by *Philadelphia* magazine

Years in business: 3½

Most requested table:
#21 (nonsmoking);
#13 (smoking)

Menu:
Nuevo Latino

Chef: Paul Trowbridge

Chef's training:
Philadelphia's Restaurant School

Pancetta Seared Squab Salad with Golden Beets and Warm Walnut Pesto Vinaigrette

Sous Chef Bruce Giardino
Marco's Restaurant, Philadelphia, PA

1 to 1½ pounds small golden beets
2 tablespoons vegetable oil
Salt and pepper
2 squabs, halved and boned
4 thin slices pancetta
1 head frissee
2 heads baby red oak
4 sprigs mâche
6 to 8 ounces Red Onion Compote (Recipe appears on page 300.)
¼ cup sherry vinegar
1 to 2 tablespoons Walnut Pesto (Recipe appears on page 300.)
12 tear drop tomatoes, peeled
Tarragon leaves

Preheat oven to 350°. Wash and season beets with 1 tablespoon oil and salt and pepper. Wrap individually in foil and roast for 20 to 40 minutes until tender. Let cool.

Reheat oven to 300°. Wrap each squab piece in pancetta. Heat remaining oil in an ovenproof skillet over medium-high heat. Add squab and sear on each side. Transfer skillet to oven and bake until medium rare, about 10 to 15 minutes.

Chop and combine greens. Slice beets and place in centers of 4 plates. Top with greens and onion compote. Remove squab from pan and place on greens.

Reheat pancetta fat in pan over medium heat. Add sherry vinegar and simmer. Stir in walnut pesto. Dress greens with warm vinaigrette. Garnish with tomatoes and tarragon leaves.

Serves 4

Pan-seared Duck Breast with Caramelized Pears, Mâche, and Goat Cheese

Executive Chef Joel Gaughan
Braddock's Tavern, Medford, NJ

2 tablespoons unsalted butter
2 pears, peeled and quartered
2 tablespoons sugar
2 tablespoons water
2 duck breasts
4 handfuls mâche
6 ounces goat cheese, sliced into 12 thin rounds
Ginger Vinaigrette (see recipe)

Melt butter in a skillet over medium-high heat. Add pears and cook on one side until golden brown, about 4 minutes. Turn and cook on other side, about 4 minutes. Add sugar and water and cook until syrup turns a rich golden brown. Remove from heat and keep warm.

Split duck breasts in half and make 3 slits in skin, making sure not to cut into breast meat. Heat a large skillet over medium-high heat. Add breasts, skin side down, and cook for about 6 minutes or until breast is a deep golden brown. Turn and cook for 3 minutes more. Remove from pan and let rest for 3 minutes.

Carve duck breast across the grain into very thin slices. Set aside. Ladle vinaigrette onto bottoms of 4 plates. Divide duck between plates, placing slices on top of vinaigrette. Place 1 handful mâche, 3 slices goat cheese, and 2 pear quarters on each plate.

Serves 4

Ginger Vinaigrette

½ cup ground ginger
1 cup grapeseed oil
½ cup simple syrup
½ cup rice vinegar
2 scallions, finely chopped
Salt and pepper

Whisk together vinaigrette ingredients. Season to taste with salt and pepper.

Fried Crawfish Salad with Tomato-Leek Vinaigrette

Chef/Owner Joe Brown
Melange Café, Cherry Hill, NJ

3 eggs
1 cup milk
1 pound crawfish, peeled and cooked
1 cup flour
2 cups breadcrumbs
1 pound mesclun or your choice of salad greens
Tomato-Leek Vinaigrette (see recipe)
6 cups oil
2 cups crumbled Gorgonzola

Whisk together eggs and milk. Dip crawfish in flour and then in egg wash. Coat crawfish in breadcrumbs, tapping off excess. Refrigerate until ready to cook.

Toss mesclun with vinaigrette and divide among 4 plates. Refrigerate.

Heat oil to 350° in a large cast-iron pan or mini fryer. Carefully place crawfish in oil and fry until golden brown, about 5 minutes. Remove and drain on paper towels. Immediately place crawfish on mesclun and top with crumbled Gorgonzola.

Serves 4

Melange Cafe

Known for:
Louisiana-Italian fusion

Years in business: 5

Most requested table:
#17

Menu:
The Big Easy meets Italy: an original mixture of authentic Louisiana dishes and Italian classics

Chef: Joe Brown

Chef's training:
The Restaurant School; family; on-the-job

Chef's hobbies/ accomplishments:
music, playing piano and drums, sports, hanging out with Jordan

Chef's favorite foods:
rustic food

Chef's favorite cookbook:
Escoffier (1941 version)

Tomato-Leek Vinaigrette

3 cups chopped ripe Jersey tomatoes
¼ cup minced onion or shallot
2 tablespoons minced fresh garlic
2 leeks, whites only, julienned
2 tablespoons chopped fresh basil
Juice of 1 lime
½ cup balsamic vinegar
1 cup extra virgin olive oil
Salt and pepper to taste

Combine all ingredients in a bowl except oil and salt and pepper. Slowly whisk in oil until vinaigrette is emulsified. Season to taste with salt and pepper.

Fried Oyster Tostada Salad

Chef/Owner Derek Davis
Arroyo Grille, Philadelphia, PA

½ cup sour cream
Juice of ½ lime
Salt and pepper
Peanut oil
3 cups flour
1 cup cornmeal
⅔ cup kosher salt
½ cup cayenne pepper
½ cup New Mexico chili powder
24 standard shucked oysters
6 blue corn tortillas (6-inch size)
1½ cups shredded Cheddar cheese
1 cup chopped fresh plum tomatoes
3 cups mixed salad greens
Toasted Pumpkin Vinaigrette (see recipe)
1 tablespoon chopped cilantro

Combine sour cream and lime juice. Season to taste with salt and pepper. Reserve.

Heat peanut oil to 350° in a deep fryer or heavy pot. Combine flour, cornmeal, salt, cayenne pepper, and chili powder. Lightly coat oysters with flour-cornmeal mixture and shake off excess. Deep fry oysters, a few at a time, for 1½ minutes until crisp. Drain on paper towels. Deep fry tortillas for 2 minutes. Season with salt and pepper while hot.

Preheat oven to 350°. Place 4 oysters on each tortilla and sprinkle evenly with Cheddar cheese. Top with tomatoes. Bake until cheese melts. Cut each tostada into 4 pieces.

Toss greens with vinaigrette. (Be careful not to use too much or it will weigh salad down.) Divide greens between 6 chilled plates, placing greens in center of plates. Top greens with 4 tostada pieces. Sprinkle with chopped cilantro and drizzle with reserved sour cream crema. Serve immediately.

Serves 6

Toasted Pumpkin Vinaigrette

1 cup corn oil
½ cup cider vinegar
Juice of ½ lime
¼ teaspoon fresh thyme
1 tablespoon salt
1 teaspoon black pepper
½ cup pumpkin seeds, toasted

Combine all ingredients, except pumpkin seeds, in a blender. With motor running, slowly add seeds until dressing is nice and smooth.

soups

Tomato Onion Soup

Executive Chef David Young
Chadds Ford Inn, Chadds Ford, PA

2 large onions, sliced
1 tablespoon chopped garlic
1 teaspoon brown sugar
¼ cup chopped basil
2 teaspoons thyme
1 bay leaf
¼ cup port wine
2 cans peeled tomatoes (16 ounces each)
2 cans chicken stock (16 ounces each)
Salt and pepper

Sauté onions, garlic, sugar, basil, thyme, and bay leaf in a stockpot until onions begin to brown. Add wine, tomatoes with juice, chicken stock, and salt and pepper to taste. Bring to boil. Reduce heat and simmer until ready to serve. Serve with garlic Parmesan croutons.

Serves 6 to 8

Chadds Ford Inn

Known for:
The Inn has seen a great parade of American history from Indians to officers of the American Revolution and Martha Washington.

Years in business: 264

Most requested table:
The Wyeth table (#23)

Menu:
American — both traditional and creative

Chef: David Young

Chef's training:
classically trained with European chefs from the age of 14

Chef's hobbies/ accomplishments:
golfing and spending time with family

Chef's favorite cookbook:
Philadelphia Flavor

Vegetarian Minestrone Soup

President Jack Kramer
Jack Kramer's Catering, Philadelphia, PA

2 tablespoons extra virgin olive oil
1 small onion, chopped
2 cloves garlic, minced
1 large carrot, peeled and chopped
1 medium celery stalk with leaves, minced
½ small head green cabbage, chopped
½ pound green beans, cut
¼ cup mixed chopped fresh oregano, basil, and parsley
1 can red kidney beans (16 ounces), drained and rinsed
1 can whole peeled plum tomatoes (14 ounces), chopped
4 cups tomato juice
6 cups vegetable stock
¼ cup sugar
1 bay leaf
1 small zucchini, diced
1 small yellow squash, diced
2 cups uncooked pasta
Salt and pepper
Grated cheese

Heat oil in a 6-quart stockpot over medium heat. Add onion, garlic, carrot, celery, cabbage, green beans, and herbs and sauté until almost tender. Puree half of kidney beans and add to pot. Add remaining whole kidney beans, tomatoes, tomato juice, vegetable stock, sugar, and bay leaf. Bring to a boil. Reduce heat and simmer for about 15 minutes. Add zucchini and squash and simmer for 15 minutes. Add pasta and simmer for 15 minutes. Season to taste with salt and pepper. Serve with grated cheese.

Serves 4 to 6

White Bean Escarole Soup

Executive Chef/Co-owner Anne-Marie Lasher
Fork, Philadelphia, PA

1 pound dried great Northern beans
¼ cup olive oil
½ pound pancetta, diced
1 large white onion, diced
1 bulb fennel, cored and diced
2 tablespoon minced garlic
1 bay leaf
1 cup white wine
8 cups chicken stock or canned chicken broth
6 large plum tomatoes, diced
¼ head escarole, washed and coarsely chopped
1 tablespoon chopped fresh thyme
Salt and pepper

Pick through beans for stones. Soak in cold water for 4 hours or overnight.

Drain beans and place in a medium saucepot. Add enough fresh water to cover beans by 2 inches. Cook over medium-high heat until tender, approximately 1 hour. (The cooking time will depend on how long the beans soaked and how old they were.) Remove from heat and drain, reserving the excess water.

Heat olive oil over medium-high heat in a large saucepot. Add pancetta and cook, stirring frequently, until fat is rendered, about 5 minutes. Add onion, fennel, garlic, and bay leaf. Cook for about 5 minutes until vegetables are softened. Add white wine and cook for about 5 minutes. Add cooked beans, chicken stock or broth, and tomatoes. Simmer for about 15 minutes.

Add escarole and thyme and cook for 5 minutes. Add reserved bean water and/or more stock if soup needs more liquid. Season with salt and pepper. (Remember that pancetta is salty; and if you use canned broth, you might not need as much salt as you think.)

Yields 12 cups

Fork

Known for:
elegant yet casual atmosphere with decor that reflects the neighborhood's history as an artists' community

Years in business: 3

Most requested table:
window

Menu:
new American bistro

Chef: Anne-Marie Lasher

Chef's training:
10 years of hard labor in the restaurant industry

Chef's hobbies: choral singing, movies, reading

Chef's favorite foods:
vegetables, risottos, bread, cheese

Chef's favorite cookbook:
anything by Alice Waters, Perla Meyers, Joyce Goldstein

Grandma's Escarole and Fagioli

Owner John J. Garagozzo
Blue Moon Restaurant & Café, Haddon Heights, NJ

3 to 4 heads escarole
3 slices bacon or 1 tablespoon olive oil
2 sticks pepperoni
6 cloves garlic, crushed
Crushed red pepper, optional
Salt and pepper
2 cans cannellini beans (15.5 ounces each)

Clean escarole well. Cut off base and place wet leaves in a large stockpot. Cover and steam over medium heat until water from leaves evaporates.

Cook bacon (or heat olive oil) in a 4-quart pot. Skin and cut pepperoni into 1- to 2- inch pieces. Place in pot with bacon or olive oil. Add garlic. Cook until pepperoni is well cooked — almost burned. Place enough water in pot to cover pepperoni plus an additional half amount. Bring to a boil. Cover, reduce heat, and simmer for 1 hour.

Pour pepperoni mixture into stockpot with escarole. Season with crushed red pepper and salt and pepper. Simmer for 15 minutes. Add beans. (Do not drain liquid from cans.) Cook for 5 to 10 minutes. Serve with crusty Italian or French bread.

Serves 4 to 6

Wine Notes

Recommended Wine: Valori, Montepulciano d'Abruzzo 1998 ($12.00)

Description: Solid wines with plenty of tannins and sharp edges used to come from this wine district in central Italy. Today the situation has changed dramatically, and this is a superb example of new style Montepulciano. Low yield, total destemming, more attention to tannins and a cleaner, spicy finish are now features of this wine, an ideal companion of flavorful but not necessarily heavy vegetarian and meat dishes.

Sommelier: Frank Splan, Moore Brothers Wine Co.

Vegetarian Borsht

Chef/Owner Tracey Slack
The Red Hen Café, Medford, NJ

1 small onion, diced
½ pound mushrooms, any variety, sliced
1 pound fresh beets, peeled and diced small
1 carrot, peeled and diced
1 small purple turnip, peeled and diced
½ parsnip, peeled and diced
½ celery root knob, peeled and diced
8 cups water
¼ head savoy cabbage, shredded
2 tablespoons tomato paste
1½ teaspoons chopped garlic
⅓ cup red wine vinegar or to taste
⅛ cup sugar or to taste
Salt and pepper
Sour cream
Chopped fresh dill

Sauté onion and mushrooms in a soup pot until just browned. Add beets, carrot, turnip, parsnip, celery root, and water. Simmer for 5 minutes. Add savoy cabbage, tomato paste, and garlic and simmer for 30 minutes. Add vinegar and sugar, adjusting amounts to suit your sweet and sour preference. Season with salt and pepper. Serve hot with a dollop of sour cream and sprinkle of dill.

Serves 6 to 8

The Red Hen Café

Known for:
European cuisine emphasizing German and Hungarian food

Years in business: 1½

Most requested table:
They're all good!

Menu: Eastern European influences

Chef: Tracey Slack

Chef's training:
The Restaurant School in Philadelphia

Chef's hobbies/ accomplishments:
eating

Chef's favorite foods:
any seafood

Chef's favorite cookbook:
The Hungarian Cookbook, La France Gastronomique, Please to the Table

Snowflake Soup

Executive Chef Wallapa Suksapa
East of Amara, Philadelphia, PA

½ cup ground chicken
1 egg
Pinch of black pepper
1 tablespoon minced garlic
1 tablespoon minced ginger
¼ cup soy-mushroom sauce
1 cup jasmine rice
8 to 10 cups hot chicken broth
3 teaspoons spicy pepper vinegar
1 teaspoon julienned ginger
1 scallion, diced
1 tablespoon Rice Krispies cereal

Mix ground chicken in a bowl with egg, black pepper, garlic, ginger, and soy-mushroom sauce. Cover and refrigerate for 30 minutes.

Wash rice. Bring 8 cups stock to a boil in a stockpot. Add rice, cover, and boil until rice is very soft, about 30 minutes. Whisk rice into a coarse puree. (Add more stock if you prefer soup to have a thinner consistency.) Bring puree to a boil. Add chicken mixture. Stir until cooked and incorporated, about 2 minutes. Serve in large soup bowls. Garnish with a splash of vinegar, a pinch of ginger, scallions, and Rice Krispies.

Serves 6

East of Amara

Known for:
pad Thai, roast duck in spicy hot pepper sauce

Years in business: 10

Most requested table:
corner near window

Menu:
Thai and contemporary cuisine

Chef:
Wallapa Suksapa

Chef's training:
professionally trained in Thailand — always 1st in class!

Chef's hobbies/ accomplishments:
1999 Zagat survey "Best Thai in the City"

Chef's favorite foods:
Thai noodle dishes, various delightful Thai concoctions

Parsnip Soup

Chef/Instructor Philip G. Pinkney
The Restaurant School, Philadelphia, PA

2 tablespoons butter
1½ pounds parsnips, peeled and roughly chopped
5 cups vegetable stock
4 sage leaves
⅔ cup light whipping cream, optional
Salt and pepper

Melt butter in a large saucepan over medium heat. Add parsnips and cook for 10 minutes, stirring occasionally. Add stock and sage leaves and bring to a boil. Reduce heat and simmer until parsnips are tender. Remove from heat and cool slightly. Puree with an immersion blender or in a food processor.

Return soup to saucepan, add cream, and reheat over medium heat. Season to taste with salt and pepper. Serve hot, garnished with croutons and minced sage or parsley.

Serves 6

Chef's Note

Other vegetables may be substituted for parsnips. Carrots, leeks, onions, potatoes, pumpkin, or any member of the squash family would make good alternatives. Try apples! If you don't have vegetable stock available, you may use water instead. Just add half an onion and 2 diced ribs of celery.

Walnut and Eggplant Soup

Executive Chef Jeffrey Gutstein
Cresheim Cottage Cafe, Philadelphia, PA

2 medium eggplants, stems removed
2 tablespoons olive oil
3 cloves garlic, minced
1 Spanish onion, diced
1 tablespoon chopped fresh rosemary
1 quart vegetable or chicken stock
1 cup walnuts
3 tablespoons butter
3 tablespoons all-purpose flour
Salt and pepper

Preheat oven to 400°. Cut eggplants in half lengthwise. Place eggplants, flesh sides down, on a greased baking sheet. Bake for 15 to 20 minutes. Let cool. Scrape out pulp. Discard skin. Coarsely chop pulp and reserve.

Heat oil in a large saucepan over medium heat. Add garlic and sauté for about 30 seconds. Add onion and sauté for 3 to 4 minutes or until onions become transparent. Stir in rosemary and cook for 1 minute. Add eggplant, stir to combine, and cook for 5 minutes. Add stock and bring to a boil. Reduce heat and simmer for 20 minutes. Meanwhile, grind walnuts in a food processor and reserve.

Remove stock and eggplant from heat. Strain through a fine strainer. Pour stock back into pan. Place eggplant mixture in a food processor and puree. Add back to stock.

Melt butter over low heat in a small saucepan. Stir in flour with a wooden spoon. Turn heat up and continue to stir for 4 to 5 minutes to form a roux. Remove from heat and cool for 5 minutes.

Whisk roux into stock mixture. (Whisk rather quickly to prevent lumps.) Increase heat to high and bring soup to a boil. Reduce heat and simmer for 15 to 20 minutes. Season to taste with salt and pepper. Stir in walnuts and enjoy!

Serves 4

Watermelon Soup

Chef/Nutritionist/Owner Joseph K. K. Poon
Joseph Poon Asian Fusion Restaurant, Philadelphia, PA

1½ pounds spare ribs
1½ gallons water
1 pound watermelon, skinned and diced
3 slices fresh ginger
3 dried figs, diced

Cut ribs into 1-inch cubes. Heat a skillet or wok over high heat and stir-fry ribs for 1 minute.

Bring water to a boil in a large stockpot. Add ribs and remaining ingredients. Reduce heat and cook for 45 to 60 minutes. Remove stockpot from heat. Skim oil from top. Season with a pinch of salt, if desired.

Serves 6

Grilled Shrimp and Pineapple Soup

Executive Chef Gerald Dougherty
Moshulu, Philadelphia, PA

1 cup sliced pineapple
12 medium shrimp, peeled, deveined, tails off
1 cup shrimp stock
¾ cup sugar
2 tablespoons julienned ginger
1 teaspoon julienned jalapeño pepper
1 cup diced tomato
1 cup mint leaves

Grill pineapple on preheated hot grill until charred.
Dice into ½-inch squares. Allow some juice to drain
from pineapple. Discard juice. Grill shrimp for about 3
to 5 minutes or until done. Cut in half lengthwise.

Heat stock, sugar, and ginger in a stockpot over medium heat. Add jalapeño and tomatoes and simmer for 2
minutes. Stir in shrimp and pineapple and heat through.
Stir in mint leaves and serve.

Serves 4

Moshulu

Known for:
oldest operational 4
masted ship

Years in business: 3

Most requested table:
captain's table

Menu:
"new American"
featuring market fresh
seafood

Chef: Gerald Dougherty

Chef's training:
trained 3 years under a
master chef

Chef's favorite food:
Thai, Vietnamese,
Provençal, Moroccan

**Chef's favorite
cookbook:**
*Larousse, Escoffier, Art
Culinaire*

Bouillabaisse

Executive Chef David Grear
La Terrasse, Philadelphia, PA

10 cloves garlic, crushed

1 medium Spanish onion, diced

4 stalks celery, thinly sliced

1 head fennel, sliced

1 pound fish bones or shrimp shells

2 quarts water

3 bay leaves

Pinch of saffron

Pernod liqueur

2 ounces small shrimp

12 large mussels

3 ounces fish fillet (your choice)

2 large shrimp (U-15)

8 medium clams

2 large sea scallops

1 baby lobster

4 tomatoes, julienned

Sauté garlic and half of onion in a medium saucepan for 2 minutes. Add celery and half of fennel and sweat for 2 minute. Add bones/shells and sweat for 5 minutes. Add water, bay leaves, saffron, and Pernod to taste. Bring to a boil. Reduce heat and simmer for about 1 hour.

Strain to remove solids. Transfer stock to a large sauce-pan and heat over medium heat. When stock begins to simmer, add remaining onion and fennel, all seafood, and tomatoes. Cover and poach seafood for about 2 minutes.

Serve in deep bowls, dividing seafood pieces evenly.

Serves 4

La Terrasse

Known for:
live olive tree growing in lower terrace dining room

Years in business:
originally opened 1966; reopened 1998

Most requested table:
by the windows in the lower terrace

Menu: French/American

Chef: David Grear

Chef's training:
self taught — learned "in the field"

Chef's hobbies/ accomplishments:
weight lifting, sports, recipe development/my son!

Chef's favorite foods:
anything I don't have to cook myself!

Chef's favorite cookbook:
Gotham Bar & Grille

Lobster Bisque

Executive Chef Robert Cloud
The Oak Grill at the Marshalton Inn, West Chester, PA

2 shallots, peeled and minced
1 cup sherry
12 cups lobster stock
1 tablespoon cayenne pepper
1 teaspoon paprika
2 ounces tomato paste
½ to ¾ pound lobster meat, diced
1 cup heavy whipping cream

Sauté shallots in a large pot until translucent. Add sherry and simmer until it reduces by half. Add stock, cayenne pepper, paprika, and tomato paste. Simmer until liquid is reduced by one-third. Add lobster and cook until heated through. Stir in cream just before serving.

Serves 6 to 8

The Oak Grill

Known for:
listed on the national register of historic buildings

Years in business:
since 1841

Most requested table:
#11 — right in front of the fireplace

Menu: traditional

Chef: Robert Cloud

Chef's training:
been in the restaurant business since the age of 14

Chef's hobbies/ accomplishments:
golf

Chef's favorite foods:
anything prepared by a chef other than himself

Chef's favorite cookbook:
Le Bec-Fin Recipes by Georges Perrier

Shrimp and Asparagus Bisque

Executive Chef Brandon Carter
David's Yellow Brick Toad, Lambertville, NJ

1 pound shrimp
2 bunches asparagus
3 teaspoons sweet butter
1 teaspoon salt and pepper
1 cup Chardonnay
1 quart heavy cream

Peel shrimp and asparagus. Place shells and peelings into a large pot. Add 8 cups cold water and bring to a boil. Boil until liquid is reduced by two-thirds. (You will have about 1 cup of stock.) Strain and set aside.

Melt butter in a soup pot over medium heat. Add shrimp, asparagus, and salt and pepper and cook for 15 minutes.

Add strained stock, wine, and cream and bring to a boil. Cook until asparagus is mushy. Strain and return liquid to pot. Transfer solids to a food processor and puree. Add back to pot and stir to combine. Reduce, if necessary. Season to taste with salt and pepper. Serve hot or try it cold with crème frâiche.

Serves 8

David's Yellow Brick Toad

Known for:
ambiance and food

Years in business: 22

Most requested table:
by the window

Menu:
New World cuisine

Chef: Brandon H. Carter

Chef's training:
Academy of Culinary Arts

Chef's hobbies/ accomplishments:
roller blading, hiking, skiing/2 gold medals and 1 bronze from various culinary competitions

Chef's favorite foods:
steak and bar food

Chef's favorite cookbook:
La Cuisine de France

Crab and Tomato Bisque

Executive Chef Mustapha Rouissiya
Rococo, Philadelphia, PA

½ pound butter
1 onion, roughly chopped
2 ribs celery, roughly chopped
1 red pepper, roughly chopped
1 poblano pepper, roughly chopped
1 teaspoon minced garlic
Flour
1 tablespoon Old Bay Seasoning
2 cans crushed tomatoes (16 ounces each)
1 can diced tomatoes or whole tomatoes (16 ounces)
½ cup white wine
2 quarts chicken stock or chicken broth
1 teaspoon chopped thyme
1 pound jumbo lump crabmeat, shells removed
1 cup heavy cream
Worcestershire sauce
Salt and pepper
½ pound crabmeat, optional

Melt butter in a large pot. Add onion and celery and cook until soft. Add peppers and garlic and cook briefly. Stir in enough flour to absorb butter. Stir in Old Bay, crushed and diced tomatoes, white wine, chicken stock, and thyme. Heat soup thoroughly. Add lump crabmeat.

Whisk in heavy cream. Season to taste with Worcestershire and salt and pepper. Puree soup in a blender. Garnish with optional crabmeat, if desired.

Serves 4 to 6

Crock of Gold

Executive Chef John Salerno
Pirates Inn, Mount Laurel, NJ

½ cup butter
2 ribs celery, chopped
¼ medium onion, diced
2 sprigs parsley, chopped
1 quart milk
1 cup heavy cream
Salt and pepper
Seafood seasoning
¼ cup flour
1 tablespoon cognac
4 ounces steamed shrimp, chopped
4 ounces steamed lobster tail, chopped
4 ounces steamed clams, chopped
4 ounces cooked crabmeat

Melt ¼ cup butter in a skillet over medium heat. Add celery, onion, and parsley. Sauté until onion is transparent. Add milk, cream, salt and pepper, and seafood seasoning to taste. Heat to a warm temperature.

In a separate saucepan, melt remaining butter. Add flour and stir constantly until mixture is creamy and thick like paste but not too thick to stir.

Strain milk mixture to remove solids and slowly add to flour and butter mixture. Stir in cognac. Add shellfish, warming gently until fish is heated through.

Serves 4

Pirates Inn

Known for:
fresh seafood

Years in business: 26

Most requested table:
window view

Menu:
seafood, Continental

Chef: John Salerno

Chef's training:
Philadelphia's
Restaurant School and
self taught

**Chef's hobbies/
accomplishments:**
fishing

Chef's favorite foods:
Italian and seafood

**Chef's favorite
cookbook:**
Wenzel's *Outerbridges
Original Cookbook*

Bacalao Stew

Chef/Owner Guillermo Pernot
¡Pasión!, Philadelphia, PA

2 pounds bacalao fillets
¼ cup extra virgin olive oil
1 large Spanish onion, diced
2 large red bell peppers, diced
4 cloves garlic, minced
3 cups diced plum tomatoes (Canned is ok.)
1 teaspoon crushed red pepper flakes
Salt
2 tablespoons chopped fresh Italian parsley

Soak bacalao overnight in cold water; then cut into 6 portions.

Place bacalao in a large pot and cover with cold water. Bring to a boil, reduce heat, and simmer for 20 minutes. Drain and repeat the process two more times.

Heat olive oil in a heavy, ovenproof casserole dish. Add onions and sauté until lightly browned. Add red bell peppers and garlic. Cook for 2 to 3 minutes. Stir in tomatoes and red pepper flakes. Simmer for 30 minutes.

Add drained bacalao to stew, mixing gently so fish does not break apart. Cover and simmer for 20 minutes. Season with salt and parsley. Serve with steamed potatoes.

Serves 6

Philly Foodie Fact

Bacalao (baccalá in Italian) is dried salt cod. Choose segments with white — not yellow — flesh and skin attached. Wrap and store in an airtight container in a cool, dark place. Soaking softens the flesh and each time you change the water the salt is reduced. It is available in most specialty stores, including Antonio Freire Grocery in Philadelphia.

Bayou Oyster Stew

Executive Chef Patrick Bradley
Buckley's Tavern, Centreville, DE

2 leeks, white and light green part only
Salt and pepper
1 tablespoon oil
½ gallon oysters
½ cup butter plus 2 tablespoons
5 cups half-and-half
4 cups whole milk
4 tablespoons Worchestershire sauce
¾ teaspoon cayenne pepper
1½ teaspoons Old Bay Seasoning

Preheat oven to 425°. Cut leeks in half lengthwise; then crosswise. Wash thoroughly. Sprinkle with salt and pepper and oil. Roast until lightly golden, about 15 minutes.

Shuck oysters and strain to reserve oyster liquid. Scrape strainer with a rubber spatula to remove all liquid. Heat oyster liquid and ½ cup butter over a double boiler, stirring occasionally. Add remaining ingredients and simmer for 20 minutes. (Do not boil.) Add leeks and simmer for 20 minutes. Place oysters and remaining butter in a saucepan over medium heat and cook until butter is melted. Add oyster broth and bring to a strong simmer. Stew is done when oysters become plump.

Serves 8

Wine Notes

Recommended Wine: Jean-Marc Brocard Petit Chablis 1998 ($14.00)

Description: A flinty, crisp wine with notes of tropical fruits and citrus will effectively cut through the milk and spice of this dish.

Sommelier: John McNulty, Triangle Liquors

Vegetable Paella

Chef/Proprietor Alfonso Contrisciani
Opus 251, Philadelphia, PA

2 or 3 saffron threads
¼ cup hot water
2 teaspoons chopped garlic
2 teaspoons diced shallot
1 cup julienned red onion
4 cups short-grain brown rice, parcooked
2 cups cooked chickpeas
Salt and pepper
3 cups vegetable stock
2 tablespoons canola oil
1 cup mixed chopped spring vegetables, such as asparagus, blanched fava beans, pea
    shoots, morels
2 cups mixed sliced fennel, eggplant, and portobello mushrooms
½ cup slow roasted plum tomatoes
Red curry oil
Fennel fronds

Steep saffron in hot water. Sauté garlic, shallot, and onion in a large lidded sauce-pan. Stir in brown rice and chickpeas. Season to taste with salt and pepper. Add steeped saffron and 1½ cups vegetable stock. Cover and cook for about 3 to 5 minutes.

Heat canola oil in a sauté pan. Add vegetables and roasted tomatoes and sauté. Add remaining vegetable stock as needed to keep vegetables moist. Season to taste with salt and pepper.

Plate brown rice mixture and top with vegetables. Garnish with red curry oil and fennel fronds.

Serves 6

pastas

Penne Rigate

Executive Chef Ernie Varalli
Upstares at Varalli, Philadelphia, PA

12 ounces penne pasta
2 cups heavy cream
6 tablespoons diced plum tomatoes
2 ounces fresh mozzarella, cut into strips
2 ounces smoked mozzarella, cut into strips
2 ounces grated Parmesan
2 teaspoons chopped parsley

Cook penne al dente according to package directions. Drain.

Heat cream in a saucepan over medium heat. Cook until liquid is reduced by half. Add penne, tomatoes, fresh and smoked mozzarella, and Parmesan. Toss lightly so that mozzarella is heated through but not melted.

Garnish with parsley and serve immediately.

Serves 2

Wine Notes

Recommended Wine: Cascina val del Prete Barbera d'Alba 1997 ($13.00)

Description: Incredible intensity and richness with moderate tannin that ensure this wine will stand up to this hearty, cream-laden dish.

Sommelier: John McNulty, Triangle Liquors

Fettuccine Alla Boscaiola

Executive Chef Ernie Varalli
Upstares at Varalli, Philadelphia, PA

12 ounces fettuccine

6 tablespoons extra virgin olive oil

1 teaspoon chopped garlic

4 ounces wild mushrooms, sliced (Button, oyster, shiitake, and portobello mushrooms work well.)

8 sun-dried tomatoes, cut into strips

3 ounces Marsala wine

1 cup chicken stock

2 teaspoons chopped parsley

2 teaspoons chopped basil

2 tablespoons grated Romano cheese

2 tablespoons butter

Cook fettuccine al dente according to package directions. Drain and reserve.

Heat oil in a large skillet or sauté pan over medium heat. Add garlic and mushrooms and sauté for 1 to 2 minutes. Stir in sun-dried tomatoes and Marsala wine. Cook until liquid is reduced by half. Stir in chicken stock, parsley, basil, cheese, and butter. Cook until slightly thickened. Add fettuccine and toss to coat. Serve immediately.

Serves 2

Wine Notes

Recommended Wine: Delcetto d'Alba Del Pino 1998 ($13.50)

Description: A 6-hectare new estate with old vineyards situated in the Ovello cru of Barbaresco is responsible for this juicy, concentrated, delicious varietal Dolcetto wine. The young wine maker Renato Vacca blends the experience gained in ten years at the Cooperativa Produttori with inventive vinification techniques aimed at maximizing extraction and harmonization of tannis while keeping fragrant and very attractive fruit. This is a supple and full-bodied interpretation of a remarkably versatile variety.

Sommelier: Luca Mazzotti, Moore Brothers Wine Co.

Cavatappi Stir-Fry

Executive Chef Thomas Geneviva
Thommy G's Restaurant, Burlington, NJ

1 pound cavatappi or penne pasta
2 tablespoons olive oil
1 pound boneless, skinless chicken breasts, sliced and
    cubed
1 pound London broil, sliced and cubed
½ cup sliced red onions
2 cups sliced roasted red peppers
½ cup crumbled Gorgonzola cheese
1 cup freshly grated Pecorino Romano cheese
1 quart heavy cream
½ cup unsalted butter
2 tablespoons chopped fresh parsley
Salt and pepper

Cook pasta in boiling salted water according to package
directions.

Heat oil in a skillet. Add chicken and beef and sauté
until browned. Add red onions and sauté until transparent. Add roasted peppers, cheeses, and heavy cream.
Simmer for 5 minutes. Add butter and parsley. Season to
taste with salt and pepper. Toss with pasta and serve.

Serves 4

Thommy G's Restaurant

Known for:
restaurant is housed in a
bank built in 1929

Years in business: 1

Most requested table:
private vault table

Menu:
fine Italian cuisine with a
New Orleans flair

Chef: Thommy Geneviva

Chef's training:
Culinary Institute of
America

**Chef's hobbies/
accomplishments:**
playing pool/Star Chefs of
New Jersey 1999

Chef's favorite foods:
any kind of pasta

**Chef's favorite
cookbook:**
La Cucina, books by
Paul Prudhomme

Penne with Chicken, Broccoli, Artichokes, and Bacon

President Jack Kramer
Jack Kramer's Catering, Philadelphia, PA

1 pound skinless, boneless chicken breasts
2 teaspoons herbes de Provence
Salt and pepper
1 pound penne pasta
½ pound sliced bacon
1 teaspoon olive oil
1 can artichoke hearts (14 ounces), drained
2 cups chicken stock
Bouquet garni
2 cups heavy cream
6 ounces broccoli florets, blanched
Chopped fresh parsley

Preheat oven to 450°. Season chicken with herbes de Provence and salt and pepper. Roast chicken for 12 to 18 minutes. Cool slightly and cut into ¼-inch strips.

Cook pasta according to package directions and drain. Cook bacon until crisp and drain off fat. Roughly chop bacon and reserve. Heat olive oil in sauté pan over medium heat. Halve artichokes and sauté. Season with salt and pepper.

Heat chicken stock and bouquet garni in a saucepan over medium-high heat. Simmer until liquid is reduced by half. Stir in heavy cream. Raise heat and bring to a boil. Reduce heat and simmer until liquid is reduced by half. Remove and discard bouquet garni. Season to taste with salt and pepper.

Combine chicken, pasta, artichokes, and broccoli in a large serving bowl. Pour cream sauce over pasta mixture and toss to combine. Top with chopped bacon and parsley.

Serves 6

Chef's Note

The term, bouquet garni, refers to a bunch of herbs (such as the classic parsley, thyme, and bay leaf) that are tied together or wrapped in cheesecloth. The herbs are used to flavor soups, stews, and broths. Because it's tied or bagged, it's easy to remove from the pan.

Penne Smoked Chicken

Executive Chef Shawn Sollberger
Davio's, Philadelphia, PA

1 Spanish onion, diced
1 clove garlic, minced
1 shallot, minced
¼ cup white wine
2 pints heavy cream
3 sprigs thyme, destemmed and chopped
1 tablespoon butter
12 ounces smoked chicken breast or thigh, julienned
4 ounces sun-dried tomatoes, julienned
1 leek, julienned
4 ounces spinach, blanched and squeezed dry
1 pound penne pasta, cooked al dente
¼ cup grated Romano cheese
Chopped fresh Italian parsley
Salt and pepper

Davio's

Years in business: 1

Menu:
Northern Italian
steakhouse

Chef: Shawn Sollberger

Chef's training:
International Culinary
Academy, Pittsburgh, PA

**Chef's hobbies/
accomplishments:**
dining out with my wife,
outdoor activities with my
dog

Chef's favorite foods:
Indian, Vietnamese, BBQ,
burgers

**Chef's favorite
cookbook:**
*Thrill of the Grill, Your
Place or Mine*

Sauté onion, half of minced garlic, and half of shallot in a skillet over medium-high heat until brown. Add wine and cook until liquid is reduced by three-quarters. Stir in cream and thyme. Reduce heat to medium and simmer for 20 minutes. (Cream should start to thicken.)

In a separate pan, heat butter over medium-high heat. Add remaining garlic and shallot and sauté until brown. Add smoked chicken, sun-dried tomatoes, and leek. Sauté for 2 minutes. Add spinach and cream reduction. (If sauce gets too thick, add a little more cream.)

Toss in penne pasta, Romano cheese, and parsley. Season to taste with salt and pepper. Serve garnished with additional Romano cheese and parsley leaves.

Serves 4

Rosemary Chicken over Pasta

Executive Chef Daniel D. Bethard
Iron Hill Brewery and Restaurant, West Chester, PA

12 ounces tomato linguine or your favorite pasta
5 or 6 boneless chicken breasts, cut into strips
1 cup all-purpose flour
6 tablespoons vegetable oil
2 cups sliced mushrooms, such as crimini, shiitake, and
   oyster
1 tablespoon minced fresh garlic
6 ounces sherry wine, pale dry
1 cup chicken broth
1 cup mushroom broth
1 tablespoon chopped fresh rosemary
1 tablespoon lemon juice (fresh squeezed, if possible)
10 tablespoons salted butter
Pinch each salt and pepper

Iron Hill

Known for:
award-winning beers and
Thursday cuisine nights

Years in business: 3

Most requested table:
booths

Menu: regional American

Chef: Daniel Bethard

Chef's training:
self educated and
restaurant trained

**Chef's hobbies/
accomplishments:**
music, playing sports/not
paying for an education
and becoming the chef
that I am

Chef's favorite foods:
inventive seafood, Thai,
authentic Mexican

**Chef's favorite
cookbook:**
Bold America and
Mexican Kitchen

Bring salted pasta water to a boil and cook linguine according to package directions.

Meanwhile, dredge chicken in flour and shake off excess. Heat oil in a large sauté pan. When oil begins to shimmer, add chicken and mushrooms. Brown chicken on one side; then turn and continue cooking. Add garlic and sauté briefly. Deglaze pan with sherry wine. Add both broths. Bring to a boil and cook until liquid is reduced by one-quarter.

Add rosemary and lemon juice and cook for 1 minute. Add butter and salt and pepper. Sauce will begin to thicken. Taste and add additional salt, pepper, lemon, or rosemary, if desired.

Divide prepared pasta between 4 plates. Place chicken strips on linguine and cover with sauce.

Serves 4

Herb Battered Soft-shell Crabs over Spinach Linguini

Executive Chef Alfonso Contrisciani
circa, Philadelphia, PA

6 eggs
¼ cup chopped parsley
¼ cup snipped chives
¼ cup destemmed and finely sliced basil leaves
1½ teaspoons salt
1 teaspoon white pepper
¼ cup grated Parmesan cheese
½ cup heavy cream
8 jumbo soft-shell crabs, cleaned and dressed
Seasoned flour
Olive oil
1 pound fresh spinach linguini, cooked al dente
Broccolini and Plum Tomato Sauce (Recipe appears on page 295.)

Combine eggs, parsley, chives, basil, salt, pepper, and Parmesan in a mixing bowl. Whip in heavy cream and reserve in a cool place.

Preheat oven to 300°. Dredge crabs in flour and then dip in egg mixture. Heat oil in a nonstick sauté pan over medium heat. Add crabs to pan and sauté until each is golden brown. Transfer to a baking sheet and bake for 10 to 12 minutes.

Serve crabs over cooked pasta and top with sauce. Garnish with additional chopped parsley, if desired.

Serves 4

Wine Notes

Recommended Wine: Castello di Monterinaldi Chianti Classico Riserva 1995 ($15.00)

Description: Rich and supple with plenty of earth notes, it will combine well with the Italian elements of this dish.

Sommelier: John McNulty, Triangle Liquors

Jazzy Lasagna

Chef Jillian Louis
Severino Pasta Manufacturing Company, Westmont, NJ

½ cup olive oil
1 pound lamb sausage
2 quarts ricotta cheese
3 eggs, beaten
¼ cup grated Romano cheese
Salt and pepper
1½ quarts fresh Severino tomato sauce
2 pounds fresh Severino Garlic Basil Lasagna pasta sheets
1 jar Sonoma Muffaletta mix
1 box frozen spinach, thawed and drained
1 pound Severino homemade meatballs, cut in half
Fresh basil leaves
6 ounces fresh mozzarella balls, sliced in half

Place 2 tablespoons olive oil in a sauté pan. Add sausage and sear on all sides. Let cool and cut into thin slices.

Combine ricotta cheese, eggs, and Romano cheese. Season with salt and pepper.

Preheat oven to 350°. Cover bottom of a lasagna pan with remaining oil. Pour in 1 cup tomato sauce. Layer one sheet of fresh pasta. Evenly spread half of ricotta mixture on pasta. Spread half of muffaletta mix over cheese, followed by half of spinach. Add a layer of sausage and meatballs. Sprinkle on some basil leaves. Cover with a second layer of pasta and then 2 cups sauce. Repeat with a layer each of remaining ricotta mixture, muffaletta mix, spinach, sausage and meatballs, and basil. Finish with a final layer of pasta. Cover with remaining tomato sauce and fresh mozzarella. Garnish with basil leaves.

Cover with foil and bake for 45 to 60 minutes. Cool slightly before serving so that lasagna will "set" and slice easily.

Serves 6 to 8

Severino Pasta Manufacturing Company

Years in business: 29

Chef: Jillian Louis

Chef's training: graduated from The Restaurant School back in the dark ages

Chef's hobbies/ accomplishments: I am part of a group that recreates life in the Middle Ages. When the need arises, I put on 65 pounds of armor and "become" a medieval warrior.

Chef's favorite foods: goat vindaloo, eel sushi, collard greens, macaroni and cheese

Chef's favorite cookbook: *Taste of New Orleans*

Timballo alla Teramamo

Chef/Owner Anthony Stella
L'Osteria Cucina Italiana, Wilmington, DE

2 pounds ground veal
1 teaspoon salt
1 teaspoon garlic powder
3 tablespoons chopped parsley
2 eggs, beaten
1¼ cups grated Pecorino Romano cheese
1 cup plus 3 tablespoons breadcrumbs
Marinara Sauce (Recipe appears on page 295.)
Fried Zucchini (Recipe appears on page 215.)
L'Osteria Crêpes (Recipe appears on page 248.)
Sautéed Spinach (Recipe appears on page 211.)
20 ounces fresh mozzarella, cut into ½-inch cubes
6 eggs
½ cup heavy cream

Preheat oven to 350°. Mix veal, salt, garlic powder, parsley, eggs, ¼ cup grated cheese, and 1 cup breadcrumbs in a mixing bowl. Spread on a cookie sheet to form one giant burger. Bake for 30 minutes. Cool and cut into 1-inch cubes. Mix with marinara sauce.

Cut zucchini into 1-inch cubes. Butter a 12 x 10-inch baking dish and sprinkle with remaining breadcrumbs. Cover bottom of dish with 4 crêpes, overlapping as you go. Spread one-quarter of spinach into a thin layer with your hands. Follow with thin layers of one-quarter amounts of veal cubes, zucchini cubes, grated cheese, mozzarella, and egg-cream mixture. Repeat process, beginning with crêpes, three more times, pressing down each layer with hands before beginning another.

Finally, cover with remaining crêpes and brush with remaining egg wash. Bake in reheated 350° oven for 60 minutes. Allow to cool for 15 minutes before cutting. Serve as is or with tomato or white sauce. At the restaurant, we use both.

Serves 8 to 10

L'Osteria Cucina Italiana

Known for: pasta gnocchi

Years in business: 5

Most requested table: #3

Menu:
multiregional Italian specializing in Abruzzo region

Chef: Anthony Stella

Chef's training:
valedictorian graduate from The Restaurant School in Philadelphia

Chef's hobbies/ accomplishments:
cooking/guest chef on the PBS series "Ciao Italia" with MaryAnn Esposito

Chef's favorite foods:
pasta, Southern food,

Chef's favorite cookbook:
The Classic Italian Cookbook, The Cake Bible

Chef's Note

From one hillside town to another in Abruzzo, great debates take place among the women who do the cooking regarding cooking technique and terminology. I was present one day in Ofena, Italy, while my grandmother and three of her dearest and oldest friends argued heatedly over the proper way to make gnocchi. In my restaurant, customers always remind me how their grandmothers made ravioli, gnocchi, or lasagne. I guess there are no definitive answers to these all important questions except that the final products, no matter what they are called or how they are made, are always unbelievably delicious and as diverse as are personalities.

The same goes for timballo or timpano or lasagne or pasticcio — whatever you want to call it. Very basically, they are all molded and baked pasta dishes, often with the addition of meat, cheese, and vegetable. In Ofena, one lady will call it lasagna while her next door neighbor will call it timballo. I believe, however, that there is a difference. In my opinion, lasagne are layered pasta dishes while timballi are a celebration and the mother of all lasagne. I also believe that timballi came about from the necessity of the often poor southern Italians to use up leftovers so as to stretch out their meals.

Timballo Alla Teramano is a dish taught to me by my cousin's wife, Rosalba, who is from Teramo, a relatively large city in Abruzzo. Undoubtedly, this recipe was handed down by many generations, and I consider myself very blessed to have learned it and to be able to share it.

The recipe, on its face, seems quite complicated and time-consuming, but many of the steps may be done ahead of time. In fact, this dish is very well suited to entertaining. It can be prepared well ahead of time and put in the oven to bake while you enjoy arguing with your friends over how you make your gnocchi. It is also substantial enough for a one-course meal, served with a salad and dessert.

vegetarian entrees

Breaded Cabbage Cutlet

Chef/Owner Fritz Blank
Deux Cheminées, Philadelphia, PA

1 medium-size head white or savoy cabbage (Look for a 2- to 3-pound head about 6 inches in diameter.)
2 quarts water
1 tablespoon salt
1 to 2 cups peanut oil
½ cup all-purpose flour
Salt and pepper
2 eggs
2 tablespoons water or milk
1½ cups fresh white breadcrumbs
Creamy Cheddar Sauce with White Wine (Recipe appears on page 293.)
Cherry tomatoes

Slice cabbage into quarters or sixths through the core so that each slice has the core holding it together. Bring water and salt to a rolling boil in a 5-quart pot. Place cabbage into boiling water and cook until just tender, about 4 to 6 minutes. Drain cabbage well and place on a clean cloth or paper towels. Cover with a large tray or sheet pan and weigh it down with bricks or large-size containers of canned goods. (This pressing is an important step.) Allow cabbage to cool completely.

Heat oil in a large, preferably cast-iron, skillet over medium-high heat. Season flour with salt and pepper and place in a shallow bowl. Beat eggs with water or milk and place in a separate shallow bowl. Place breadcrumbs in a third shallow bowl or plate. Dust cabbage cutlets with flour and pat off excess. Dip into egg wash and shake off excess. Coat with fresh breadcrumbs. Place breaded cutlets into hot oil and fry until golden brown, about 3 to 4 minutes on each side. Drain on paper towels to remove fat. Serve hot napped with cheese sauce and garnish with cherry tomatoes.

Serves 4 to 6

Chef's Note

Breaded and fried, this "meaty" main course is usually a welcome respite from the steamed, stewed, boiled, and raw items which so often dominate vegetarian menus. Almost any sauce suitable for veal, chicken, turkey, or even steak can be a candidate for this dish — provided, of course, that no meat stocks are used.

Goat Cheese Tart

Chef/Owner Christopher Todd
Fourchette 110, Wayne, PA

2 cups all-purpose flour
6 ounces cold butter
¼ teaspoon salt
⅓ cup cold water
½ yellow onion, diced small
1 tablespoon chopped garlic
3 cups heavy cream
1 pound goat cheese
6 egg yokes
Salt and pepper

Place flour, butter, and salt in a food processor. Start machine and slowly pour water in until mixture forms a ball. Use hands to form dough into a cylinder. (Do not overwork it.) Let dough rest for 30 minutes in refrigerator.

Preheat oven to 350°. Slice dough into ¼-inch rounds and then roll into ⅛-inch-thick circles. Press into individual tart shells. Bake for 10 minutes.

Sauté onion and garlic lightly over medium heat. Add heavy cream and simmer for 5 to 10 minutes. Add goat cheese and stir to thoroughly combine. Remove from heat. In a separate bowl, whisk egg yolks. Slowly add egg yolks to goat cheese mixture. Season with salt and pepper. Ladle into tart shells. Bake for 12 to 15 minutes.

Serves 8

Fourchette 110

Known for:
hip atmosphere on the Main Line

Years in business: 1

Most requested table:
our custom made banquette

Menu:
modern American grill

Chef: Christopher Todd

Mushroom Roll

Chef/Owner Olivier De Saint Martin
Dock Street Brasserie, Philadelphia, PA

2 tablespoons butter
2 cups sliced mushrooms (at least three varieties)
1 shallot, minced
Salt and pepper
2 tablespoons tomato sauce
2 ounces Swiss cheese, grated
2 tablespoons chopped parsley
8 sheets phyllo dough
Clarified or melted butter
Parmesan cheese

Heat butter in a large skillet until foamy. Add mushrooms and cook in bubbling butter. Add shallot and season with salt and pepper. When mushrooms are brown and dried of natural water, add tomato sauce and cook for 1 minute. Add Swiss cheese and turn heat off. Mix very well and let cool a bit. Add parsley.

Preheat oven to 350°. Lay flat 4 sheets phyllo dough on a clean work surface. Brush each sheet with clarified or melted butter and place carefully in a stack. Place half of mushroom mixture on lower edge of dough. Roll into a cylinder. Brush top with butter and sprinkle with Parmesan cheese. Repeat with remaining phyllo and mushroom mixture. Place seam sides down on a baking sheet and bake for 15 to 20 minutes. Use a serrated knife to cut ½-inch-wide slices. Serve hot.

Serves 4

Wine Notes

Recommended Wine: Sancerre Domaine du Carrou ($16.50)

Description: The best Sauvignon Blanc in the world is produced in Sancerre at the western end of the Loire valley. The subdistrict of Bué, a hamlet where 400 people live and 350 are involved in the making of wine, is famous for producing the richest and fullest Sancerres. This is wine of very elegant bouquet and palate, with mineral and citrusy flavors that produce a very fleshy mouthfeel and leave a persistent and pleasant aftertaste.

Sommelier: Megan Shawver, Moore Brothers Wine Co.

Vegetable Roulade

Executive Chef Andrew Maloney
Nodding Head Brewery & Restaurant, Philadelphia, PA

1 tablespoon olive oil
¼ cup EACH finely diced zucchini, yellow squash,
   Roma tomato, crimini mushrooms, baby spinach,
   and broccoli florets
1 tablespoon finely diced scallions
2 cloves garlic
2 tablespoons chopped fresh sage
18 sheets phyllo dough
Melted butter
1 egg, beaten
Smoked Tomato Sauce (Recipe appears on page 294.)
Chopped chives or fresh oregano

Heat oil in a large sauté pan. Add vegetables, scallions, garlic, and sage. Sauté for 2 to 3 minutes to sweat out some excess moisture. (Don't overcook or the roulade will be very soggy.) Remove vegetables from pan with a slotted spoon and reserve.

Preheat oven to 325°. Lay 1 phyllo sheet out on a clean work surface. Brush with melted butter and cover with another sheet. Repeat until you have a stack of 6 sheets. Place one-third vegetable mixture along lower edge of stack, leaving a 1-inch margin on each side. Roll to resemble a sushi roll or a log. Repeat process two more times with remaining dough and filling.

Place the 3 logs on a baking sheet and brush with egg wash. Bake for 15 to 20 minutes.

Slice logs at an angle into thirds. Spoon 2 ounces smoked tomato sauce into centers of plates. Arrange 3 slices roulade on sauce. Garnish with chives or fresh oregano.

Serves 2 to 3

Nodding Head Brewery & Restaurant

Known for:
collection of nodding head
dolls; brewery

Years in business: 1

Most requested table:
the church pews in
nonsmoking

Menu:
American and vegetarian
and brewpub

Chef: Andrew Maloney

Chef's training:
Barbados and Philly

**Chef's hobbies/
accomplishments:**
creating flavorful and
beautiful vegetarian meals

Chef's favorite foods:
jerked chicken and other
island food

Chef's favorite cookbook:
Local Flavor

Portobello "Bruschetta"

Owner John J. Garagozzo
Blue Moon Restaurant & Café, Haddon Heights, NJ

4 large portobello mushrooms
2 cups white wine
6 tablespoons olive oil
4 cloves garlic, minced
2 small shallots, minced
2 pints grape tomatoes, halved
½ teaspoon dry or 1 teaspoon fresh thyme
8 basil leaves, chopped
Salt and pepper
1 cup grated cheese, such as provolone or Asiago
Parsley

Place portobellos in a shallow bowl. Combine 1½ cups wine, 4 tablespoons olive oil, and half of minced garlic. Pour over portobellos and marinate for 30 to 60 minutes.

Preheat grill or broiler. Heat remaining olive oil in a sauté pan over medium-high heat. Add shallots and sweat a few minutes. Add remaining garlic and cook until light gold in color. Add tomatoes and cook until tender but not saucy. Add remaining wine, thyme, and basil. Cook until alcohol is burned off. Season to taste with salt and pepper.

Grill or broil portobellos, being careful not to burn them. Remove from grill. Top with grated cheese and melt under broiler.

Top with tomato mixture and garnish with parsley.

Serves 4

Riot of Wild Mushrooms

Executive Chef/Co-owner Jack Gudin
The Black Walnut, Doylestown, PA

¼ cup hoisin sauce
¼ cup low-sodium soy sauce
¼ cup balsamic vinegar
¼ cup water
2 tablespoons Worcestershire sauce
1 tablespoon honey
1 teaspoon rice wine vinegar
1 teaspoon lemon juice
Dash of sherry vinegar
¼ teaspoon minced fresh ginger
¼ teaspoon minced garlic
Pinch of red pepper flakes
1 to 2 tablespoons sesame oil
4 medium portobello mushrooms, cleaned
2 handfuls mushrooms (shiitake, oyster, cremini) cleaned
Minced fresh garlic and ginger, optional

Combine first 12 ingredients in a covered jar. Store covered in refrigerator overnight or 24 hours.

Heat sesame oil in a skillet over high heat. Add mushrooms, garlic, and ginger and sauté until brown and caramelized. Whisk refrigerated sauce ingredients to recombine. Add enough sauce to cover bottom of pan. Heat through. Serve with sturdy greens.

Serves 2 as an entree
Serves 4 as an appetizer or side dish

Bavarian Spinach Dumplings with Bechamel Sauce

Executive Chef Harry Burns
Ludwig's Garten, Philadelphia, PA

2 loaves French, Levian, or Alsatian bread
2 cups milk
2 bags spinach, stemmed and cooked
2 white onions, minced
2 tablespoons garlic powder
1 tablespoon ground caraway seed
1 tablespoon tarragon
1 tablespoon marjoram
Salt and pepper
4 eggs
1 cup breadcrumbs
½ cup flour
Bechamel Sauce (Recipe appears on page 292.)

Break bread into small pieces. Place pieces in a large mixing bowl and let sit, uncovered, for 2 days until stale.

When ready to prepare dumplings, scald milk and pour over stale bread. Let stand for 20 minutes. Grind bread mixture until well blended, using a mixer set on medium speed.

Sauté spinach, onions, and seasonings until onions are translucent. Add to bread mixture. Add eggs and mix well. Add breadcrumbs and flour.

Dip hands in cold water; then form mixture into 3-ounce balls. (Balls should be bigger than a golf ball but smaller than a baseball.)

Bring a large pot of salted water to a boil. Roll balls in additional flour and place in boiling water. Cook until balls float. Serve hot with bechamel sauce.

Serves 4 to 6

Potato, Spinach, and Mushroom Pierogies

Chef Marie Jarzenski
Warsaw Cafe, Philadelphia, PA

1½ cups unsifted flour
1 whole egg plus 4 egg yolks
1 tablespoon sour cream
¼ cup cold water
7 medium potatoes, peeled, boiled, and drained
2 tablespoons butter
½ medium onion, minced
¼ teaspoon minced garlic
Handful of fresh spinach, coarsely chopped
¼ pound mushrooms, coarsely chopped
Pinch of dried thyme
1 tablespoon grated Parmesan cheese
Salt and pepper
1 tablespoon oil
Sour cream
Chopped scallions

Combine flour, egg, egg yolks, and sour cream in a deep 3- to 4-quart mixing bowl. Gradually stir in water until mixture sticks together. (You may not need to use all the water.) Turn mixture onto a floured work surface and knead for 2 to 3 minutes until smooth and pliable. Wrap in plastic wrap and refrigerate for 20 minutes.

Mash potatoes and set aside. Melt butter in a saucepan over medium heat. Add onions, garlic, spinach, and mushrooms and sauté until onions are transparent. Sprinkle in thyme. Combine spinach mixture with mashed potatoes. Stir in Parmesan cheese and salt and pepper to taste.

Unwrap dough and place on a floured work surface. Form dough into ½-inch round balls. Dust balls with flour and roll out to flatten. Place 1 full teaspoon potato filling in middle of each pancake. Fold in half and pinch edges together to seal tightly.

Bring 3 quarts water to a boil in a large pot. Drop dough balls into water and reduce heat to medium. Cook until all pierogies rise to the top. Strain and rinse gently with cold water. Heat oil in a large skillet over medium heat. Add pierogies and brown on all sides. Serve garnished with sour cream and scallions. (Dough and filling may be prepared up to 3 days in advance and refrigerated.)

Yields 15 to 18 pierogies

Classic Polenta

Proprietor Antonio "Toto" Schiavone
Toto, Philadelphia, PA

½ cup blended oil
1 cup diced white onion
2 tablespoons finely diced garlic
1 gallon milk
1 quart chicken stock
¼ cup chopped parsley
1½ tablespoons chopped oregano
Salt and cayenne pepper
4 cups cornmeal
1 cup ricotta cheese
¾ cup grated Parmesan cheese

Heat oil in a saucepan over medium heat. Add onion and garlic and sauté until translucent. Stir in milk, stock, and herbs and bring to a boil. Add salt and cayenne pepper to taste. Slowly add cornmeal, whisking constantly to maintain a creamy texture and avoid lumps. (This should take 5 to 8 minutes.)

Remove from heat and let stand for 3 to 4 minutes. Fold in ricotta and Parmesan cheeses.

Serves 4 to 8

Chef's Note

Serve polenta hot and either plain or topped with tomato sauce. Or press into a loaf pan, chill, slice into wedges, and grill. Delicious topped with sautéed broccoli rabe or diced hot or sweet Italian sausage.

Risotto Primaverile

Executive Chef Gino Sena
La Famiglia, Philadelphia, PA

1 large eggplant, cut into cubes
Salt
½ cup olive oil
3 tablespoons salted butter
1 Spanish or white onion, diced
½ pound champignon mushrooms, cleaned, dried, and
   thinly sliced
2 ripe tomatoes, seeded and cut into cubes
Salt and pepper
4 cups Arborio rice
4 cups water
½ cup Parmigiano cheese

Place eggplant cubes in a colander. Cover with salt and
let stand, covered, for at least 30 minutes so that all
water drains out. Rinse eggplant well and set aside.

Heat olive oil and 1 tablespoon butter in a skillet over
medium heat. Add onion and sauté for 5 minutes. Stir
in eggplant and mushrooms. Add tomatoes and salt and
pepper to taste. Cover and cook for 15 to 20 minutes.

Meanwhile, boil rice in water, covered, until al dente,
about 15 to 20 minutes. Drain rice and rinse under cold
water.

Heat oven to 150°. Line a baking sheet with parchment
paper. Spread rice over paper. Cover with another sheet
of parchment paper. Bake for 15 minutes. (The rice
should be dry when it comes out of the oven.) Transfer
rice to a serving bowl. Stir in remaining butter. Gently
stir in vegetable mixture and cheese. Buon appettito.

Serves 4

La Famiglia

Known for:
wine cellar, food

Years in business: 24

Most requested table:
12

Menu:
regional Italian

Chef: Gino Sena

Chef's training:
in Italy

**Chef's hobbies/
accomplishments:**
tennis

Risotto with Wild Leeks, Fresh Herbs, and Goat Cheese

Executive Chef Chris Scott
The Latest Dish, Philadelphia, PA

6 tablespoons butter
1 cup chopped wild leeks
1 cup chopped onion
1 cup chopped carrot
1 teaspoon chopped garlic
2 cups Arborio rice
3 cups vegetable or chicken stock
¾ cup crumbled goat cheese
¾ cup chopped thyme, parsley, and rosemary
½ cup heavy cream
Salt and pepper

Melt butter in a large skillet. Add leeks, onions, carrots, and garlic and sauté until onions are transparent. Add rice and stir to coat with butter. Cook until rice is toasty. Add 1½ cups stock and stir continuously until liquid is evaporated. Add remaining stock and stir continuously until liquid is evaporated. Add remaining ingredients and cook until rice is creamy and soft.

Serves 4

The Latest Dish

Known for:
Chef Chris Scott's aphrodisiac cocktail party

Years in business: 3

Most requested table:
#1 — the chef's table

Menu:
upscale comfort food

Chef: Chris Scott

Chef's training:
The French Culinary Institute

Chef's hobbies/ accomplishments:
photography/top 200 finish in 1998 Boase D'Or

Chef's favorite foods:
cheeseburgers, sushi, seafood, good red wine

Chef's favorite cookbook:
Cooking with Patrick Clark, Vegetables by Charlie Trotter

Spanish Risotto with Charred Tomato Coulis

Executive Chef Daniel D. Bethard
Iron Hill Brewery and Restaurant, West Chester, PA

½ cup salted butter
¼ cup diced Spanish onion
1 large ear white corn, kernels only
1 teaspoon minced garlic
¼ teaspoon Spanish paprika
¼ pound cooked chorizo, chopped
4 saffron threads
3 cups Arborio rice
1 cup sherry
6 cups vegetable or chicken broth, hot
4 ounces Manchego cheese, freshly grated
Salt and pepper
Charred Tomato Coulis (Recipe appears on page 298.)

Melt ¼ cup butter in a 14-inch skillet over medium heat. Add onion, corn kernels, and garlic and sauté for 4 minutes. Add paprika, chorizo, saffron, and rice. Stir to coat all ingredients with butter. Add sherry and cook until liquid is reduced by half. Add 2 cups hot chicken broth and cook, stirring frequently, until liquid is reduced by three-quarters. Repeat process two times until all broth has been added. Add remaining butter and 2 ounces cheese. Stir until butter is incorporated into rice. Season to taste with salt and pepper. Spoon onto plates and top each serving with ¼ ounce cheese. Ladle coulis around risotto and serve.

Serves 8 as an appetizer
Serves 4 as an entree

Philly Foodie Fact

Manchego is Spain's most famous cheese. Originally made only from the milk of the Manchego sheep that grazed on the plains of La Mancha, you can find it locally at Fresh Fields and Chestnut Hill Cheese Shop, among others.

Horseradish Mashed Potatoes with Spaghetti Vegetables and Scallion Butter Sauce

Executive Chef John Anderson
Solaris Grille, Philadelphia, PA

1 medium carrot
1 medium zucchini
1 medium yellow squash
2 Idaho potatoes, peeled and quartered
¾ cup heavy cream
2 tablespoons prepared horseradish
1¼ cups unsweetened butter
Salt and Pepper
1 cup spinach
1 bunch scallions, finely chopped
4 tablespoons white wine vinegar
2 tablespoons tomato paste

Use a mandolin or box grater to cut carrot, zucchini, and yellow squash into 4-inch-long and ⅛-inch-wide sticks. Mix together and reserve.

Place potatoes in a saucepan with a small amount of salt and enough water to cover. Bring to a boil and cook until potatoes are tender. Strain.

Mash potatoes and return to saucepan. Add ¼ cup cream, horseradish, and 2 tablespoons butter. Heat, stirring occasionally, until ingredients are incorporated. Season to taste with salt and pepper. Keep warm.

Melt 2 tablespoons butter in a skillet. Add vegetable mixture and spinach. Sauté until tender. Reserve and keep warm.

Place ½ cup butter and scallions in a food processor. Pulse until completely mixed and butter is green.

Place ¼ cup heavy cream and 2 tablespoons vinegar in a small saucepan. Place ¼ cup heavy cream, 2 tablespoons vinegar, and tomato paste in a separate saucepan. Heat

Solaris Grille

Known for:
outdoor patio

Years in business: 2

Menu:
American grille

Chef: John Anderson

Chef's training:
CIA

Chef's hobbies/ accomplishments:
my son Danny (age 4) and daughter Josie (10 months)

Chef's favorite foods:
French and Asian

Chef's favorite cookbook:
Charlie Trotter's

both pans over medium heat until mixtures are both reduced by half. Whisk remaining ½ cup butter into pot with tomato paste mixture. Whisk scallion butter into pot with cream and vinegar mixture. Season each with salt and pepper.

Ladle a small portion of each sauce onto plates. Top with mashed potatoes and vegetables.

Serves 4

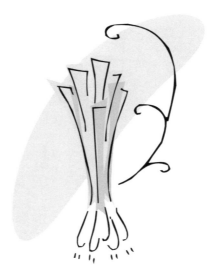

Chef's Note

We serve this dish with grilled salmon at Solaris Grille, and it has become our signature dish. If you'd like to serve it this way as well, grill the fish last — right before you are ready to serve — so it doesn't overcook.

poultry

Fox Briar Chicken

Executive Chef Joseph Becker
Cock 'n Bull in Peddler's Village, Lahaska, PA

4 skinless, boneless chicken breasts
Flour
1 ounce sesame seed oil
½ cup julienned onion
½ cup sliced mushrooms
2 tablespoons chopped garlic
4 ounces sherry
4 ounces chicken stock
4 ounces oyster sauce
8 ounces Monterey Jack cheese, sliced

Dredge chicken in flour. Heat oil in a large sauté pan over medium-high heat. Add chicken and sauté for about 5 minutes. Turn chicken and add onion, mushrooms, and garlic. Deglaze pan with sherry and cook until liquid is reduced by half. Stir in chicken stock and oyster sauce. Cover chicken with cheese slices. Serve when cheese has melted.

Serves 4

Cock 'n Bull

Known for:
quaint country setting

Years in business: 38

Most requested table:
window seat with view of gardens

Menu:
American

Chef: Joseph Becker

Chef's training:
Johnson & Wales University

Chef's hobbies/ accomplishments:
cooking for Chaine dinners, food competitions

Chef's favorite foods:
Italian, eclectic, all food!

Chef's favorite cookbook:
CookWise, Classic and Contemporary Italian Cooking

Chicken Tapenade

Executive Chef Eric Hall
La Campagne, Cherry Hill, NJ

4 boneless chicken breasts (8 ounces each)
Flour
2 tablespoons olive oil
1 small onion, minced
2 teaspoons chopped garlic
1 small red pepper, finely diced
½ cup pitted and chopped black olives
4 anchovy fillets, minced
2 teaspoons chopped parsley
1 tablespoon capers, rinsed
1 teaspoon chopped fresh thyme
1 teaspoon crushed red pepper
¼ cup water
Salt and pepper

Dredge chicken in flour, shaking off excess. Heat oil in a large sauté pan over medium-high heat. Place chicken in pan and cook until golden on one side. Turn breasts and add onion, garlic, and red pepper. Cook for 2 minutes. Add remaining ingredients, except salt and pepper, and simmer until liquid has evaporated and chicken is cooked through, about 5 to 8 minutes. Season to taste with salt and pepper and serve.

Serves 4

Wine Notes

Recommended Wine: Les Bau de Provence Mas de la Dame "Cuvée Gourmande" 1998 ($11.00)

Description: Located in the idyllic village of Les Baux, this beautiful estate has captured the imagination of many travelers, including Vincent Van Gogh who immortalized the eastern side of the *mas* in a 1889 painting. Organically grown Grenache, Carignan, and Syrah provide a bright, fruity wine that offers a good amount of spices and a clean, fragrant finish and aftertaste.

Sommelier: Dale Belville, Moore Brothers Wine Co.

Chicken Frutta Secca

Executive Chef Frank Buchler
Viana's Italian Cuisine, Voorhees, NJ

4 boneless chicken breasts
4 tablespoons flour
3 tablespoon oil (or butter)
½ cup dried fruit (raisins, berries, or apricots)
1 tablespoon whole butter
1½ ounces Marsala wine
1 ounce chicken, veal, or vegetable stock
Salt and pepper

Dust chicken with flour. Heat oil in a skillet over medium heat. Add chicken and
sauté until brown on both sides. Add fruit and whole butter and sauté briefly. Add
Marsala wine and stock. Continue cooking until liquid thickens. Season to taste
with salt and pepper. Serve alone or over rice.

Serves 4

Wine Notes

Recommended Wine: Linardi, Ciró Rosso Superiore 1997 ($10.50)

Description: This intriguing wine from the Calabria region of southern
Italy combines ripe concentrated and spicy flavors with a food-friendly
degree of acidity and full body. From 100% old vines of
Gaplioppo grape (an antique and rare grape variety
known since Ancient Greece as Cremissa and served to
Olympians to celebrate their victories), this wine is
perfect for aged *provolone* and *caciocavallo* cheeses,
balsamic vinegar reductions, and Mediterranean
dishes like *penne all'arrabbiata* and *pasta puttanesca*.

Sommelier: Christian Lane, Moore Brothers Wine Co.

Rosemary-scented Chicken Breasts with Blueberry Gastrique

Executive Chef Paul L. Henderson
Rembrandt's Restaurant and Bar, Philadelphia, PA

4 large skinless, boneless chicken breasts
1 stalk fresh rosemary, stripped and chopped
Salt and pepper
Flour
1 tablespoon vegetable oil
Blueberry Gastrique (see recipe)

Rub chicken breasts with rosemary and salt and pepper. Lightly coat with flour. Heat oil in skillet and sauté chicken until golden brown.

Arrange on serving plate and top with blueberry gastrique. Serve immediately with wild rice or mashed potatoes and the seasonal vegetable of your choice.

Serves 4

Blueberry Gastrique

1 pint blueberries, rinsed and drained
1 cup sugar
1 cup balsamic vinegar
½ cup water

Place all ingredients in a deep saucepan and bring to a boil. Reduce heat and simmer for 20 minutes or until sauce thickens to a glaze consistency.

Wine Notes

Recommended Wine: Gasiner, Chinon VV 1997 ($14.50)

Description: Low yielding 50-year-old vines of Cabernet Franc (locally known as Breton) give aromatically complex fruit that is carefully vinified in large wood barrels to produce a very attractive wine with the scents and flavors of the Loire valley.

Sommelier: Luca Mazzotti, Moore Brothers Wine Co.

Barbecued Chicken Breasts

Director of Culinary Arts Joseph E. Shilling
The Art Institute of Philadelphia, Philadelphia, PA

2 tablespoons oil
½ pound bacon, finely chopped
1 cup chopped onion
2 tablespoons chopped garlic
1 cup ketchup
1 cup chili sauce
¼ cup molasses
¼ cup honey
1 tablespoon chili powder
1 teaspoon Tabasco sauce
1 tablespoon Worcestershire sauce
1 teaspoon thyme
Salt and pepper
10 skinless, boneless chicken breast halves

Heat oil in a large sauté pan. Add bacon and cook until crisp. Stir in onion and garlic and cook until tender. Add remaining ingredients, except chicken. Simmer for 30 minutes. Transfer to a shallow bowl. Marinate chicken for at least 60 minutes.

Grill or bake in a preheated 400° oven for 6 to 8 minutes per side, basting with sauce.

Serves 10

Moroccan Chicken

Chef/Manager Nina Kouchacji
Marrakesh, Philadelphia, PA

1 whole chicken (approximately 4 pounds)
2 tablespoons ground onions
2 tablespoons ground parsley
1 tablespoon ground garlic
1 tablespoon ground cilantro or coriander
Pinch of saffron
2 tablespoons salt
1 tablespoon black pepper
1 tablespoon powdered ginger
1 lemon, cut into wedges, seeds removed
1 handful olives

Preheat oven to 400°. Place chicken in a deep baking dish. Fill dish with enough water so that three-quarters of chicken is submerged. In a separate bowl, combine all ingredients, except lemon and olives, and mix well. Baste chicken with mixture. Bake for 90 minutes, basting occasionally. Add lemon wedges and olives when chicken starts to brown on top. Serve with Moroccan bread for dipping.

Serves 4

Wine Notes

Recommended Wine: Balthasar Hess Scloss Reichartshausen Riesling Kabinett 1997 ($12.50)

Description: Crisp, fresh green apple and mineral flavors will cool down the heat and will work well with the cilantro or coriander.

Sommelier: John McNulty, Triangle Liquors

Chicken Dijon

Executive Chef Chuck II
Friday Saturday Sunday, Philadelphia, PA

2 to 3 pounds skinless, boneless chicken breasts
1 cup flour
1 cup milk
1 egg
2 cups breadcrumbs
2 tablespoons chopped fresh tarragon
1 tablespoon chopped fresh parsley
Melted butter
Dijon Sauce (Recipe appears on page 291.)

Trim fat from chicken breasts. Place flour in a shallow bowl. Whisk together milk and egg in a second bowl. Combine breadcrumbs, tarragon, and parsley in a third bowl. Coat each breast with flour. Dip in egg wash and then coat with breadcrumbs. (You will find breading easier if you use one hand to dip the chicken into the milk and the other hand to do the flour and breadcrumb coating.)

Preheat oven to 375°. Butter a baking sheet. Lay breasts on the sheet and drizzle with melted butter. Bake for 25 minutes or until cooked through. Serve with Dijon sauce.

Serves 8 to 10

Friday Saturday Sunday

Years in business: 27

Most requested table: #12

Menu: American/Asian

Chef: Chuck II

Chef's training: 5 years in Thailand; 16 years at Friday Saturday Sunday

Chef's hobbies/ accomplishments: computers, model airplanes

Chef's favorite foods: Asian fusion

Chef's favorite cookbook: *Le Bec-Fin Recipes*

Chicken MontSerrat

Owner Harris Eckstut
MontSerrat, Philadelphia, PA.

2 chicken cutlets (4 to 6 ounces each), trimmed and flattened
3 tablespoons Parmesan cheese
4 tablespoons Clarified Butter (Recipe appears on page 299.)
2 cloves garlic, crushed
6 white mushrooms, washed and trimmed
6 strips roasted pepper, canned or home roasted
2 tablespoons spicy Dijon mustard
6 ounces heavy cream
6 ounces cooked white rice
2 bunches fresh spinach, washed
4 slices tomato
Parsley

Coat chicken cutlets with Parmesan cheese. Melt butter in a nonstick skillet over medium heat. Place cutlets in pan and cook until Parmesan browns slightly. Turn cutlets over and add garlic, mushrooms, and roasted pepper strips. When Parmesan has browned, whisk together mustard and cream and add to skillet.

Arrange cooked rice in center of 2 serving plates. Place spinach on top to cover rice. Remove chicken from skillet and place atop spinach. Arrange mushrooms and peppers around each cutlet.

Increase heat under skillet to medium-high and cook cream sauce until slightly thickened. Top each cutlet with tomato slices and sauce. Garnish with parsley.

Serves 2

MontSerrat

Known for:
South Street sidewalk cafe, fun and sophisticated atmosphere

Years in business: 20

Most requested table:
sidewalk cafe, Bruce Springsteen booth

Menu:
eclectic with moderate prices

Chef: Fernando Cruz

Chef's training:
School of Hard Knocks (self taught)

Chef's hobbies/ accomplishments:
cooking, watching Food Channel/ family

Chef's favorite foods:
everything

Chef's favorite cookbook:
Emeril's

Coq au Vin

Chef/Proprietor Philippe Chin
Philippe's Bistro, Philadelphia, PA

2 pounds chicken thighs
2 cups red wine
1 large onion, diced
1 large carrot, diced
1 clove garlic, chopped
1 bouquet garni
2 tablespoons olive oil
2 slices bacon
½ pound button mushrooms, quartered
¼ cup brandy
1 tablespoon cornstarch
2 tablespoons cold water
¼ cup chopped bitter chocolate
Salt and pepper

Place chicken, wine, onion, carrot, garlic, and bouquet garni in a bowl. Cover and refrigerate for 24 hours.

Remove chicken from marinade. Strain and reserve marinade and vegetables. Pat chicken dry with paper towel. Heat oil in a large skillet over medium-high heat. Sear chicken until golden brown. Add marinated vegetables, bacon, and mushrooms. Add brandy and marinade liquid. Reduce heat to low. Cover and cook for about 2 hours until chicken is tender.

Remove chicken and keep warm. Discard bouquet garni. Strain broth and return it to pan. Dilute cornstarch with cold water. Stir into broth to thicken. Stir in chocolate and season to taste with salt and pepper.

Serves 4

Wine Notes

Recommended Wine: Domaine Berrod Beaujolais "Fleurie" 1999

Description: Pure classic French combination for this dish with a "Crus" of Beaujolais. Big, rich, and ripe flavors of red/purple berries with intensity and length. A delicious pairing.

Sommelier: John McNulty, Triangle Liquors

Pan-fried Chicken with Asian Far-Dill Wine

Chef/Nutritionist/Owner Joseph K. K. Poon
Joseph Poon Asian Fusion Restaurant, Philadelphia, PA

6 ounces chicken
1 tablespoon light soy sauce
⅛ teaspoon pepper
1¼ teaspoon salt
1 teaspoon sesame oil
1 tablespoon soy bean oil
2 tablespoons cornstarch
2 scallions, cut into 2-inch lengths
3 slices ginger, shredded
¼ cup far-dill wine
¼ cup chicken broth
1½ teaspoon sugar

Slice chicken into strips. Combine soy sauce, pepper, 1 teaspoon salt, sesame oil, soy oil, and 1 tablespoon cornstarch. Mix with chicken.

Heat wok or skillet over high heat. Add chicken and stir-fry until three-quarters cooked. Remove from wok and reserve.

Add scallions and ginger to wok. Add remaining salt, far-dill wine, chicken broth, and sugar. Stir for 2 to 3 minutes. Dissolve remaining cornstarch in 2 ounces water and stir in. Return chicken to wok. Stir occasionally until chicken is cooked through.

Serves 2

Pheasant with Red Fruits

Owner John Byrne
La Campagne, Cherry Hill, NJ

½ cup red wine vinegar
3 tablespoons sugar
1 cup red wine
2 tablespoons chopped shallot
1 pint mixed berries
4 tablespoons butter
2 pheasants (2 to 2½ pounds each), quartered
Salt and pepper

Combine vinegar and sugar in a saucepan over medium-high heat and cook until liquid reduces to a syrup. In a separate saucepan, combine red wine and shallots and cook until liquid is reduced by two-thirds. Add red wine to syrup and cook for 2 minutes. Strain liquid into a pot. Add berries and simmer for 5 minutes. Reserve.

Preheat oven to 425°. Melt butter in a skillet over medium-high heat. Season pheasant pieces with salt and pepper and add to pan. Pan sear on both sides until brown. Transfer pheasants to oven. Bake breasts for about 4 minutes or until medium. Bake legs for 10 minutes or until cooked through. Transfer pheasant pieces to a warm serving platter.

Deglaze pan with sauce. Serve sauce over pheasants.

Serves 4

Reprinted from *From The Cooking School at La Campagne* by John Byrne (Small Potatoes Press, copyright 1999). Reprinted with permission of the publisher.

Kriek Duck

Chef/Owner Tom Peters
Monk's Café, Philadelphia, PA

½ cup dried cherries
1 bottle Boon Kriek (Belgian ale)
1 dried ancho chili pepper or 1 teaspoon ancho powder
1 teaspoon finely grated ginger
1 teaspoon flour
Pinch of ground cinnamon
2 tablespoons sugar
2 tablespoons water
1 teaspoon sliced sorrel
2 duck breasts

Soak dried cherries overnight in half of Boon Kriek. Reserve remaining ale for later use. (Of course, you could just drink it and open another bottle later!)

Pour remaining ale into a saucepan. Add dried ancho chili pepper and ginger. Simmer over low heat for about 10 minutes to infuse flavors. Remove pan from heat and allow chili to steep in liquid for 10 minutes. Remove chili from liquid.

Return pan to heat and add flour and cinnamon. Cook over low heat, stirring occasionally, until flour dissolves, about 2 to 3 minutes. Remove from flame.

Place sugar in a separate saucepan. Add water and cook over low heat. Stir until sugar dissolves. Increase heat. Boil mixture until it begins to turn golden brown, about 3 to 5 minutes. DO NOT STIR! (Be very careful with the hot sugar. If spilled on skin, it will cause severe burns. You may omit this step if you don't feel totally comfortable.)

Remove pan from heat. Add soaked cherries and sorrel. Set aside to cool and thicken. (If mixture it too thick for basting, add more Boon Kriek. If too thin, puree a few rehydrated cherries and add to mixture.)

Preheat oven to 350°. Prick duck skin a with fork. (More perforation equals crispier skin.) Baste duck with the cherry sauce. Roast duck, skin side up, for 45 minutes. Baste every 15 minutes with cherry sauce. (For crisper skin, place duck under broiler for 2 to 4 minutes to finish.)

Slice duck and fan out on serving plates. Ladle 2 ounces cherry sauce over slices. Serve with a farmhouse ale such as Saison Dupont from Belgium or an Oregon Pinot Noir or even a California/Australian Syrah.

Serves 2 to 4

meats

Grilled Skirt Steak

Chef/Owner Fritz Blank
Deux Cheminées, Philadelphia, PA

¼ cup Kitchen Bouquet® browning sauce
2 tablespoons peanut oil or other vegetable oil
6 cloves garlic, crushed
2 strips trimmed skirt steaks (about 3 pounds)
Chef's Salt (Recipe appears on page 301.)

Mix together browning sauce, oil, and crushed garlic. Season skirt steaks with chef's salt and then rub with browning sauce mixture. Refrigerate for 1 hour or more.

Preheat grill or a cast-iron skillet until very hot. Sear steaks on both sides and cook until medium-rare or rare. (Well-cooked steak, especially skirt steak, is not recommended.)

Transfer meat to a warm serving platter and allow to rest for at least 15 minutes before carving. Slice into very thin strips and serve au jus.

Potatoes of any kind and a small green salad are my partners-of-choice for this dish.

Serves 2

Chef's Note

Affectionately called *La Bavette* in French, skirt steak, along with skillet sautéed potatoes, have a little-known history of being a favorite breakfast dish for French chefs in France as a finale to their daily early morning marketing chores. Most every town and city in France has a *marché* or market. Chefs usually arrive at these markets at three or four in the morning and spend a lot of time, effort, and expertise shopping. They look, sniff, poke, feel, and taste, and IF they are interested in buying, they haggle for the "right" price. This is hard work, and empty bellies soon begin to grumble for attention. At nearby bistros on the periphery of the marketplace, Cognac, coffee, grilled garliced skirt steak, pan-fried potatoes, and more Cognac provide the needed repast. Gastronomic conversation abounds and conviviality reigns.

Filet of Beef Niçoise

Executive Chef Eric Hall
La Campagne, Cherry Hill, NJ

4 beef filet mignons (6 ounces each)
Salt and pepper
2 tablespoons olive oil
1 onion, finely diced
1 tablespoon chopped garlic
1 can whole peeled plum tomatoes (28 ounces), drained and chopped
½ cup pitted black olives
4 tablespoons fresh basil, cut into ribbons

Season steaks on both sides with salt and pepper. Heat olive oil in a sauté pan over medium-high heat. Add filets and sear each side until brown. Remove from pan and set aside. In same pan, sauté onion and garlic until lightly browned. Add tomatoes and simmer for 15 to 20 minutes or until tomatoes are reduced and concentrated. Add olives and basil. Return steaks to pan and simmer covered for about 5 minutes or until steaks reach desired doneness. Remove steaks from pan. Season sauce with salt and pepper and serve immediately on top of steaks.

Serves 4

Wine Notes

Recommended Wine: Côtes de Provence "Cuvée Privee" Domaine Sorin 1997 ($16.00)

Description: A robust blend of 50% Syrah and 50% Mourvédre, the noble varietal of Badol is the "private" wine of Luc Sorin, a young and ambitious wine maker in St. Cyr Sur Mer who uses rotofermenters to maximize extraction and *barriques* to mature the wine for 9 months prior to bottling. This is rich, flavorful, and expressive *vin de Provence*, endowed by finely grained tannins and capable of accompanying a meat or game dish admirably.

Sommelier: Greg Moore, Moore Brothers Wine Co.

Kansas City Prime's Cowboy Steak with Roquefort Gratinee

Chef/Owner Derek Davis
Kansas City Prime, Philadelphia, PA

½ cup Roquefort cheese, room temperature
½ cup toasted breadcrumbs
½ teaspoon chopped garlic
¼ cup heavy cream
1 teaspoon cracked black pepper
1 standing rib roast (7 bone)
Kosher salt and fresh black pepper

Place first 5 ingredients in a mixer and combine until well incorporated. Lay out 3 sheets parchment paper. Divide mixture into thirds and place one-third mixture on lower third of each sheet. Shape into logs and roll up like you would refrigerator cookies. Twist paper ends and refrigerate.

Trim roast of all exterior fat. Cut between bones to get 7 equal-size steaks. Season steaks with kosher salt and fresh black pepper. Grill steaks on preheated grill until desired doneness.

Unwrap cheese logs and cut into ¼-inch disks. Place 2 or 3 cheese disks on top of each steak and brown under broiler.

Serves 7

Wine Notes

Recommended Wine: Côte de Roussillon La Casenove 1996 ($11.50)

Description: A supple and spicy blend of fragrant Carignan, Syrah, and Grenache, this is a classic from the *Sud-Ouest*, meant to be happily drunk with Mediterranean food. Owner and wine maker Etiènne Montes has partially abandoned his brilliant photographic career to invest his money and energy in the family farm and has since then produced the most interesting wines on the French side of the Spanish border.

Sommelier: Greg Moore, Moore Brothers Wine Co.

Thai Peanut Filet Mignon

Director of Culinary Arts Joseph E. Shilling
The Art Institute of Philadelphia, Philadelphia, PA

3 tablespoons peanut oil
2-inch piece fresh ginger, finely chopped
4 cloves garlic, finely chopped
1 stick lemon grass, finely chopped
¼ cup soy sauce
½ cup peanut butter, smooth or crunchy
¼ cup coconut milk
2 pounds beef tenderloin

Place oil, ginger, garlic, and lemon grass in a hot sauté pan and sauté until tender.
Add remaining ingredients, except beef. Simmer for 10 to 15 minutes. Cut filet
into 2-inch-long strips. Skewer each strip of steak. Rub Thai peanut sauce on steak.
Grill or bake in a preheated 375° oven for 12 to 16 minutes for medium rare.

Serves 4 to 6

Chef's Note

This Thai peanut sauce is great with noodles and any
type of meat, chicken, or vegetable as a main course
or as a tasty appetizer. Garnish with snow peas,
carrots, and scallions for flavor and contrast.

Bistecca Balsamico

Owner John J. Garagozzo
Blue Moon Restaurant & Café, Haddon Heights, NJ

2 filet mignon or sirloin steaks (8 to 10 ounces each)
1 tablespoon olive oil
Cracked pepper
1 cup good balsamic vinegar
¼ to ½ teaspoon butter
Salt

Brush steaks with olive oil. Press cracked pepper into both sides of steak. Set aside.

Heat balsamic vinegar and butter in a saucepan over medium heat. Reduce by almost half but be careful not to let vinegar caramelize. (Vinegar should be like a syrup but not too thick.) Season to taste with salt and pepper.

Grill or broil steaks to desired doneness. Drizzle balsamic reduction over steaks or place reduction on bottom of plates.

Serves 2

Wine Notes

Recommended Wine: Corteforte, Valpolicella Classico Superiore 1995 ($18.00)

Description: Superior quality Valpolicella produced with fruit grown in the *podere* (vineyard) *Bertarole* in the commune of Fumane by a tiny winery located inside a 14th century walled court (*Corteforte*). An explosive blend of Corvina Veronese (60%), Rondinella (25%), and Molinara refermented on the lees and in the barrels used for Amarone, this is a supple, concentrated, aristocratically rich wine ideal for meat entrees and seasoned cheeses.

Sommelier: Frank Splan, Moore Brothers Wine Co.

London Broil
with Herbed Wild Mushroom Stuffing

President Jack Kramer
Jack Kramer's Catering, Philadelphia, PA

1 flank steak (3 to 4 pounds)
½ cup Worcestershire sauce
½ cup prepared steak seasoning, such as Montreal steak seasoning
Pinch of cumin
¼ cup vegetable oil
3 pounds mixed wild mushrooms, sliced
1 shallot, minced
1 tablespoon minced garlic
3 ounces beef stock
2 ounces herbes de Provence
¼ cup Dijon mustard
Salt and pepper

Butterfly steak. Combine Worcestershire sauce, steak seasoning, and cumin and pour over steak. Marinate for 20 to 60 minutes.

Heat oil in a sauté pan over medium heat. Add mushrooms and sauté until soft. Add shallot and garlic and sauté for 3 to 5 minutes. Stir in beef stock and herbs. When stock begins to simmer, stir in mustard. Season to taste with salt and pepper. Remove from heat and cool slightly.

Preheat oven to 350°. Spread mushroom mixture on inside of flank steak and roll up jelly-roll style. Wrap tightly in plastic wrap and then securely in foil. Cook for 30 minutes to medium rare. Cool, slice, and serve.

Serves 8

Philly Foodie Fact

Herbes de Provence is an herbal blend used in Provençal cooking. Although rosemary, lavender, thyme, fennel, basil, and bay leaf typically make up the combination the blend can vary. Herbes de Provence can be found in most grocery and specialty stores, such as The Spice Terminal in the Reading Terminal Market and Haddonfield Gourmet in Haddonfield, NJ.

London Broil Jack Daniel's

Chef/Owner Tony Daggett
Daggett's Catering, Washington Township, NJ

3 pounds top round London broil
Olive oil
Cracked black peppercorns
½ teaspoon cayenne pepper
1 medium onion, finely diced
Chopped fresh parsley
Splash of Kentucky Bourbon (Pretend it's vinegar for a salad.)

Rub meat with olive oil and coat with remaining ingredients. Marinate meat overnight in baking dish, turning a few times. Grill on high heat to sear in juices; turn and sear other side. Lower flame to medium. Baste with juices from marinade. Cook for 10 minutes on each side or to desired doneness. Slice at an angle across the grain.

Serves 10

Wine Notes

Recommended Wine: Château de Belingard, Côtes de Bergerac 1998 ($12.00)

Description: Made mostly from Merlot old vines in an area contiguous to Saint-Emilion, this wine offers potent aromatics of ripe fruit and rich, full-bodied palate with a spicy finish and persistent aftertaste. This is a style of wine that requires food pairings of a certain complexity and richness for a reciprocal enhancement of flavor.

Sommelier: Chris Kurlakovsky, Moore Brothers Wine Co.

Four-Onion Pot Roast with Beer

Executive Chef Jim Coleman
Treetops in the Rittenhouse Hotel, Philadelphia, PA

2 tablespoons olive oil
4- to 5-pound chuck roast, boned and tied
Salt and pepper
1 tablespoon dried thyme
1 tablespoon dried sage
2 large onions, peeled and thinly sliced
1 pound leeks, washed and thinly sliced
1 cup pearl onions
1 carrot, peeled and diced
1 celery stalk, diced
2 large potatoes, peeled and cut into 1½-inch cubes
2 shallots, chopped
½ cup chopped fresh parsley
1 tablespoon molasses
1 bay leaf
2 12-ounce bottles of dark beer
2 tablespoons Dijon mustard
1 tablespoon cider vinegar
½ bunch scallions, chopped

In a roasting pan large enough to hold the roast, heat the olive oil over medium-high heat. Season the roast with salt, pepper, thyme, and sage. Place the roast in the pan and sear on all sides.

Remove the roast, add all the vegetables, and sauté for about 2 minutes. Add the molasses and continue to cook for about 5 minutes, stirring to prevent burning.

Place the roast back in the pan and add the bay leaf and the beer. Cover and cook for about 1½ to 2 hours over low heat, until the meat is tender. Remove the meat and keep it warm.

Degrease the liquid in the pan and stir in the mustard and vinegar. Reduce the liquid until it is thick enough to coat the back of a spoon. Adjust the seasoning and add the scallions. Slice the roast and serve it with the sauce and vegetables.

Serves 6

Reprinted from *Flavors of America* by Jim Coleman and Candace Hagan (Camino Books, Inc., copyright 1999). Reprinted with permission of the publisher.

Five Spiced Braised Beef Short Ribs

Executive Chef Michael Yeamans
Rouge, Philadelphia, PA

2 tablespoons oil
2 tablespoons butter
12 beef short ribs
1⅓ cups EACH diced carrots, onion, and celery
6 garlic cloves, chopped
1 piece ginger, about finger length, chopped
1 tablespoon Szechuan peppercorns
1 tablespoon star anise
1 teaspoon cloves
4 cinnamon sticks
2 cups red wine
2 cups red wine vinegar
1 cup brown sugar
8 cups veal stock
1 cup Thai chili sauce
½ cup sriracha sauce
½ cup soy sauce
Chinese hot oil, optional
Scallions, optional

Rouge

Known for:
outside seating on
Rittenhouse Square

Years in business: 2

Most requested table:
the window table

Menu:
French bistro

Chef: Michael Yeamans

Chef's training:
Johnson & Wales
University

**Chef's hobbies/
accomplishments:**
playing with Andrew
Yeamans

Chef's favorite foods:
pastrami reubens

**Chef's favorite
cookbook:**
Making of a Cook by
Madeleine Kamman

Heat oil and butter in a large ovenproof saucepan or casserole. Add short ribs and brown on all sides. Remove from pan. Add carrots, onion, celery, garlic, ginger, peppercorns, star anise, cloves, and cinnamon sticks and sauté. Deglaze pan with wine and vinegar. Add remaining ingredients and stir to combine.

Preheat oven to 300°. Return ribs to pan and bring to a simmer. Cover and bake for 3 hours until meat falls off bone. Remove ribs. Strain sauce and adjust seasonings. Serve with mashed potatoes and glazed baby carrots. Garnish with Chinese hot oil and scallions.

Serves 6

Hot and Sour Baby Short Ribs

Chef/Nutritionist/Owner Joseph K. K. Poon
Joseph Poon Asian Fusion Restaurant, Philadelphia, PA

1 pound baby short ribs, cut into 2-inch lengths
1 tablespoon light soy sauce
1¼ teaspoons salt
Dash of pepper
4 cups oil
1 tablespoon Zechun bean sauce
1½ tablespoons Chinese red wine vinegar
½ tablespoon sugar
1 tablespoon cornstarch
¼ cup water

Combine ribs with soy sauce, 1 teaspoon salt, and pepper. Marinate for at least 30 minutes.

Heat oil in a wok over high heat to 350°. Add ribs and deep fry for 25 to 35 minutes until well done. Remove ribs from wok and reserve. Discard oil.

Add remaining salt, bean sauce, red wine vinegar, and sugar to wok. Stir and cook over medium heat. Dissolve cornstarch in water, add to wok, and stir to combine. Add ribs and coat well.

Enjoy!

Serves 2

Joseph Poon Asian Fusion Restaurant

Known for:
dim sum, Peking duck, Wok and Walk culinary tours of Chinatown

Years in business: 3

Menu: Asian fusion

Chef: Joseph K.K. Poon

Chef's training:
B.S. in Nutrition; continuing education at CIA

Chef's hobbies/ accomplishments:
ping pong, testing recipes/ teaching and sharing

Chef's favorite foods:
dim sum, pasta, Asian noodles

Chef's favorite cookbook:
All — any one can enrich my knowledge of culinary skill!

Escalope of Veal Neri

Owner/Director Charlotte-Ann Albertson
Charlotte-Ann Albertson's Cooking School, Wynnewood, PA

8 slices veal, pounded thin*
Unseasoned breadcrumbs
Salt and pepper
Flour
1 egg, beaten
4 tablespoons sweet butter
2 tablespoons olive oil
8 slices lemon, thinly sliced and peeled
8 slices Swiss cheese, thinly sliced
1 tablespoon fresh lemon juice
1 cup half-and-half
¼ cup chicken stock
Sweet paprika
Parsley, optional
Pitted black olives, optional

Preheat oven to 350°. Dry veal slices on a paper towel. Season breadcrumbs with salt and pepper. Dip veal first in flour; then egg; and finally breadcrumbs.

Melt butter and oil in a sauté pan. Add veal, 2 pieces at a time, and brown for about 2 minutes. Place browned veal in a baking dish. Place lemon slices on veal; then cover with Swiss cheese slices, 1 slice on at a time.

Add lemon juice to half-and-half and allow to curdle. Stir in stock. Pour over veal. Sprinkle with paprika. Bake for 20 minutes. (Do not overcook.) Garnish with parsley and black olives, if desired.

Serves 4

*Thin strips of boneless chicken or turkey cutlets may be substituted for veal.

Veal Bernard

Chef/Owner Jean Sarne
JeanneNatalia Bistro, Philadelphia, PA

1 pound veal medallions, thinly pounded
Flour
¼ cup Clarified Butter (Recipe appears on page 299.)
¼ cup crumbled blue cheese
¼ cup crème fraîche or sour cream
Pepper, black or white

Lightly coat medallions with flour. Melt butter in a skillet over medium heat. Add medallions and sauté for 2 minutes on each side. Add blue cheese. Stir in crème fraîche. Season to taste with pepper. Nap medallions with sauce and serve with your favorite green vegetable.

Serves 4

Wine Notes

Recommended Wine: Chinon "Les Graves" Gasnier ($12.00)

Description: The wine Rabelais loved above any other and that inspired some of his best works is made of 100% Cabernet Franc from the very prestigious appellation in the Loire valley. The 1998 vintage has gifted us a wine of fragrant, juicy fruitiness; soft tannin structure; velvety mouthfill; and clean, fresh finish.

Sommelier: Megan Shawver, Moore Brothers Wine Co.

Braised Osso Buco with Tomato-Marsala Jus

Chef/Proprietor Alfonso Contrisciani
Opus 251, Philadelphia, PA

12 veal shanks
Garlic powder
Salt and pepper
Seasoned flour
½ cup plus 1 tablespoon olive oil
2 teaspoons chopped garlic
2 cups rough cut onions
1 cup rough cut carrots
1 cup rough cut celery
6 ounces tomato paste
8 ounces red wine (Burgundy preferred)
1 gallon veal stock
1 bouquet garni (see Chef's Note)
¼ cup diced sweet onions
½ teaspoon roasted garlic paste
2 cups peeled, seeded, and chopped plum tomatoes
1 ounce brandy
4 ounces Marsala wine
1 tablespoon julienned basil
4 tablespoons whole butter

Preheat oven to 325°. Rub shanks well with garlic and salt and pepper. Dust with seasoned flour. Heat ½ cup oil in a large braising pan or stockpot with tight-fitting lid over medium-high heat. Add shanks and sear in hot oil. Remove and reserve on a baking sheet. Add garlic to pot and lightly brown. Add onions, carrots, celery, and tomato paste and cook until lightly browned.

Chef's Note
Bouquet garni is a bunch of herbs tied together or wrapped in cheesecloth. For this recipe, wrap 1 tablespoon peppercorns, a sprig of thyme, 2 bay leaves, and 2 marjoram leaves in cheesecloth.

Deglaze with wine. Add veal stock. Add shanks and bouquet garni. Cover and bake in oven for 2½ hours or until fork tender.

Remove shanks from liquid and reserve. Discard bouquet garni. Strain, reserve vegetables, and return braising liquid to pot. Simmer over medium-high heat. Puree vegetables and stir into liquid.

Heat remaining olive oil in a large sauté pan. Add sweet onions and garlic paste and sauté until onions are translucent. Add tomatoes. Add brandy and ignite to flambé. Add braising liquid, veal shanks, and Marsala wine. Simmer for 2 to 3 minutes. Swirl in basil and butter. Season to taste with salt and pepper.

Serves 12

Wine Notes

Recommended Wine: Cascina Val del Prete "Vigna de Lino" Nebbiolo 1997 ($22.00)

Description: A barrique-aged, hearty red from the Italian Northwest's Piedmont region. Full and lush with good intensity and medium to full body. A classic pairing.

Sommelier: John McNulty, Triangle Liquors

Roulade of Pork Tenderloin with Caramelized Shallot and Clementine Sauce

Executive Chef David Stoltzfus
The Ivy Grille at The Inn at Penn, Philadelphia, PA

2 cups chopped fresh basil
2 tablespoons chopped toasted walnuts
1 teaspoon chopped garlic
2 tablespoons olive oil
1 ounce Montrachet cheese
1 pork tenderloin (16 ounces)
¼ pound spinach, wilted
1 roasted red pepper, cut into thin strips
1 lobster tail (6 ounces), poached
1 to 2 tablespoons flour
1 teaspoon vegetable oil
Caramelized Shallot and Clementine Sauce (Recipe
   appears on page 296.)
1 clementine orange, segmented

Combine chopped basil, walnuts, garlic, olive oil, and Montrachet in a food processor and pulse to form a wet pesto. Set aside.

Trim tenderloin and butterfly. Pound flat. Spread pesto over tenderloin, leaving a ½-inch border on all sides. Layer spinach on top of tenderloin. Cover spinach with roasted red pepper strips. Slice lobster tail in half and place on top of peppers. Roll tenderloin up tight and secure with butcher's twine. Coat with flour.

Preheat oven to 395°. Heat oil in a large ovenproof skillet. Sear tenderloin in oil. Place skillet in oven and roast until pork is cooked through, about 12 minutes. Remove pork from oven and let stand for 5 minutes. Slice on a bias. Pour warm sauce over slices and garnish with clementine segments and additional basil.

Serves 4

The Ivy Grille

Known for:
show kitchen, tin ceiling, community table

Years in business:
opened October 1999

Most requested table:
#230

Menu:
America bistro — regional cuisine with eclectic flair

Chef: David Stoltzfus

Chef's training:
Culinary Institute of America plus 21 years on the job

Chef's hobbies/ accomplishments:
2nd degree black belt

Chef's favorite foods:
Caribbean and American blends

Chef's favorite cookbook:
Sugar Reef Cookbook

Southwestern Cracked Black Pepper Tenderloin

Executive Chef Patrick Bradley
Buckley's Tavern, Centreville, DE

1 cup red wine vinegar
¼ cup honey
1½ teaspoons minced garlic
1 tablespoon minced shallots
2 tablespoons cracked black pepper
1½ teaspoons cumin
2 tablespoons cayenne pepper
2 tablespoons coriander
2 tablespoons chopped fresh chives
½ cup oil
1 pork tenderloin (about 3 pounds)

Combine all ingredients, except tenderloin, in a mixing bowl and mix thoroughly. Place tenderloin in a baking dish and cover with marinade. Refrigerate for 2 hours.

Preheat oven to 350°. Sear pork in a cast-iron skillet until golden brown on both sides. Transfer to a baking sheet and bake until barely pink in the middle, about 15 to 20 minutes.

Serves 6 to 8

Wine Notes

Recommended Wine: Les Baux de Provence Reserve Mas de la Dame 1997 ($13.50)

Description: The "Reserve" wine produced by this lovely estate nestled in the rocky landscape of Les Baux en Provence among cypresses, pines, and bushes of lavender and thyme is a blend of Cabernet Sauvignon and Grenache, hand-harvested, softly pressed, and vinified in stainless steel vats after extended maceration. Ideally suited for lamb or roasted birds served with *herbs de Provence.*

Sommelier: Kevin McCann, Moore Brothers Wine Co.

Pork Cézanne

Chef/Owner Jean Sarne
JeanneNatalia Bistro, Philadelphia, PA

1 pork loin (2 pounds), trimmed of fat
Flour
Salt and pepper
2 tablespoons olive oil
½ pound fresh mushrooms, sliced
½ cup white wine
2 tablespoons whole jellied cranberries
2 tablespoons crème fraîche or sour cream

Preheat oven to 400°. Cut loin into ½-inch slices. Lightly coat both sides of slices with flour. Season with salt and pepper to taste. Heat oil in a large ovenproof skillet. Add pork slices and cook for 3 minutes on each side. Add mushrooms and wine and cook until liquid begins to reduce. Add cranberries and crème fraîche. Transfer skillet to oven and bake for 8 minutes.

Serves 4

Wine Notes

Wine: Coteaux d' Aix-en-Provence Château Calissanne "Cuvée du Chateau" ($10.50)

Description: Cézanne too would agree that the best view of Mont-St.-Victoire is from the mistral-swept cliff towering on this beautiful estate located just outside Aix-en-Provence. Authentic *garrigue* flavors (Grenache) and good structure (Cabernet Sauvignon) with supple tannins and some spices (Syrah) make this soft and vibrant wine an ideal complement to medium fare and Mediterranean dishes.

Sommelier: Megan Shawver, Moore Brothers Wine Co.

Pan-seared Pork Chops with Cider Sauce

Chef/Instructor Philip G. Pinkney
The Restaurant School, Philadelphia, PA

Flour
Salt and pepper
3 tablespoons corn oil
6 double cut loin pork chops (8 ounces each)
3 tart apples, peeled, cored, and sliced ¼-inch thick
1½ quarts apple cider
Ground cinnamon
⅜ cup pumpernickel breadcrumbs
Assorted herbs
Green Apple Salsa (Recipe appears on page 299.)

Preheat oven to 400°. Season flour with salt and pepper. Heat oil in an ovenproof skillet over high heat. Dust chops with seasoned flour, add to skillet, and sear on both sides. Place skillet in oven and bake for 5 minutes. Remove from oven. Stack sliced apples around chops. Return to oven and bake for 5 to 7 minutes or until fully cooked.

Remove chops and apples from skillet and reserve. Warm pan over medium heat on stovetop. Deglaze pan with cider. Season with cinnamon. Stir in breadcrumbs. Allow sauce to reduce and thicken. Season to taste with salt and pepper.

Spoon sauce onto serving plates. Place chop in center of plate and arrange apples around each chop. Garnish with herbs and green apple salsa.

Serves 6

Wine Notes

Recommended Wine: (White) Balthasar Ress Hattenheimer Schutzenhaus Riesling Kabinett 1997 ($11.00)

Description: Crisp and lean with plenty of green apple flavor — what's better than apples with pork?

Recommended Wine: (Red) Bethel Heights Estate Pinot Noir 1997 ($21.00)

Description: Rich, ripe, and focused with bold, powerful berry flavors and medium tannin.

Sommelier: John McNulty, Triangle Liquors

Moroccan Lamb Tajine

Chef/Owner Michèle R. Haines
Spring Mill Café, Conshohocken, PA

⅓ cup olive oil

4 onions, finely chopped

5 pounds lamb shoulder, cut into 2-inch pieces

2 pounds fresh tomatoes, peeled, seeded, and chopped

3 tablespoons ground cumin

2 tablespoons turmeric

1 tablespoon freshly grated ginger

Pinch of salt

1 heaping teaspoon red pepper flakes

1 bunch cilantro, finely chopped

5 cups couscous

5 cups chicken stock

½ cup golden raisins

½ cup slivered almonds, toasted

½ cup EACH chopped dried apricots, dried figs, and dried dates

½ cup Moroccan black olives

½ cup sliced Mandarin oranges

Harissa, optional

Heat olive oil in a large earthenware pot over medium heat. Add onions and lamb and cook for 5 minutes. Add tomatoes, cumin, turmeric, ginger, salt, red pepper flakes, and three-quarters of cilantro. Stir, cover, and cook very slowly until lamb is tender, about 45 minutes.

Prepare couscous according to package instructions, replacing water with chicken stock. When couscous is ready, toss with raisins and almonds.

Mound couscous on a serving tray. Cover with lamb tajine. Garnish with remaining cilantro, apricots, figs, dates, black olives, and oranges. Serve harissa on the side.

Serves 6 to 8

Philly Foodie Fact

Harissa is a fiery-hot sauce that is usually served with couscous but also makes a nice addition to soups and stews. It is available in cans and jars in Middle Eastern stores, such as Bitar's in Philadelphia and Norma's in Cherry Hill, NJ.

Lamb Shank Provencal

Chef/Owner Olivier De Saint Martin
Dock Street Brasserie, Philadelphia, PA

4 lamb shanks
Salt and pepper
½ cup olive oil
1 onion, sliced
8 garlic cloves, cracked
1½ cups white wine
4 ripe tomatoes, chopped
1 bay leaf
½ red pepper, sliced
½ green pepper, sliced
⅓ cup black olives with pits
1 tablespoon basil pesto
5 sprigs thyme, stemmed
1 sprig rosemary, stemmed
1 teaspoon fresh lavender flower

Preheat oven to 375°. Season shanks with salt and pepper. Heat ¼ cup olive oil in a large skillet over medium-high heat. Add shanks and pan sear until browned on each side. Add onion and garlic and cook for 5 minutes. Deglaze with wine and cook until liquid is reduced by half. Add tomatoes and bay leaf and cook for 10 minutes. Add enough water to cover. Place lid on skillet and bake in oven for at least 1 hour or until meat falls off bone.

Heat remaining oil in a skillet over medium-high heat. Add peppers and brown for 4 minutes. Season with salt and pepper. Add cooked meat and olives.

Combine pesto, thyme, rosemary, and lavender and add to pepper mixture. Incorporate sauce from bottom of shank pan.

Spoon sauce onto bottom of each plate and place shank majestically on top.

Serves 4

Buffalo Meatloaf
with Apple Cider Reduction

Chef/Owner Brian W. Duffy
Kristopher's, Philadelphia, PA

2 pounds ground buffalo
¼ cup chopped green onions
¼ cup diced carrots
3 tablespoons chopped shallots
1 teaspoon chopped garlic
¼ cup breadcrumbs
2 eggs
½ cup thinly sliced roasted red peppers
3 fresh egg-size mozzarella balls, thinly sliced
Olive oil
Salt and pepper
Apple Cider Reduction (Recipe appears on page 299.)

Combine first 7 ingredients in a mixing bowl. Use palms of hands to form mixture into four ½-inch-thick patties. Lay peppers and mozzarella in center of each patty. Roll into mini-loaves, making sure entire loaf is sealed around edges. Drizzle with olive oil. Season to taste with salt and pepper.

Preheat oven to 350°. Grill meatloaf on a preheated grill or in a grill pan. Grill to mark loaves, about 2 minutes per side. Transfer to a baking tray and bake for 12 to 15 minutes. Remove meatloaf from oven and slice into 1-inch-thick diagonal slices. Drizzle some cider reduction onto 4 plates. Fan meatloaf slices on sauce. Drizzle with remaining reduction.

Serves 4

Philly Foodie Fact

You'll find buffalo meat (actually American bison) on more and more restaurant menus and at specialty meat markets. A tasty and tender alternative to beef, buffalo has more iron than beef and less fat and cholesterol than most cuts of beef and chicken. You can buy it at D'Angelo Brothers Meat Market in South Philadelphia and Fresh Fields markets.

Shepherd's Pie

Executive Chef David Young
Chadds Ford Inn, Chadds Ford, PA

5 pounds ground lamb
2 onions, chopped
4 carrots, chopped
½ stalk celery, chopped
¼ cup chopped garlic
1 tablespoon fresh rosemary
1 cup tomato paste
2 quarts beef stock
Salt and pepper
4 cups mashed potatoes

Cook lamb in a large skillet until brown. Drain excess fat. Add vegetables, garlic, rosemary, tomato paste, and beef stock. Season to taste with salt and pepper. Bring to a boil. Lower heat and simmer until thickend, about 30 minutes.

Preheat oven to 400°. Place in a 10 x 16-inch baking dish. Cover with mashed potatoes. Bake for 30 minutes or until potatoes are golden.

Serves 12

Wine Notes

Recommended Wine: Premières Côtes de Bordeaux Chateau de Juge "Cru Quinette" 1996 ($13.50)

Description: Fleshy, vibrant Merlot from the single vineyard Quinette in the commune of Cadillac is from where the most convivial and fine Côtes de Bordeaux wines come. This is a bright, aromatic, and succulent example produced by the 28-hectare estate owned by Pierre Dupleich and Denis Dubourdieu, head of Oenology at the world famous institute in Bordeaux.

Sommelier: Christian Lane, Moore Brothers Wine Co.

fish

Grilled Salmon 156

Grilled Salmon with Champagne and Leek Sauce 157

Bruce Lim's Roasted Salmon with Artichokes 158

Tea Poached Salmon 160

Potato-Crusted Salmon with Mustard Sauce 161

Salmon Casino 162

Grilled Sea Bass with Olive Relish and Roasted Tomato Coulis 163

Pan Roasted Chilean Sea Bass with Ceci and Potatoes Morzello 164

Poached Chilean Sea Bass with Shrimp in Saffron Broth 165

Swordfish and Rosemary Sauté 166

Grilled Swordfish with Spicy Black Bean Sauce 167

Prosciutto Seared Red Snapper with Fennel and Tomato Broth 168

Sun-dried Tomato Crusted Snapper with Fennel, Artichokes, and Olives 169

Crispy Red Snapper with Chili Lime Sauce 170

Sautéed Red Snapper with Crabmeat 171

Sesame-Crusted Tuna Loin with Ponzu-Wasabi Vinaigrette 172

Tuna Tempura with Pepper Jelly Sauce 173

Tuna Sambuca 174

Grilled Tuna Steak with Mango Salsa 175

Baked Flounder with Lobster Aïoli 176

Braised Monkfish with Portobello Mushrooms 177

Crispy Whole Black Bass 178

Baccala Regannet 179

Grilled Salmon

Executive Chef Micheal Giletto
Cater 2U, Mount Laurel, NJ

2 salmon fillets (about 8 ounces each)
1 cup vegetable oil
1 cup white wine
Juice of 1 lemon
Juice of 1 lime
⅔ teaspoon EACH salt, pepper, fresh lemon thyme,
    fresh basil, fresh parsley, and minced fresh garlic
2 leaves red leaf lettuce
2 scallion flowers or parsley
2 wedges lemon

Place fillets in a shallow bowl. Combine oil, white wine,
lemon and lime juices, salt, pepper, herbs, and garlic and
pour over fish. Refrigerate for 1 to 2 hours.

Heat grill or grill pan. Remove salmon from marinade
and grill until desired doneness. Lay lettuce on serving
plate. Cover with salmon. Garnish with scallion flower
or parsley and lemon wedge. Finito!

Serves 2

Cater 2U

Known for:
theme parties

Years in business: 7

Menu:
Island, Caribbean

Chef: Michael Giletto

Chef's training:
Culinary Institute of
America and 33 years in
the culinary field

**Chef's hobbies/
accomplishments:**
certified executive chef

Chef's favorite foods:
everything but liver

**Chef's favorite
cookbook:**
Each day another book
comes to life. I never
stop learning.

Grilled Salmon
with Champagne and Leek Sauce

Executive Chef Luigi Baretto
Ram's Head Inn, Absecon, NJ

6 salmon fillets (8 ounces each)
2 tablespoons butter
1 teaspoon flour
1 cup fish stock
½ cup champagne
¼ teaspoon Worcestershire sauce
1 teaspoon lemon juice
Salt and pepper
2 tablespoons heavy cream
½ baby leek, julienned and blanched

Preheat oven to 350°. Preheat grill. Grill salmon on each side until marked. Transfer to oven and bake for about 10 minutes or until desired doneness.

Melt butter slowly in a saucepan over medium heat. (Be careful not to let it burn.) Add flour and stir until a thick roux forms. Gradually add fish stock and champagne, whipping constantly until smooth. Add Worcestershire, lemon juice, and salt and pepper. Lower heat and simmer for 6 to 8 minutes. Remove from heat and strain through a fine strainer. Stir in heavy cream and baby leek and cook until heated through. Serve fillets topped with sauce.

Serves 6

Wine Notes

Recommended Wine: Thierry Triolet, Grande Reserve Champagne ($29.50)

Description: The blend of three vintages (1989, 1990, and 1991), this *blanc des blancs* is wine of traditional, mature, biscuity flavors admirably combined with fresh, aromatic, and soft fruit. This wine has spent eight years on the lees to provide structure and richness integrated with finesse, still worth aging.

Sommelier: Christian Lane, Moore Brothers Wine Co.

Bruce Lim's Roasted Salmon with Artichokes

Chef/Owner Bruce Lim
Ciboulette, Philadelphia, PA

1 tablespoon olive oil
½ onion, chopped
Salt and pepper
4 whole artichokes, cleaned
12 cloves garlic
2 plum tomatoes, chopped
1 carrot, sliced
½ celery root or parsnip, peeled
1 bulb fennel, sliced
2 cups white wine
½ cup water
1 bunch thyme
1 stalk basil
1 bay leaf
½ cup extra virgin olive oil
Lemon juice
4 pieces Atlantic salmon (about 6 ounces each), skin on
1 head Chinese Napa cabbage
Butter
Basil oil

Ciboulette

Known for:
Chinese cuisine with French flair

Years in business: 12

Most requested table:
in the "back room"

Menu:
French cuisine

Chef: Bruce Lim

Chef's training:
trained under Chef Jean-Louis Palladin and Jean-Marie Lacroix; former personal chef for George Harrison

Chef's hobbies/ accomplishments:
travel/recipient of numerous culinary awards

Heat 1 tablespoon olive oil in a saucepan over medium heat. Add onion and salt and pepper and sauté until soft. Add artichokes, garlic, tomatoes, carrot, celery root, and fennel. Sauté for 2 to 3 minutes. Add wine, water, thyme, basil, and bay leaf. Cover and cook until tender.

Transfer 3 artichokes, garlic, and celery root to a blender. (Reserve 1 artichoke for garnish.) Add ½ cup stewing liquid and mix until well blended. Add extra virgin olive oil. Add a touch of lemon juice and salt and pepper to taste. Blend and pass through a strainer. Reserve.

Preheat oven to 425°. Heat an ovenproof skillet or sauté pan over medium-high heat. Coat lightly with oil. Sear salmon, skin side down. Transfer to oven and bake until opaque, about 10 to 12 minutes.

Place cabbage in a saucepan with a little butter and enough water to cover. Cover saucepan and cook over high heat until just tender, about 2 to 3 minutes. Drain and sauté in butter for about 3 minutes. Season to taste with salt and pepper.

Lay cabbage on a serving plate. Cover with roasted salmon. Slice remaining artichoke and place on top of fish. Pour sauce around salmon and drizzle with basil oil.

Serves 4

Wine Notes

Recommended Wine: Jean-Georges, Chenas 1997 ($16.00)

Description: This elegant Beaujolais is revered as a celebratory wine and was said to have graced the table of Louis XIII. This varietal Gamay from southern Burgundy has delicate floral and spicy aromas and refined black fruit on the palate. This distinctive deep purple wine comes from fruit grown on manganese-enriched, salmon-pink granitic soil. While this wine has many characteristics in common with those of Burgundy, it is not for long keeping.

Sommelier: Kevin McCann, Moore Brothers Wine Co.

Tea Poached Salmon

Chef Alan Lichtenstein
Food for Thought, Marlton, NJ

2 salmon fillets (8 ounces each)
2 Earl Grey or Jasmine tea bags
2 tablespoons Chardonnay or Pinot Grigio
⅛ stick vanilla bean
1 tablespoon chopped white onion
1 rib celery
⅛ lemon pith and rind
1 sprig fresh basil
Fresh cracked pepper
Water or light stock

Preheat oven to 375°. Place all ingredients in a saucepot
or small roasting pan. Add enough water or light stock
to cover fillets. Bring to a simmer on stovetop. Transfer
to oven and bake for 8 to 10 minutes or to desired
doneness. Remove salmon from stock and serve over
rice or with new potatoes.

Serves 2

Food for Thought

Known for:
fresh improvisation of
highest quality ingredients

Years in business: 7

Most requested table:
#40

Menu:
upscale international
cuisine

Chef: Alan Lichtenstein

Chef's training:
Penn State

Chef's favorite foods:
sushi

**Chef's favorite
cookbook:**
Art Culinaire

Potato-Crusted Salmon with Mustard Sauce

Executive Chef Frank Buchler
Viana's Italian Cuisine, Voorhees, NJ

2 salmon fillets (8 ounces each)
1 tablespoon flour
4 red bliss potatoes, shredded
2 eggs
Salt and pepper
2 tablespoons butter
1 teaspoon vegetable oil
1½ teaspoons chopped shallots
2 tablespoons whole grain or Dijon mustard
2 ounces heavy cream
1 ounce white wine

Preheat oven to 350°. Lightly dust fillets with flour. Combine potatoes, eggs, and salt and pepper to taste. Coat fillets with potato mixture, molding and patting to get an even coating. Melt butter in an ovenproof skillet over medium-high heat. Add fish and cook for 2 minutes on each side. Transfer skillet to oven and bake for 8 to 10 minutes.

Heat oil in a separate skillet over medium heat. Add shallots and sauté for 1 minute. Whisk in mustard, cream, and wine and cook until combined and heated through. Serve fillets topped with sauce.

Serves 2

Viana's Italian Cuisine

Known for: garnishing, taste, fish

Years in business: 23

Menu:
Italian — meat, fish, pasta

Chef: Frank Buchler

Chef's training:
23 years of cooking

Chef's hobbies/ accomplishments:
cooking for the stars, ATV riding

Chef's favorite foods:
fish, lamb, meat

Chef's favorite cookbook:
The Art of Grilling

Salmon Casino

Executive Chef Daniel Dogan
The Terrace at Greenhill, Wilmington, DE

2 slices bacon, diced
½ cup butter, softened
1 small can chopped clams
½ cup chopped green bell pepper
½ cup chopped red bell pepper
¼ cup chopped white onion
1 shallot, minced
1 clove garlic, minced
1 teaspoon chopped parsley
Pinch of cayenne pepper
Pinch of salt
½ cup white breadcrumbs
2 salmon fillets (6 ounces each)
Salt and pepper
Lemon wedges

Cook bacon in a medium sauté pan until brown. Discard fat. Add butter, clams, peppers, onion, shallot, garlic, and parsley. Cook until onion becomes translucent. Season with cayenne pepper and salt. Stir in breadcrumbs. Mixture will tighten and resemble stuffing. Set aside to cool.

Preheat oven to 350°. Season each fillet with salt and pepper and place in a baking dish. Divide stuffing mixture in half. Place atop each fillet and spread evenly. Bake for 10 to 15 minutes, depending on desired doneness. Serve with lemon wedges.

Serves 2

The Terrace at Greenhill

Known for:
al fresco dining overlooking the Wilmington skyline

Years in business: 15

Most requested table:
any table overlooking the golf course

Menu:
new regional American

Chef: Daniel Dogan

Chef's training:
Philadelphia's Restaurant School

Chef's hobbies/ accomplishments:
extreme sports/ father to baby Joseph

Chef's favorite foods:
anything grilled with a lot of spice!

Chef's favorite cookbook:
Thrill of the Grill

Grilled Sea Bass with Olive Relish and Roasted Tomato Coulis

Executive Chef Nick Lo Bianco
Tuscan Twenty at Korman Suites Hotel, Philadelphia, PA

⅓ cup kalamata olives, pitted and sliced lengthwise
⅓ cup pincholine olives, pitted and sliced lengthwise
⅓ cup Sicilian olives, pitted and sliced lengthwise
Juice of ½ lemon
Chopped fresh basil
Chopped fresh mint
2 teaspoons olive oil
4 Chilean sea bass fillets (6 ounces each)
2 tablespoons extra virgin olive oil
Salt and pepper
Roasted Tomato Coulis (see recipe)

Toss together olives, lemon juice, basil, mint and olive oil. Reserve.

Prepare grill or heat grill pan over high heat. Lightly coat fish with extra virgin olive oil and salt and pepper. Grill, flesh side down, for 4 minutes. Turn over, cover, and cook for 4 minutes or until fish is firm to touch.

Top fish with generous spoonfuls of coulis and olive relish.

Serves 4

Roasted Tomato Coulis

2 pounds Roma tomatoes
2 shallots, peeled and halved
4 cloves garlic, peeled
1 sprig fresh rosemary, destemmed
2 sprigs fresh thyme, destemmed
2 ounces extra virgin olive oil
Salt and pepper

Preheat oven to 375°. Place all ingredients on a sheet pan and roast for 30 minutes. Carefully transfer ingredients to a blender or a food processor. Pulse until smooth. Strain.

Pan Roasted Chilean Sea Bass with Ceci and Potatoes Morzello

Executive Chef Donna Ewanciw
Toto, Philadelphia, PA

6 Chilean sea bass fillets (6 ounces each)
Salt and pepper
6 tablespoons extra virgin olive oil
6 cups julienned Swiss chard
½ cup coarsely chopped tomato
Ceci and Potatoes Morzello (Recipe appears on page 209.)
3 teaspoons chopped fresh chives

Preheat oven to 350°. Rub sea bass with salt and pepper. Heat 4 tablespoons olive oil in an ovenproof sauté pan over medium-high heat. Add fillets and sear for about 2 minutes per side. Transfer to oven and bake for 8 to 10 minutes.

In a separate sauté pan, heat remaining olive oil over medium heat. Gently sauté Swiss chard and tomatoes until heated through.

Place ceci and potatoes in a serving bowl or on plates. Cover with Swiss chard mixture. Place fillets on top. Garnish with chopped chives.

Serves 6

Wine Notes

Recommended Wine: Coteaux d' Aix-en-Provence "Cuvée Prestige Rose" Château Calissanne ($15.00)

Description: The largest single estate in the area with the best view of Mont-St.-Victoire in the vicinity of Aix-en-Provence also makes some of the most refined and elegant wines. This is a blend of Cabernet Sauvignon and Syrah in equal proportions, vinified with the typical *saignée* method and uncompromised by barrel elevation. A true *rosé de repas*, it is complex and full-bodied with a beautiful long, clean finish.

Sommelier: Jonathan Read, Moore Brothers Wine Co.

Poached Chilean Sea Bass with Shrimp in Saffron Broth

Chef William K. DeVore
L'Osteria Cucina Italiana, Wilmington, DE

2 cups white wine
2 cups seafood or vegetable stock
2 cups water
1 tomato, diced
2 shallots, peeled and thinly sliced
½ teaspoon saffron
½ teaspoon minced shallots
4 pieces Chilean sea bass (8 ounces each)
12 large shrimp, peeled and deveined
1 carrot, thinly sliced
⅛ cup peas
4 slices polenta (available premade in stores)
12 grape tomatoes, quartered
Chopped parsley
Salt and pepper

Combine wine, stock, and water in a medium pot and bring to a boil. Boil for 3 minutes. Add diced tomato and sliced shallots. Return to a boil and add saffron. Reduce heat to medium and simmer for 25 to 30 minutes. (Broth will be a vibrant yellow to orange color.) Remove from heat and let sit for 1 to 2 minutes. Strain and save liquid. Discard cooked vegetables.

Transfer liquid to a large lidded sauté pan. Add minced shallots and bring to a boil. Add sea bass, cover, and poach for 3 to 4 minutes. Remove lid, add shrimp, carrot, and peas. Replace lid and cook for 4 minutes or until shrimp are poached.

Warm polenta for about 30 to 45 seconds in microwave on high heat. Place 1 slice in each serving bowl. Bring broth back to a boil and add grape tomatoes and parsley. Season with salt and pepper. Carefully remove sea bass, placing each portion atop polenta. Divide shrimp and vegetable between bowls. Ladle hot broth into each bowl. Enjoy!

Serves 4

Swordfish and Rosemary Sauté

Executive Chef William Carroll
Sotto, Philadelphia, PA

½ cup extra virgin olive oil
1 pound swordfish, cut into 2-inch cubes
12 ounces red potatoes, blanched and cut into 2-inch cubes
2 tablespoons chopped shallots
2 tablespoons chopped garlic
2 tablespoons whole capers
2 medium tomatoes, peeled, seeded, and cut in 1½-inch squares
4 tablespoons chopped fresh rosemary
Juice of 2 lemons
1 cup dry white wine
6 slices yellow squash
6 slices zucchini
4 tablespoons chopped fresh Italian parsley
Salt and pepper
2 to 4 sprigs rosemary

Preheat oven to 400°. Heat oil in a medium ovenproof skillet over medium-high heat until oil reaches its smoking point. Add swordfish and potatoes and brown lightly on all sides. Add shallots, garlic, and capers. Cook until shallots and garlic start to brown, about 2 minutes. (Do NOT burn.) Add tomatoes and rosemary and cook for 1 minute. Add lemon juice and wine and cook until liquid begins to simmer. Transfer skillet to oven and cook for 4 minutes.

Grill or oven roast squash and zucchini. Place vegetables on serving plates. Place fish and potatoes atop vegetables. Season with parsley and salt and pepper to taste. Garnish each plate with sprig of rosemary.

Serves 2 to 4

Grilled Swordfish with Spicy Black Bean Sauce

Owner/Executive Chef Michael M. Wei
Yangming, Bryn Mawr, PA

4 center cut boneless swordfish steaks (8 ounces each)
1 tablespoon olive oil
1 teaspoon minced garlic
10 to 12 shallots, peeled and quartered
1 cup sliced shiitake mushrooms
1 cup julienned snow peas
1 cup shredded radicchio
4 tablespoons soy sauce
½ cup shrimp stock
½ cup white wine
2 tablespoons sugar
1 tablespoon cooked black beans
1 tablespoon hot pepper oil
1 teaspoon salt
1 teaspoon white pepper
½ teaspoon cornstarch
½ teaspoon water

Grill swordfish on hot grill (or broil) for 4 minutes per side, turning only once. Reserve.

Heat sauté pan over medium-high heat. Add olive oil, garlic, and shallots and stir-fry for 3 to 5 seconds. Add shiitakes, snowpeas, and radicchio and stir for 30 seconds. Add remaining ingredients, except cornstarch and water, and bring to a boil. Combine cornstarch and water in a small bowl and stir in. Season with additional salt and pepper, if needed.

Top swordfish steaks with vegetables and sauce.

Serves 4

Prosciutto Seared Red Snapper with Fennel and Tomato Broth

Chef Bruce Giardino
Marco's Restaurant, Philadelphia, PA

1 Yukon gold potato
2 tablespoons butter
2 ounces haricot vert, blanched
1 cup tomato juice
2 cups shrimp stock
¼ fennel bulb with top, diced
1 small shallot, diced
1 ounce white wine
2 snapper tournados (6 ounces each), pin bone out
   and skinned
1 ounce prosciutto, thinly sliced
2 tablespoons flour
2 tablespoons oil
2 to 4 drops Pernod
Kosher salt and fresh ground black pepper
1 teaspoon chopped fennel tops

Use a melon baller to scoop out potato and blanch. Melt butter, toss with potatoes and haricot vert, and reserve.

Heat tomato juice and stock in separate saucepans over medium heat. Cook until tomato juice is reduced to one-third and stock to one-half.

Lightly sauté fennel and shallot. Deglaze pan with wine. Add stock and heat until liquid is reduced by one-third.

Preheat oven to 400°. Top fish with prosciutto and lightly flour. Heat oil in an ovenproof skillet over high heat. Sear fish on one side, transfer to oven, and cook until heated through.

Place fish on serving plates. Top with buttered vegetables, sauce, and drops of Pernod. Season with salt and pepper. Garnish with drops of tomato juice and fennel tops.

Serves 2

Marco's Restaurant

Known for:
affordable, eclectic, tapas-style menu

Years in business: 2½

Most requested table:
30 and #10

Menu: international, fresh

Chef: Bruce Giardino

Chef's training:
The Restaurant School; 20 years of cooking

Chef's hobbies/ accomplishments:
coin collecting/finalist in 1998 Indian Rock Salad Toss

Chef's favorite foods:
Mediterranean, Asian, Greek, squid, lamb, pork

Chef's favorite cookbook:
any by Julia Child, Alice Waters, Paula Wolfert, Jacques Pepin

Sun-dried Tomato Crusted Snapper with Fennel, Artichokes, and Olives

Chef/Proprietor Alfonso Contrisciani
Opus 251, Philadelphia, PA

4 red snapper fillets (6 to 8 ounces each), scales removed and skin on
Kosher salt
Freshly ground black pepper
2 ounces sun-dried tomatoes, finely ground
2 tablespoons canola oil
2 tablespoons olive oil
½ teaspoon minced garlic
1 tablespoon minced shallots
¼ cup diced onions
1 cup julienned fennel
½ tablespoon julienned basil
¼ teaspoon fresh thyme
1 cup cleaned, quartered, and cooked baby artichokes
2 ounces Chardonnay
6 ounces chicken stock
4 tablespoons whole butter
¼ cup calamata olives, pits removed

Preheat oven to 350°. Season fish with salt and pepper. Cover with sun-dried tomato dust.

Heat canola oil in a skillet over high flame. Add fish, skin side down, and cook for 3 to 5 minutes. Turn fish and sear flesh side for 2 to 3 minutes or until a dark caramel color. Transfer to a baking sheet and bake for 10 to 12 minutes or until done.

In same skillet, heat olive oil over medium heat. Add garlic and shallots and sauté until golden. Add onion, fennel, basil, and thyme and cook for 2 to 3 minutes. Add artichokes and wine and cook until liquid is reduced by half. Add chicken stock and cook until liquid is reduced by two-thirds. Stir in butter. Season to taste with salt and pepper. Serve sauce over fish and sprinkle with olives.

Serves 4

Ca Chien Saigon
Crispy Red Snapper with Chili Lime Sauce

Executive Chef Hoc Van Tran
Le Colonial, Philadelphia, PA

½ cup water
2 ounces fish sauce
2 tablespoons sugar
3 tablespoons lime juice
2 teaspoons chili pepper paste
2 cups vegetable oil
1 whole red snapper (1 to 1½ pounds)
Salt and pepper
2 tablespoons all-purpose flour
2 teaspoons rice flour
2 teaspoons minced garlic
2 scallions, chopped
Cilantro
Fresh lime wedges

Combine water, fish sauce, sugar, lime juice, and chili pepper paste. Reserve. (For a spicier sauce, add more chili paste.)

Heat oil in a large sauté pan over medium-high heat. Season fish with salt and pepper. Combine flours, sprinkle over fish, and shake off excess. Place fish in pan and cook for 5 minutes on each side. Transfer fish to a serving plate.

Remove all but 1 tablespoon oil from pan. Return pan to heat, add garlic, and brown lightly. Add scallions and reserved sauce. Bring to a boil. Pour sauce over fish. Garnish with cilantro and lime wedges.

Serves 2

Sautéed Red Snapper with Crabmeat

Executive Chef Jeffrey Gutstein
Cresheim Cottage Cafe, Philadelphia, PA

1 tablespoon butter
1 teaspoon minced garlic
1 medium tomato, diced
½ teaspoon fresh thyme
2 ounces dry white wine
4 ounces crabmeat (preferably jumbo lump), shells
  removed
Salt and pepper
Flour
4 red snapper fillets (6 to 8 ounces each)
3 tablespoons olive oil
2 tablespoons pine nuts, toasted

Melt butter in a small skillet. Add garlic and cook until lightly browned. Add tomato and thyme and cook for 1 minute. Add white wine and cook for 1 minute. Stir in crabmeat and heat through. Season to taste with salt and pepper and keep warm.

Season flour with a little salt and pepper. Dredge fillets lightly in flour and shake off excess. Heat olive oil in a sauté pan over high heat. Place fillets in pan, one at a time, flesh side down. Fry for 3 to 4 minutes and turn over. Cook for 3 to 4 minutes more or until cooked to desired doneness.

Place fillets on plates and top with crabmeat mixture. Sprinkle with pine nuts. Enjoy!

Serves 4

Cresheim Cottage Cafe

Known for:
comfortable historical
setting circa 1748

Years in business: 4

Most requested table:
by the large colonial
fireplace

Menu:
regional American

Chef: Jeffrey Gutstein

Chef's training:
Culinary Institute of
America

**Chef's hobbies/
accomplishments:**
fishing/local awards, TV

Chef's favorite foods:
French, Caribbean

**Chef's favorite
cookbook:**
*Larousse
Gastronomique*

Sesame-Crusted Tuna Loin with Ponzu-Wasabi Vinaigrette

Chef/Proprietor Philippe Chin
Philippe on Locust, Philadelphia, PA

1 pound sushi-grade tuna loin, cleaned
Salt and pepper
2 tablespoons black sesame seeds, toasted
2 tablespoons white sesame seeds, toasted
1 tablespoon ponzu
1 tablespoon wasabi, diluted
½ tablespoon rice vinegar
½ tablespoon sesame oil
1½ tablespoons extra virgin olive oil
2 tablespoons olive oil
¼ pound mixed greens

Season tuna on each side with salt and pepper. Mix black and white sesame seeds and roll tuna in mixture. Set aside.

Whisk together ponzu, wasabi, and vinegar in a mixing bowl. Slowly whisk in sesame oil and extra virgin olive oil. Set aside.

Heat olive oil in a large skillet over high heat. When oil reaches smoking point, sear tuna for about 2 minutes per side. Slice tuna into 12 medallions.

Arrange 3 medallions on each plate and drizzle with vinaigrette. Serve with a bouquet of greens tossed with remaining vinaigrette.

Serves 4

Philly Foodie Fact

Ponzu is a Japanese sauce made from lemon juice, soy sauce, mirin, and dried bonito flakes. It is used as a dipping sauce. You can find it at most grocery stores and specialty markets, such as Hanyang Food Market in Cherry Hill, NJ.

Tuna Tempura

Executive Chef David Grear
La Terrasse, Philadelphia, PA

1 pound saku tuna
1 cup cornstarch
1 cup flour
½ cup pureed cilantro
8 ounces soda water
½ cup sugar
Salt and pepper
Canola oil
Pepper Jelly Sauce (see recipe)
Pickled ginger, optional

Cut tuna into 4-ounce pieces. Mix cornstarch and flour together. Add pureed cilantro and soda water and stir until consistency is close to heavy cream. Stir in sugar and salt and pepper to taste.

Heat oil in a deep fryer or heavy bottomed pan to 350°. (If using a pan, add enough oil to measure ½-inch deep.) Dip tuna into batter and let excess drain off. Fry tuna until desired doneness. (Ninety seconds will give you a nice rare tuna.) Drain on paper towel.

Spoon some pepper jelly sauce in middle of each plate. Slice tuna diagonally and place on top of sauce. (I like to serve this with pickled ginger.)

Serves 4

Pepper Jelly Sauce

2 cups pineapple juice
1 cup clear Karo syrup
1 teaspoon pectin
1 EACH red, yellow, and jalapeño pepper, diced
½ teaspoon cracked black pepper
¼ teaspoon red pepper flakes

Cook pineapple juice and Karo syrup in a saucepan over medium heat until liquid is reduced by half. Slowly stir in pectin, stirring until smooth. Add diced peppers, black pepper, and red pepper flakes. Keep warm until ready to use.

Tuna Sambuca

Chef/Owner Joseph Tucker
Pompeii Restaurant, Philadelphia, PA

2 red peppers
7 tablespoons olive oil
Salt and freshly ground pepper
1 pound fresh cut tuna steak
Blackening Seasoning Mix (Recipe appears on page 301.)
¼ cup pitted kalamata olives
2 cloves garlic, finely chopped
¼ cup thinly sliced white button mushrooms
3 ounces sambuca
1 cup fish stock or chicken broth
1 tablespoon butter
4 basil leaves, roughly chopped

Preheat oven to 350°. Cut peppers in half and discard green interiors, stems, and seeds. Julienne peppers and place in a shallow baking dish. Sprinkle with 2 tablespoons olive oil and salt and pepper. Bake for approximately 20 minutes until peppers are soft.

Meanwhile, rinse tuna and pat dry with paper towels. Dredge in blackening seasoning.

Heat 4 tablespoons olive oil in sauté pan over medium-high heat until oil is hot but not smoking. Place tuna in pan and cook for 1 minute on each side. Remove tuna from pan and reserve.

Discard used oil from sauté pan and add 1 tablespoon fresh olive oil. Heat over medium-high heat. Add roasted red peppers, olives, garlic, and mushrooms. (Be sure to add mushrooms last.) Sauté for 3 minutes until mushrooms soften. Remove vegetables. Deglaze pan with sambuca. Add butter and stock and cook for 3 minutes, bringing to a boil and then simmer.

Serve tuna topped with vegetables and sauce. Garnish with basil.

Serves 2

Pompeii Restaurant

Known for:
stuffed veal chops and light sauces

Years in business: 2

Most requested table:
chef's table by the kitchen

Menu:
multi-regional Italian

Chef: Joseph Tucker

Chef's training:
self taught

Chef's hobbies/ accomplishments:
golf and giving cooking classes/opened several successful restaurants

Chef's favorite foods:
seafood and veal chops

Chef's favorite cookbook:
Multo Mario

Grilled Tuna Steak with Mango Salsa

Executive Chef Andrew Maloney
Nodding Head Brewery & Restaurant, Philadelphia, PA

1 cup peeled, pitted, and diced into ¼-inch cubes ripe mango
¼ cup finely diced red onion
2 tablespoons coarsely chopped cilantro
1 tablespoon fresh lime juice
1 jalapeño pepper, minced (seeds and vein removed)
4 tuna steaks (6 to 8 ounces each)
Seasoned or herbed olive oil
Salt and pepper
Zucchini and/or yellow squash medallions
Strips of red peppers

Place first 5 ingredients in a bowl and combine thoroughly. Refrigerate. (Best when made 1 day in advance.)

Heat grill to medium-high. Brush steaks with oil. Sprinkle both sides with salt and pepper. Grill fish for a few minutes on each side. Do not overcook: fish can dry out very quickly on a char grill. Toss vegetable medallions and peppers with seasoned oil and grill.

Place fish on serving plates. Top fish with mango salsa and serve with grilled veggies.

Serves 4

Chef's Note

This dish is the essence of simplicity and beauty. It gives you time to mingle with your guests and talk with your family rather than slave over the grill for hours. The final dish will have your guests convinced that you did work on this for hours. Choose any firm-fleshed fish. We often use tuna, mahi mahi, and sometimes even salmon. You can use a whole fish, steak cuts, or fillets. Plan on serving 6 to 8 ounces per guest.

Baked Flounder with Lobster Aïoli

President Jack Kramer
Jack Kramer's Catering, Philadelphia, PA

3 pounds flounder
3 tablespoons lemon juice
Old Bay Seasoning
Salt and pepper
1 tablespoon whole butter, softened
1 teaspoon minced garlic
8 to 10 ounces lobster meat
2 ounces white wine
2 egg yolks
2 drops hot sauce
4 tablespoons unsalted butter, melted
Italian parsley leaves

Preheat oven to 350°. Season flounder with lemon juice, Old Bay, and salt and pepper to taste. Let rest for 10 minutes. Bake for 8 to 10 minutes or until just done.

Sauté 1 tablespoon whole butter and garlic in a large sauté pan until bubbly. Add lobster meat and sauté for 5 minutes. Deglaze pan with white wine and simmer for 2 minutes. Beat egg yolks until light yellow in color, about 2 minutes. Reduce heat under pan. Add Old Bay to taste, hot sauce, and melted butter. With flame low, stir in a little of egg yolk mixture. Incorporate and stir in remaining yolks. Remove from stove.

Place flounder on a serving plate with lobster aïoli. Garnish with Italian parsley leaves.

Serves 6

Jack Kramer's Catering

Known for:
considered to be one of Philadelphia's foremost caterers, featuring a thoroughly professional staff well versed in American, Russian, and French service

Years in business: 30

Menu:
eclectic

Chef: Jasper Reid

Chef's hobbies/ accomplishments:
collector of music and movies/has been with Kramer's for over 20 years

Chef's favorite cookbook:
Joy of Cooking

Braised Monkfish with Portobello Mushrooms

Executive Chef/Owner Marco Carrozza
Marco's Restaurant, Philadelphia, PA

2 monkfish fillets (about 7 ounces each), cleaned
½ cup all-purpose flour
2 tablespoons olive oil
2 tablespoons minced garlic
Pinch of salt and pepper
2 large portobello mushrooms, sliced
4 whole oven-dried plum tomatoes
4 ounces fennel bulb, roughly chopped
2 tablespoons chopped chives
12 ounces Saffron Shellfish Stock (Recipe appears on page 303.)
1 tablespoon butter

Preheat oven to 500°. Lightly flour fillets. Heat oil in an ovenproof skillet over medium-high heat. Add fillets and sear for 1 minute on each side. Add garlic and sauté for 1 minute. Add salt and pepper, portobellos, tomatoes, fennel, chives, and stock. Stir and place skillet in oven. Bake for 13 minutes or until fish is firm to the touch. Remove pan from oven. Swirl in butter. Serve fillets topped with vegetables and skillet sauce.

Serves 2 to 3

Chef's Note

To oven dry tomatoes . . . wash and dry ripe plum tomatoes. Cut in half lengthwise and place on a baking sheet. Sprinkle with a little salt and sugar. Bake in a 175° to 200° oven for 12 to 16 hours. Cool and peel off skin.

Crispy Whole Black Bass

Executive Chef Carolynn Angle
Fishmarket, Philadelphia, PA

1 cup balsamic vinegar
1 cup rock shrimp
6 spears asparagus, peeled
8 red grape tomatoes, sliced
8 yellow grape tomatoes, sliced
Chopped fresh garlic
Salt and black pepper
Vegetable oil
2 whole black bass (1 to 1½ pounds each)
1 cup cornstarch
2 potatoes
Beurre Blanc (Recipe appears on page 292.)
Fresh chopped parsley

Cook balsamic vinegar over medium heat until reduced and very syrupy. Reserve.

Sauté shrimp, asparagus, tomatoes, and garlic to taste over medium heat until shrimp is just cooked. Season with salt and pepper and reserve.

Heat oil in a deep fryer to 325°. Dredge bass in cornstarch and shake off excess. Spread fins and insert potato into each mouth. Place bass in fryer and fry for 4 to 5 minutes until cooked. Season with salt and pepper.

Ladle beurre blanc onto centers of serving plates. Place fish on top, sitting up. Place sautéed mixture on either side of fish. Drizzle fish and mixture with reduced balsamic vinegar. Sprinkle with parsley.

Serves 2

Fishmarket

Known for:
freshest seafood in town

Years in business: 6 months

Most requested table:
booths that seat 6

Menu:
all-seafood menu with bold and fresh flavors

Chef: Carolynn Angle

Chef's training:
12 years in the business; 6 years at Striped Bass

Chef's hobbies/ accomplishments:
music

Chef's favorite foods:
Italian, Mediterranean, Malaysian

Chef's favorite cookbook:
anything by Julia Child

Baccala Regannet

Chef/Owner Salvatore DiPalma
DiPalma Ristorante & Bar, Philadelphia, PA

2 pounds baccala fillets (skinless, boneless, pliable,
   salt-dried cod)
2 cups soft breadcrumbs
6 tablespoons extra virgin olive oil
4 tablespoons minced black olives
4 tablespoons chopped rosemary
2 tablespoons chopped capers
2 tablespoons minced garlic
Red pepper flakes
Salt and pepper
1 large potato, peeled and sliced
2 tablespoons red wine vinegar

Soak baccala in cold water for 2 to 3 days, changing
water often. Drain and pat dry. Remove any small
bones. Poach in a large pot of boiling water until
baccala is firm. Drain and cool. Crumble into bite-size
pieces.

Mix breadcrumbs with 4 tablespoons oil, 2 tablespoons
each olives and rosemary, 1 tablespoon each capers and
garlic, red pepper flakes, and salt and pepper to taste.
Mix remaining olives, rosemary, capers, and garlic with
baccala.

Preheat oven to 350°. Lightly oil a 2- to 2½-quart
baking dish. Layer potato slices evenly over bottom of
dish. Sprinkle half of breadcrumb mixture over potatoes.
Top with baccala; then remaining breadcrumbs. Drizzle
with remaining oil and vinegar. Cover. Bake for 30
minutes. Uncover to brown crumbs lightly.

Serves 6

DiPalma Ristorante & Bar

Known for:
homemade pasta

Years in business: 1½

Most requested table:
#13

Menu:
modern Italian

Chef: Salvatore DiPalma

Chef's training:
Johnson & Wales
University

**Chef's hobbies/
accomplishments:**
sky diving, mountain
climbing, sailing

Chef's favorite foods:
foie gras

**Chef's favorite
cookbook:**
Madeleine Kamman's
Making of a Chef

shellfish

Gamberi al Sugo D'Aglio Arrostito 182

Skillet Seared Indonesian Shrimp Scampi 183

Jumbo Shrimp with Asparagus, Shiitake Mushroom, and Melon 184

Drunken' Whiskey Shrimp 185

BBQ Shrimp with Grits and Collards 186

Pan Roasted Lobster 187

Prize Winning Scallops 188

Pan-seared Scallops with Grilled Fennel 189

Andrew's Crab Cakes 190

Wasabi Crab Cake 191

Savona Crab Cake 192

Maryland Crab Cakes 194

Crab Cakes with Cilantro and Poblano 195

Soft-shell Crabs Oreganate 196

Seafood Risotto 197

Seafood Jambalaya 198

Beer Seafood Fest 199

Gamberi al Sugo D'Aglio Arrostito

Chef Rosario Romano, Jr.
Ristorante Panorama, Philadelphia, PA

4 heads fresh garlic
12 jumbo shrimp
2 tablespoons unsalted butter
Pinch of cayenne pepper
Dash of white pepper
Pinch of salt
½ cup low sodium chicken stock
1 pound fresh spinach, blanched

Preheat oven to 350°. Cut garlic heads in half and cover with aluminum foil. Roast in oven for 40 to 45 minutes. Allow to cool slightly.

Peel and devein shrimp. Rinse under cold water and reserve.

Squeeze garlic from papery outer shell into a medium saucepan. Turn heat to medium heat. Add butter, cayenne pepper, white pepper, and salt. When butter is melted, add chicken stock and bring to a boil. Puree mixture in a blender or with immersion blender. Strain through a sieve into a saucepan. Return pan to heat. Add shrimp and cook until just done, about 2 to 4 minutes.

Place spinach in middle of serving plates. Arrange shrimp around spinach and top with sauce.

Serves 2

Ristorante Panorama

Known for:
pasta

Years in business: 10

Most requested table:
#16

Menu: Italian

Chef:
Rosario T. Romano, Jr.

Chef's training:
self taught

Chef's hobbies/ accomplishments:
scuba, skydiving, softball

Chef's favorite foods:
fried chicken, penne and broccoli rabe, all seafood

Favorite cookbook:
Classic Techniques of Italian Cooking by Giuliano Bugialli

Skillet Seared Indonesian Shrimp Scampi

Executive Chef Mustapha Rouissiya
Rococo, Philadelphia, PA

2 cups olive oil
1 red onion, minced
¼ cup roughly chopped garlic cloves
½ cup peeled and sliced ginger
1 teaspoon salt
¼ teaspoon Tabasco
½ cup roughly chopped cashews
½ cup currants
1½ teaspoons fennel seeds
Zest and juice of 2 lemons
1 tablespoon vegetable oil
20 large shrimp
¼ to ½ cup chicken stock or chicken broth

Heat olive oil in a medium-size pot over medium heat. Sauté red onion until translucent. Add garlic, ginger, salt, and Tabasco. Cook for about 5 minutes, stirring constantly. Add cashews, currants, and fennel seeds. Remove from heat and cool. Add lemon zest and juice.

Heat vegetable oil in a sauté pan over medium-high heat. Add shrimp and sauté until cooked to desired doneness. Add about 1 cup currant sauce to shrimp and bring mixture to a boil. Add chicken stock and stir to combine well. Serve immediately.

Serves 4

Wine Notes

Recommended Wine: Vouvray Aigle Blanc Poniatowski 1996 ($14.00)

Description: A Chenin Blanc grape is a chameleon: its characteristics change with each season, giving always elegant and complex wines with a great future ahead of themselves. This is a refined, soft, and intensely floral and fruity wine with stony and mineral flavors, well balanced by the right degree of acidity and good alcoholic level. Its ripeness is very attractive now; its subtleties allude to cellaring.

Sommelier: Jonathan Read, Moore Brothers Wine Co.

Jumbo Shrimp with Asparagus, Shiitake Mushroom, and Melon

Chef/Owner Patrick Lee
Joe's Peking Duck House, Marlton, NJ

12 jumbo shrimp, peeled and deveined
½ cup vegetable oil
1 teaspoon chopped fresh garlic
12 ounces fresh asparagus tips, 2 inches long
6 ounces shiitake mushrooms
16 cantaloupe melon balls
1 cup chicken broth
2 tablespoons oyster sauce
1 tablespoon cooking sherry
1 teaspoon sesame oil
1½ tablespoon sugar
2 tablespoons cornstarch
¼ cup water

Blanch shrimp in boiling water for 2 minutes. Remove and drain.

Heat oil in a wok over high heat. When near boiling point, add garlic. Add blanched shrimp, asparagus, shiitake mushrooms, and melon balls and sauté for 2 minutes. Mix in chicken broth, oyster sauce, cooking sherry, sesame oil, and sugar. Bring to a boil.

In a small bowl, mix cornstarch with water. Add to wok. Stir until well combined and sauce thickens.

Serves 2

Joe's Peking Duck House

Known for:
Peking duck, seasonal fresh delectable seafood

Years in business: 14

Menu:
fresh ingredients and consistent cooking

Chef: Patrick Lee

Chef's training:
Special training program at CIA; 10 years airline food service

Chef's hobbies/ accomplishments:
traveling and trying different cuisines

Chef's favorite foods:
Japanese and Italian

Chef's favorite cookbook:
Four Season Cooking by Wei Chuen

Drunken' Whiskey Shrimp

Chef/Co-owner John C. Hayden
Café Nola, Philadelphia, PA

2 tablespoons butter
8 ounces tasso ham, finely diced
2 cloves garlic, diced
1 shallot, diced
2 scallions, diced
Jack Daniel's, about ½ cup or to taste
2 teaspoons Old Bay Seasoning
1 teaspoon chopped basil
1 teaspoon coriander
2 teaspoons Worcestershire sauce
1 teaspoon Angostura bitters
1 quart good veal stock
1 quart shrimp stock
Salt and pepper
Cornstarch or arrowroot
36 large prawns (jumbo shrimp)

Melt butter in a large pan over medium heat. Add tasso ham, garlic, shallot, and scallions and sauté until caramel colored. Add Jack Daniel's and cook until liquid is reduced by one-quarter. (Be careful: liquor WILL flame.) Add seasonings and stocks and bring to a boil. Reduce heat and simmer for 20 to 30 minutes. Season to taste with salt and pepper. Thicken with cornstarch or arrowroot.

In a separate pan, sauté prawns until done. Add to mixture and stir to combine well.

Serves 6

Philly Foodie Fact

Angostura is a trade name for a brand of bitters. Bitters are made from aromatic herbs, barks, roots, and plants. Not surprisingly, they have a bitter or bittersweet taste and are used to flavor cocktails and foods. You can find them at your favorite liquor store.

BBQ Shrimp with Grits and Collards

General Manager Trish Morrissey
Jack's Firehouse/Down Home Diner, Philadelphia, PA

32 large shrimp, peeled and deveined
¼ cup vegetable oil
Salt and pepper
Chipotle BBQ Sauce (see recipe)
Cheddar Grits (Recipe appears on page 240.)
Collards with Smoked Bacon (Recipe appears on page 205.)

Heat grill or grill pan to medium-high heat. Toss shrimp with oil and salt and pepper. Grill shrimp for 1 to 2 minutes. Turn and brush with BBQ sauce. Cook for 1 minute more and serve with grits and collards.

Serves 6

Chipotle BBQ Sauce

2 tablespoons vegetable oil
½ onion, diced
3 cloves garlic, smashed
1 cup chopped tomatoes
1 cup ketchup
½ to 1 cup brewed coffee, depending on desired thickness
3 tablespoons molasses
3 tablespoons brown sugar
2 tablespoons Dijon mustard
1 tablespoon Worcestershire sauce
2 chipotle peppers
Cayenne pepper, optional

Heat oil in a medium saucepan over medium heat Add onion and garlic and cook for 3 minutes. Add tomatoes and simmer for about 8 minutes. Add remaining ingredients and simmer for 15 minutes. Remove from heat and puree in a food processor. Serve right away or let cool and refrigerate.

Pan Roasted Lobster

Executive Chef William Carroll
Sotto, Philadelphia, PA

½ cup vegetable oil
2 lobsters (2 pounds each), split with claws removed
½ cup sliced shallots
2 teaspoons chopped garlic
1½ tablespoons whole capers
4 ounces bourbon whiskey
2 cups lobster stock or clam juice
Juice of 2 lemons
8 tablespoons butter
2 tablespoons EACH chopped fresh tarragon, parsley, and chives
Salt and pepper

Preheat oven to 375°. Heat oil in a medium ovenproof skillet over medium-high heat until oil reaches just below its smoking point. Add lobster, meat side down, and cook for 1 minute. Turn and cook for 1 minute more. Add shallots, garlic, and capers. Cook until shallots and garlic start to brown, about 2 minutes. (Do NOT burn.) Add bourbon and simmer until liquid is reduced by half. Add stock and lemon juice. Bring to a simmer. Transfer skillet to oven and cook for 8 minutes. Remove lobster from oven and place on a serving plate.

Return skillet to burner. Cook until remaining liquid reduces to ½ cup. Remove skillet from heat. Gradually whisk in butter. Whisk in herbs. Season to taste with salt and pepper. Pour sauce over lobster and serve immediately.

Serves 2

Wine Notes

Recommended Wine: Vouvray "Clos de l'Avenir" Poniatowski 1995 ($17.75)

Description: From one of the most prestigious walled vineyards in the region comes the full-bodied, very well structured wine that in the bouquet reveals fresh flavors of ripe, honeyed fruit, and then develops its richness and dryness on the palate, leaving a long, clean finish and a pleasantly persistent aftertaste.

Sommelier: Christian Lane, Moore Brothers Wine Co.

Prize Winning Scallops

Teacher Kristin Albertson
Incredible Edibles, Wynnewood, PA

20 Town House crackers
2 tablespoons minced fresh parsley
1 tablespoon minced fresh oregano
1 large clove garlic, minced
¼ teaspoon cayenne pepper
2 ounces butter, melted
1 pound sea scallops (cut in half, if large) or 1 pound bay scallops
4 ounces sharp Cheddar cheese, grated
Paprika

Preheat oven to 350°. Crush crackers into fine crumbs. (This can be done in a food processor or by placing crackers in a zip lock bag and crushing them with a rolling pin.) Place crumbs, parsley, oregano, garlic, and pepper in a mixing bowl and combine well. Stir in melted butter. Add scallops and cheese and mix well. Spray or butter a 2-quart baking dish or 4 individual ramekins. Fill with scallop mixture. Sprinkle with paprika. Bake for 15 minutes.

As an hors d'oeuvre, serve with toasted pita wedges or bagel chips.

Serves 4 as an entree
Serves 32 as an hors d'oeuvre

Chef's Note

I won a $1,000 saving bond for this recipe in the "Kids in the Kitchen" cooking contest sponsored by ShopRite supermarkets! Years later, I still love to serve it as a buffet entree or in individual scallop dishes or ramekins.

Pan-seared Scallops with Grilled Fennel

Executive Chef Joseph Becker
Peddler's Village, Lahaska, PA

5 ounces fennel
24 jumbo scallops
Salt and pepper
2 tablespoons olive oil
½ cup small diced onion
¼ cup minced garlic
1 cup sambuca
½ cup sherry
1 pint fish stock
2 tablespoons sliced basil
½ pound tomatoes, diced
1 tablespoon lemon zest
2 tablespoons honey
8 ounces butter, cut into chunks

Grill fennel, dice, and reserve.

Season scallops with salt and pepper. Heat oil in a skillet over medium-high heat. Sear scallops on both sides and remove from pan. Add onion and garlic to pan and cook until translucent. Stir in fennel. Deglaze pan with sambuca and sherry. Add fish stock and cook until reduced by half. Stir in basil, tomatoes, lemon zest, and honey. Season to taste with salt and pepper. Return scallops to pan and cook for about 2 minutes. Remove pan from heat. Whisk in butter. Serve alone or over pasta.

Serves 6

Wine Notes

Recommended Wine: Sancerre VV Domaine Daulny 1998 ($17.50)

Description: This single vineyard, 40-year-old Sancerre from Etiènne Daulny, is the product of careful fruit selection, vinified in stainless steel vats, and released in small quantities (about 1,500 bottles for the 1998 vintage). A crisp, complex, refined, and multi-layered wine, this would be a marvelous accompaniment to seafood.

Sommelier: Jonathan Read, Moore Brothers Wine Co.

Andrew's Crab Cakes

Executive Chef Andrew Berks
Twelve Caesars Radisson Hotel, Philadelphia, PA

1 pound jumbo lump crabmeat
3 tablespoons mayonnaise
2 medium eggs
1 tablespoon whole grain mustard
1 teaspoon Old Bay Seasoning
Pinch of cayenne pepper
½ cup Japanese-style breadcrumbs
1 tablespoon EACH minced parsley, chervil, and chives
Juice of 1 lemon
½ teaspoon Worcestershire sauce
Salt and pepper
1 teaspoon olive oil
½ lemon

Mix together all ingredients, except olive oil and lemon, being careful not to break up crab lumps too much. Divide mixture into 8 equal portions and shape each into a cake.

Preheat oven to 350°. Heat oil in a large nonstick skillet over medium heat. Place cakes in skillet and fry until just golden on each side. Transfer cakes to oven and bake for 8 to 10 minutes. Serve hot with a squeeze of lemon.

Serves 4

Wine Notes

Recommended Wine: Alsace Riesling Herrenweg Barmès-Beucher 1998 ($15.50)

Description: Situated between the villages of Turckheim and Wintzenheim, the Herrenweg vineyard has a unique microclimate with sandy, well-drained soil and plenty of sun during the year. Elegant, sensuous wines are made from fruit grown here, particularly the beautiful Riesling, so palatable young as worth cellaring for a few years.

Sommelier: Luca Mazzotti, Moore Brothers Wine Co.

Wasabi Crab Cake

Executive Chef Chris Scarduzio
Brasserie Perrier, Philadelphia, PA

6 ounces crabmeat, picked over
2 teaspoons minced fennel
2 teaspoons minced celery
2 teaspoons minced shallot
4 tablespoons wasabi mayonnaise (add more, if you like)
1 teaspoon chopped chives
1 teaspoon chopped cilantro
Salt and pepper
Drizzle of sesame oil
Japanese panko breadcrumbs
1 tablespoon blended oil
1 cup juliennned daikon radish
1 cup picked pea leaves
Olive oil

Place crabmeat in a chilled bowl. Place fennel, celery, and shallot in a food processor and pulse to combine well. Squeeze to remove excess moisture and add to crabmeat. Stir in wasabi mayonnaise, chives, and cilantro. Season to taste with salt and pepper and sesame oil. Mix in enough breadcrumbs to tighten mixture. Form mixture into 2 crab cakes and coat with additional breadcrumbs.

Heat blended oil in a sauté pan over medium-high heat. Sauté crab cakes until hot and crispy on both sides.

Combine daikon radish, pea leaves, salt and pepper, and olive oil to taste. Place crab cakes on plates and garnish with vegetables.

Serves 2

Brasserie Perrier

Known for:
Art Deco design

Years in business: 3

Most requested table:
#32

Menu:
French with Asian and Italian influence

Chef: Chris Scarduzio

Chef's training:
Culinary Institute of America

Chef's hobbies/ accomplishments:
golf

Chef's favorite foods:
pasta

Chef's favorite cookbook:
any of Joel Robuchom's books

Savona Crab Cake

Executive Chef Dominique Filoni
Savona, Gulph Mills, PA

½ cup breadcrumbs

1 teaspoon Old Bay Seasoning

1 teaspoon salt

⅛ teaspoon white pepper

1 red pepper, diced small

½ tablespoon chopped parsley

½ tablespoon chopped thyme

3 tablespoons Worcestershire sauce

1 teaspoon Tabasco sauce

1 tablespoon lemon juice

½ tablespoon chopped garlic

½ cup chopped shallots

2 cups heavy cream

2 egg yolks

1 pound jumbo lump crabmeat

2 roasted red peppers

2 tablespoons extra virgin olive oil

1 bulb fennel, thinly shaved

1 bunch arugula, chiffonade

Lemon Vinaigrette (see recipe)

Red Pepper Coulis (see recipe)

1 bunch chives, chopped

Savona

Known for:
extensive award-winning
wine list

Years in business: 2½

Most requested table:
#13

Menu: seafood inspired
by the Italian Riviera

Chef: Dominique Filoni

Chef's training:
Culinary Institute in Hyeres,
graduated with honors

**Chef's hobbies/
accomplishments:**
traveling, soccer, music,
movies, reading

Chef's favorite foods:
oven-roasted Branzino
with tomatoes, potatoes,
garlic, and olive oil

**Chef's favorite
cookbook:**
*Escoffier, Riviera of Alain
Ducasse*

Combine breadcrumbs, Old Bay Seasoning, salt, and pepper. Reserve.

In a separate bowl, combine diced red pepper, parsley, thyme, Worcestershire, Tabasco, and lemon juice. Lightly sauté garlic and shallots in a skillet for 1 minute. Add to red pepper mixture.

Heat cream in a small saucepan until reduced by half. Pour into a bowl to cool. Add egg yolks and stir to combine.

Combine red pepper mixture, cream mixture, and crabmeat. Add enough seasoned breadcrumbs to achieve desired consistency. Divide crab mixture among 8 ring molds or shape into patties. Dust with remaining breadcrumbs.

Preheat oven to 500°. Lightly sauté cakes in an ovenproof skillet over medium heat. Transfer to oven and bake for 4 minutes.

Julienne roasted red peppers. Heat olive oil in a small sauté pan over medium heat. Add peppers and sauté until warmed through. Season to taste with salt and pepper.

Place fennel and arugula in a bowl and toss with a portion of lemon vinaigrette.

Place a ring mold slightly larger than crab cake in the center of each serving plate and fill with fennel and arugula (or simply mound in the centers of plates). Place 3 julienned roasted red peppers in three spots around ring mold on each plate and fork twirl. Drizzle plate with red pepper coulis and lemon vinaigrette. Sprinkle chives around plate. Top salad with cooked crab cake. Remove ring mold and serve.

Serves 8

Lemon Vinaigrette

1 cup extra virgin olive oil
3 tablespoons lemon juice
1 tablespoon Dijon mustard
1 teaspoon salt
⅛ teaspoon pepper

Combine all ingredients and mix with a hand blender until emusified.

Red Pepper Coulis

¼ pound red peppers, halved with stems and seeds removed
3 ounces chicken stock
3 tablespoons butter
Salt and pepper

Cook peppers in chicken stock until tender and liquid is reduced by half. Transfer to a blender and puree. Season with salt and pepper to taste. Strain and serve.

Maryland Crab Cakes

Executive Chef Cary Neff
Sansom Street Oyster House, Philadelphia, PA

2 eggs
½ tablespoon dry mustard
½ teaspoon Old Bay Seasoning
Pinch of cayenne pepper
¼ teaspoon sugar
½ cup diced red pepper
½ cup diced onion
¾ cup mayonnaise
½ to ¾ cup breadcrumbs
1½ pounds lump crabmeat

Preheat oven to 350°. Mix eggs with spices and sugar. Fold in red pepper and onion. Mix in mayonnaise. Fold in breadcrumbs. Fold in crabmeat, taking care NOT to break up the lumps!

Form into cakes. Place on a sheet pan and bake for 15 minutes or sauté until golden brown.

Serves 6

Sansom Street Oyster House

Known for:
oysters and fresh seafood

Years in business: 24

Chef: Cary Neff

Crab Cakes with Cilantro and Poblano

Chef/Owner Carlo deMarco
333 Belrose Bar & Grill, Radnor, PA

1 tablespoon oil
1 rib celery, diced small
1 red pepper, diced small
1 yellow pepper, diced small
1 poblano pepper, diced small
2 jalapeño peppers, diced small
3 pounds jumbo lump crabmeat
1 cup fresh breadcrumbs
1 bunch cilantro, chiffonade (cut into thin strips)
¾ cup lime mayonnaise
Kosher salt
Fresh ground black pepper

Heat oil in a sauté pan. Add celery and peppers and sauté until just translucent. Remove from heat and let cool. Fold remaining ingredients into pepper mixture, being careful not to break up crabmeat. Form into patties.

Preheat oven to 375°. Heat sauté pan over medium high heat. Add patties and brown on each side. Transfer to oven and bake for 5 to 8 minutes or until hot.

Serves 6 to 8

333 Belrose Bar & Grill

Known for:
great food, very busy bar, outside patio dining

Years in business:
6 months

Menu:
California-inspired American cuisine

Chef: Carlo deMarco

Chef's training:
Culinary Institute of America; University of Massachusetts

Chef's hobbies/ accomplishments:
have appeared in *Esquire, Gourmet,* and *Bon Appetit*

Chef's favorite cookbook:
Chez Panisse Menu Cookbook

Soft-shell Crabs Oreganate

Executive Chef William Fischer
Caffé Aldo Lamberti, Cherry Hill, NJ

4 wale or jumbo soft-shell crabs, dressed and dry
Salt and pepper
Flour
Clarified Butter (Recipe appears on page 299.)
2 cloves garlic, sliced
4 tablespoons olive oil
4 tablespoons diced red plum tomatoes
4 tablespoons diced yellow tomatoes
2 teaspoons chopped fresh oregano
4 tablespoons rock shrimp
2 teaspoons breadcrumbs
4 ounces Chablis
1 cup clam stock or water
Red pepper flakes

Season crabs with salt and pepper. Dust with flour. Pour in enough clarified butter to cover bottom of a large sauté pan and warm over moderate heat. Add crabs and sauté for 1 to 2 minutes. Turn and sauté for 1 to 2 minutes. Drain fat. Add garlic and sauté until light brown. Add remaining ingredients and simmer for 5 minutes or until sauce is slightly thick.

Serves 2 as an entree
Serves 4 as an appetizer

Caffé Aldo Lamberti

Known for:
excellent cuisine

Years in business: 12

Most requested table:
table by front window overlooking our pond

Menu:
regional and contemporary Italian

Chef: William Fischer

Chef's training:
A.C.C. Culinary Arts with high honors; ACF certified chef de cuisine; 15 years experience

Chef's hobbies/ accomplishments:
fishing, boating/family

Chef's favorite foods:
fresh striped bass

Chef's favorite cookbook:
Art Culinaire

Seafood Risotto

Executive Chef William Fischer
Caffé Aldo Lamberti, Cherry Hill, NJ

6 cups clam stock
6 cups water
¾ cup chopped onion
2 tablespoons butter
4 tablespoons olive oil
2 cloves garlic, sliced
2 pounds Italian rice
1½ cups Chablis
½ pound EACH calamari, scallops, rock shrimp, clams, and firm-fleshed fish
1 pound mussels
½ pound plum tomatoes, chopped
½ pound yellow tomatoes, chopped
⅛ teaspoon crushed red pepper flakes
2 ounces parsley, chopped

Place stock and water in a 3-quart stockpot and bring to a boil. In a separate 3-quart stockpot, sauté onion in butter and oil until translucent. Add garlic and sauté, without browning, until aromatic. Add rice and stir to coat with oil mixture. Add wine and half of stock-water mixture. Cook over high heat and stir frequently.

Meanwhile, cook all seafood, one type at a time in sequence, in stock until just done. Remove each with a slotted spoon before adding the next and reserve.

As soon as rice is ready, add all seafood, tomatoes, pepper flakes, and parsley and blend together.

Serves 8 as an entree
Serves 12 as an appetizer

Chef's Note

As the rice cooks, you will need to add additional stock to prevent burning. The rice absorbs the liquid and will surely stick, so stir it frequently. By the time you have cooked all of the seafood, the rice will need the remainder of the stock. Add it all and test for doneness during the last stage of cooking. Rice is always served al dente so be careful not to overcook it.

Seafood Jambalaya

Chef/Owner Joe Brown
Melange Café, Cherry Hill, NJ

8 tablespoons soy oil
1 cup sliced smoked andouille sausage
1 cup diced tasso ham
20 sea scallops (20-30 count)
8 shrimp (16-20 count), peeled and deveined
8 whole crawfish, cleaned
1 cup diced green pepper
1 cup diced white onion
1 cup chopped green onion
20 mussels, cleaned and debearded
16 littleneck clams, cleaned and scrubbed
2 teaspoons chopped fresh garlic
8 tablespoons Cajun seasoning
8 cups cooked white rice
4 cups chicken stock or seafood stock

Heat oil in a 12-inch sauté pan over high heat. Add sausage and tasso ham. Sauté for 1 minute. Add scallops, shrimp, crawfish, green pepper, white onion, and green onion. Sauté for 3 minutes. Add mussels, clams, garlic, and 6 tablespoons Cajun seasoning. Sauté for 2 minutes. Add rice and chicken stock. Cover and cook until liquid is reduced by three-quarters and clams are open.

Serve in large bowls and garnish with remaining Cajun seasoning.

Serves 8

Wine Notes

Recommended Wine: Beaujolais "Tradition" Domaine du Vissoux 1998 ($12.50)

Description: Pierre Chermette reduces yield and never chaptalizes his fruit; during vinification, allows long fermentation and extraction with indigenous yeasts; ages in oak *foudres;* and bottles with no filtration. The result is a pure, ripe, flavorful wine that is to Gamay what Pauillac is to Merlot . . . a Beaujolais *d'antan* as one could have had in a café in Paris in the 1940s.

Sommelier: Jonathan Read, Moore Brothers Wine Co.

Beer Seafood Fest

Chef/Owner Olivier De Saint Martin
Dock Street Brasserie, Philadelphia, PA

12 ounces sea bass fillet, skin on (any kind of bass)
12 ounces salmon fillet, skin on
Salt and pepper
1 pound asparagus, cut in 3-inch pieces
8 oysters in shell, brushed and cleaned
1½ cups Pilsner (Bohemian) crisp, well balanced lager
¼ teaspoon caraway seeds
½ pound cleaned mussels
4 Russet potatoes, peeled, cooked, and mashed, using milk and butter as needed
1 ounce good butter, cold
2 teaspoons chopped parsley

Cut each fish fillet into 4 slices and season with salt and pepper. Reserve.

Cook asparagus al dente in salty water; then refresh in iced water.

Butter bottom of a large saucepan. Add fish pieces and oysters. Pour beer on top and sprinkle with caraway seeds. Bring to a boil, cover, and reduce heat. After 2 minutes, add asparagus and mussels. Let simmer, covered, until mussels open.

Place fish, shellfish, asparagus, and potatoes on a deep serving plate. Bring pan juices to a boil and whisk in cold butter little by little. Pour sauce over seafood and sprinkle with fresh parsley. Serve all in one dish.

Serves 4

Wine Notes

Recommended Wine: Dashwood Sauvignon Blanc New Zealand 1999 ($12)
Description: This is a crisp, zingy wine with flavors of herbs and citrus.
Recommended Wine: Chateau de la Terriere Beaujolais Vielles Vignes 1998
Description: This wine is fruity and vibrant with rich flavors of wild red berries.
Recommended Beer: Dock Street Bohemian Lager
Sommelier: John McNulty, Triangle Liquors

side dishes

Minted Green Beans and Pearl Onions in a Brown Butter Sauce 202

Hoppin' Johns 203

Brussels Sprouts with Maple Mustard Sauce 204

Collards with Smoked Bacon 205

Colombian Arepas 206

Mushrooms PA 207

Lobster Mashed Potatoes 208

Ceci and Potatoes Morzello 209

Ruby Red Grape and Roma Apple Confit 210

Sautéed Spinach 211

Sweet Potato and Apple Puree 212

Creamy Succatash 213

Zucchini with Amaretto Stuffing 214

Fried Zucchini 215

Vegetable Couscous 215

Howard's Sweet Kugel 216

Nicola Shirley's Rice and Beans 217

Minted Green Beans and Pearl Onions in a Brown Butter Sauce

Executive Chef Jim Coleman
Treetops in the Rittenhouse Hotel, Philadelphia, PA

1 pint pearl onions
2 pounds cleaned green beans
¼ cup European-style butter (such as Keller's)
¼ cup chopped fresh mint
1 tablespoon chopped fresh tarragon
Salt and pepper to taste

Bring 2 quarts of water to a boil. Add the pearl onions and cook for 2 to 3 minutes. Remove the onions from the water with a slotted spoon and cool in a bowl of ice water.

Add the beans to the boiling water and cook for about 2 minutes, or until tender but not mushy. Remove from the water and cool in the ice water. Peel the onions.

Melt the butter in a medium sauté pan. Add the onions and cook until the butter begins to brown. Add the beans, mint, and tarragon and sauté until heated through, about 1 minute. Season with salt and pepper.

Serves 6 to 8

Hoppin' Johns

Chef/Co-owner John C. Hayden
Café Nola, Philadelphia, PA

12 ounces black-eyed peas
2 pints chicken stock
1 cup long-grain rice
5 rashers streaky smoked bacon, chopped
1 small onion, finely chopped
1 small green pepper, finely chopped
1 small red pepper, finely chopped
1 stalk celery, finely chopped
4 ounces tasso or salted ham
1 teaspoon paprika
1 teaspoon garlic salt
1 teaspoon cayenne pepper
1 teaspoon white pepper
3 scallions, chopped

Soak peas in cold water for 8 hours or overnight.

Drain and boil in fresh water for 15 minutes. Drain and discard water. Add chicken stock to pot and bring to a boil. Reboil peas for 15 minutes. Cook rice in a separate pan according to package instructions. Reserve and keep warm.

In a third pan, sauté bacon, vegetables, and ham. Remove from heat and mix in seasonings. When peas are soft, add vegetable mixture and mix thoroughly. Mix in scallions. Serve over rice.

Serves 6 to 8

Café Nola

Known for:
Mardi Gras atmosphere

Years in business: 19

Most requested table:
#43 in the Garden Room

Menu: Cajun/Creole

Chef: John C. Hayden

Chef's training:
Academy of Culinary Arts;
2.5 years in Paris

Chef's hobbies/ accomplishments:
cooking at home with family/opening crew for Euro Disney

Chef's favorite foods:
a good creme brûlée, William Hill Merlot, and Steak Jack Daniels

Chef's favorite cookbook:
Hot Beignets and Warm Boudoirs by John D. Folsey and anything by Chef Charlie Trotter

Brussels Sprouts
with Maple Mustard Sauce

Owner/Director Charlotte-Ann Albertson
Charlotte-Ann Albertson's Cooking School, Wynnewood, PA

4 cups Brussels sprouts, trimmed
1 tablespoon sugar
2 tablespoons champagne vinegar
2 tablespoons balsamic vinegar
2 tablespoons maple syrup
2 tablespoons Dijon mustard
1 tablespoon coarse grain mustard
½ teaspoon salt
½ teaspoon fresh ground pepper
⅛ teaspoon nutmeg
½ cup extra virgin olive oil

Make a cut in the base of each Brussels sprout and the bitter outer leaves will fall away. Cut an "x" in the bottom of each sprout. Bring 7 to 8 quarts water to a rapid boil. Add Brussels sprouts and sugar. When water returns to a boil, reduce heat and simmer for 5 to 8 minutes. Cool sprouts in a cold water bath and drain.

Whisk together remaining ingredients, except oil. Slowly add oil in a steady stream, whisking until mixture thickens.

Toss sprouts with sauce and serve at room temperature.

Serves 4 to 6

Chef's Note

James Sherman was the owner and chef of Jamey's, the first restaurant in the newly upscaled Manayunk. He was also a popular teacher at Charlotte-Ann Albertson's Cooking School, and although he has since closed his restaurant and moved to Oregon, we still fondly remember him when we make this wonderful winter dish.

Collards with Smoked Bacon

General Manager Trish Morrissey
Jack's Firehouse/Down Home Diner, Philadelphia, PA

4 pounds collard greens
¼ pound hickory smoked bacon, diced
1 onion, diced
Hot chicken stock
3 tablespoons brown sugar
3 tablespoons cider vinegar
Salt and pepper

Rinse and trim greens. Place in a large pot of boiling water and boil for 2 minutes.
Drain and discard water.

Heat pot over medium heat. Add bacon and cook for 3 minutes. Add onion and
cook for 3 minutes. Add greens and enough chicken stock to cover them. Bring to
a boil, cover, and reduce heat. Simmer for 1 hour or until tender. Stir in brown
sugar and vinegar. Season with salt and pepper. Serve greens with juices.

Serves 6

Colombian Arepas

Chef/Owner Guillermo Pernot
¡Pasión!, Philadelphia, PA

1 pound corn kernels (about 8 ears)
½ cup cornmeal
¾ cup masa harina
6½ ounces Monterey Jack cheese, shredded
¼ cup milk
¾ cup sugar
¼ teaspoon salt
1 tablespoon butter

Cook corn kernels in a saucepan over medium heat until tender, about 5 to 10 minutes. Let cool. Place in a food processsor and grind to a rough puree. Transfer to a mixing bowl. Add remaining ingredients, except butter, and mix together very well. Cover and refrigerate for at least 1 hour.

Line a baking sheet with waxed or parchment paper. Divide corn mixture into 12 balls. Place on baking sheet and refrigerate for 30 minutes.

Heat a nonstick griddle or frying pan over medium heat. Coat pan with butter. Place corn balls on griddle. Flatten lightly with a spatula to ½-inch thick. Brown on both sides and serve immediately.

Yields 12 corn cakes

¡Pasión!

Known for:
ceviche

Years in business: 1½

Most requested table:
ceviche bar

Menu:
Nuevo Latino

Chef: Guillermo Pernot

Chef's training:
self taught

Chef's hobbies/ accomplishments:
cooking

Chef's favorite foods:
Latino

Chef's favorite cookbook:
Nuevo Latino

Mushrooms PA

Executive Chef Joseph Becker
Jenny's Bistro, Lahaska, PA

¼ pound sun-dried tomatoes
1 tablespoon plus 1 cup butter
½ cup chopped garlic
¼ cup chopped shallots
2½ pounds button mushrooms
¼ cup flour
1 tablespoon salt
1½ teaspoons black pepper
2 cups Madeira wine
2 cups heavy cream

Rehydrate sun-dried tomatoes in hot water and reserve.

Melt 1 tablespoon butter in a large skillet. Add garlic and shallots and sauté until translucent. Melt remaining butter in pan. Add mushrooms and cook until tender. Stir in flour and salt and pepper and cook for about 3 minutes. Add Madiera and cream and cook until liquid is reduced by one-quarter. Drain sun-dried tomatoes and cut into strips. Fold into mixture.

Serves 6

Lobster Mashed Potatoes

Executive Chef Joel Gaughan
Braddock's Tavern, Medford, NJ

2 pounds Idaho potatoes
¼ pound bacon, diced
2 lobster tails (8 ounces each), finely diced
½ cup chopped fresh chives
¾ cup whole milk
½ cup butter
Salt and pepper

Scrub potatoes and place in a large pot. Add enough salted water to cover by at least 1 inch. Simmer, uncovered, over moderate heat until an inserted knife comes away easily, about 20 to 30 minutes. Drain and cool to handle.

While potatoes are cooling, cook bacon until crisp in a large sauté pan over medium high heat. Add lobster. Cook for 5 to 6 minutes or until lobster is cooked through. Stir in chives. Remove from heat and reserve.

Bring milk to a boil. Remove from heat and reserve.

Peel potatoes. Pass potatoes through the finest grid of a food mill into a mixing bowl. Slowly stir in heated milk and butter. Fold in lobster mixture. Season with salt and pepper to taste.

Serves 4

Braddock's Tavern

Known for:
superb cuisine and romantic, historic ambiance

Years in business: 22

Most requested table:
on porch and near fireplace

Menu:
traditional American

Chef: Joel Gaughan

Chef's Training:
Atlantic County College

Chef's favorite foods:
French

Ceci and Potatoes Morzello

Executive Chef Donna Ewanciw
Toto, Philadelphia, PA

¼ cup diced onion
½ teaspoon minced garlic
¼ cup diced celery
1 tablespoon extra virgin olive oil
½ teaspoon chopped fresh oregano
1 anchovy fillet, chopped
¼ cup white wine
1 medium Idaho potato, peeled and diced
1 quart light fish stock or clam juice
2 cups cooked chickpeas (ceci) (Canned is fine.)

Sauté onion, garlic, and celery in a skillet in olive oil until onion is translucent. Stir in oregano and anchovy and cook for 2 minutes. Deglaze pan with white wine. Add potatoes and stock. Simmer until potatoes are firm but done. Add chickpeas and simmer slowly for 5 to 8 minutes so that flavors blend.

Yields 1 quart

Ruby Red Grape and Roma Apple Confit

President Louise Symington
Chez Amis Catering, Ltd., West Chester, PA

2 pounds red grapes, halved
1 tablespoon cornstarch
4 tablespoons butter
½ pound onion, sliced
1 ounce fresh ginger, minced
¼ cup white balsamic vinegar
¼ cup lemon juice
¼ cup honey
1½ pounds apples, sliced and chopped
½ teaspoon salt
½ teaspoon Chinese five-spice powder
½ teaspoon mustard seed

Toss grapes with cornstarch and reserve.

Melt butter in a large skillet. Add onion and ginger and sauté until onion is translucent. Add balsamic vinegar and lemon juice and cook until slightly reduced. Stir in honey. Add grapes and remaining ingredients. Stir for 5 minutes over high heat. Remove from heat and let cool.

Yields 2 quarts

Chez Amis Catering, Ltd.

Known for: chutneys and mojos, desserts and chocolate

Years in business: 13

Menu:
Continental techniques with Asian, American, and Pacific Rim accents

Chef: Louise Symington

Chef's training:
L'Academie de Cuisine, Maryland/France

Chef's hobbies/accomplishments:
female entrepreneur, classical pianist, cooking show performances

Chef's favorite foods:
those mentioned above; root vegetable garnishes

Chef's favorite cookbook:
Nuevo Latino, Creative Cuisine

Sautéed Spinach

Chef/Owner Anthony Stella
L'Osteria Cucina Italiana, Wilmington, DE

1 onion, minced
¼ cup extra virgin olive oil
1½ pounds spinach, chopped
½ teaspoon ground nutmeg
¼ teaspoon salt
¼ teaspoon pepper

Sauté onion in olive oil until soft. Add spinach and seasonings and cook until most of liquid has evaporated.

Serves 4

Sweet Potato and Apple Puree

Executive Chef Patrick Bradley
Buckley's Tavern, Centreville, DE

1½ cups butter
2 Spanish onions, chopped
8 sweet potatoes, peeled and chopped
1 quart apple juice
1 cup brown sugar
7 McIntosh apples, peeled, cored, and chopped

Melt 1 cup butter in a large skillet. Add onions and sauté until translucent. Add sweet potatoes and sauté for 3 minutes. Add juice and brown sugar and bring to a boil. When potatoes begin to get tender, add apples. Cook until potatoes are fork tender. Add remaining butter. Puree mixture in a food processor or with a hand blender until smooth and creamy. Season with salt and pepper, if desired.

Serves 8

Buckley's Tavern

Known for:
historic country tavern, relaxed atmosphere, and outdoor rooftop dining

Years in business: 60+

Most requested table:
the booths in the tavern

Menu:
creative American fare

Chef: Patrick Bradley

Chef's training:
Delaware Tech; apprenticed under Paul O'Toole

Chef's hobbies/ accomplishments:
reading, roller blading, basketball

Chef's favorite foods:
pork tenderloin

Chef's favorite cookbook:
Kitchen Sessions by Charlie Trotter

Creamy Succatash

Executive Chef Michael J. Heinle
Arroyo Grille, Philadelphia, PA

1 tablespoon oil
½ small onion, diced small
½ red pepper, diced small
6 ears corn, kernels removed
2 cups frozen lima beans
½ cup white wine
½ cup heavy cream
Salt and pepper

Heat oil in a medium skillet over medium heat. Add onion and sauté until translucent. Add corn and red pepper and cook until hot throughout. Add wine. Bring to a boil and simmer for 5 minutes. Add lima beans and heavy cream. Bring to a boil and cook until cream thickens slightly. Season to taste with salt and pepper.

Serves 6

Arroyo Grille

Known for: outdoor dining deck

Years in business: 4

Most requested table: river deck

Menu: Southwestern/Texas Barbecue

Chef: Michael J. Heinle

Chef's training: The Restaurant School, Class of 1993

Chef's hobbies/ accomplishments: collecting Wizard of Oz memorabilia

Chef's favorite foods: Tasty Klair pies from Tastycake!

Chef's favorite cookbook: anything by Bobby Flay — all of his books are good

Zucchini with Amaretto Stuffing

Executive Chef Luigi Baretto
Ram's Head Inn, Absecon, NJ

3 to 4 medium zucchini
6 amaretto cookies
6 tablespoons butter
¾ cup flour
1½ cups chicken stock or milk
1 tablespoon sugar
1 ounce amaretto liqueur
Salt and white pepper
1 tablespoon Parmesan cheese
1 to 2 tablespoons melted butter

Boil zucchini until cooked halfway. Remove from water. Cut off and reserve each end. Cut zucchini in half lengthwise and hollow out centers so that halves resemble "boats." Grind scopped out zucchini centers, reserved ends, and cookies in a food processor or a meat grinder.

Melt butter in a saucepan. Stir in flour and chicken stock until smooth. Cook for about 5 minutes. Add ground zucchini mixture, sugar, amaretto liqueur, and salt and white pepper. Cook for 5 minutes over low heat. Remove from heat and let cool. (If mixture seems too loose to keep shape, add breadcrumbs.)

Preheat oven to 350°. Put cooled stuffing in a pastry bag and fill hollowed centers of zucchini. Sprinkle with Parmesan and drizzle with 1 to 2 tablespoons melted butter. Bake for approximately 10 minutes or until golden brown.

Serves 6 to 8

Ram's Head Inn

Years in business: 21

Most requested table:
terrace in summer,
fireplace in winter

Menu:
Continental

Chef: Luigi Baretto

Chef's training:
Italy

**Chef's hobbies/
accomplishments:**
gardening

Chef's favorite foods:
Continental

**Chef's favorite
cookbook:**
professional books

Fried Zucchini

Chef/Owner Anthony Stella
L'Osteria Cucina Italiana, Wilmington, DE

5 large zucchini, cut lengthwise into ¼-inch slices
1 cup flour
Salt and pepper
3 large eggs, beaten
1 cup breadcrumbs
Peanut oil for deep frying

Salt zucchini and stand up in a bowl for 1 hour or up to 3 hours to extract excess water. Dry with towel. Season flour with salt and pepper. Dust zucchini in flour, dip in egg, and then coat with breadcrumbs. Heat oil in a large skillet over medium heat. Fry zucchini in batches until golden.

Serves 6 to 8

Vegetable Couscous

Chef/Owner Patrick Given
Church Street Bistro, Lambertville, NJ

8 ounces couscous
8 ounces chicken stock
1 cinnamon stick
2 bay leaves
1 medium onion, diced
1 carrot, diced
1 green or red bell pepper, diced
1 zucchini, diced
Salt and pepper

Place couscous in a large, lidded serving bowl and reserve.

Combine stock, cinnamon stick, and bay leaves in a saucepan. Bring to a boil. Add vegetables and boil for 2 to 3 minutes. Pour over couscous. Cover and let sit for 10 minutes. Fluff with a fork. Season to taste with salt and pepper.

Serves 2

Howard's Sweet Kugel

Owner Howard Nutinsky
Corned Beef Academy, Philadelphia, PA

4 tablespoons butter
1 cup breadcrumbs
2 pounds medium noodles
1 dozen eggs
8 ounces dry curd fruit flavored cottage cheese
24 ounces cream cheese
1 cup golden raisins
2 cups sugar

Coat an 8 x 5-inch casserole dish with butter. Sprinkle with breadcrumbs.

Preheat oven to 350°.

Cook noodles in salted water according to package instructions. Combine hot noodles with remaining ingredients and mix well. Pour into prepared dish and bake for 45 minutes. If kugel is not firm, bake for an additional 15 minutes. Cool, cut into squares, and serve.

Yields 12 to 16 pieces

Corned Beef Academy

Known for:
Philly's best deli/corned beef and turkey

Years in business: 6

Most requested table:
any booth

Menu: traditional deli

Owner:
Howard Nutinsky

Chef's training:
the best kind — on the job

Chef's hobbies/ accomplishments:
still in business after all these years

Chef's favorite foods:
too many to list

Chef's favorite cookbook:
Local Flavor, Joy of Cooking

Nicola Shirley's Rice and Beans

Chef/Owner Nicola Shirley
Jamaican Jerk Hut, Philadelphia, PA

3 cups dried kidney beans

12 cups water

1 medium yellow onion, coarsely chopped

1 cup coarsely chopped scallions

1 Scotch Bonnet pepper

4 teaspoons fresh thyme or 2 teaspoons dried thyme

¼ cup butter

½ block (or 3.5 ounces) coconut cream (I use Grace Brand.)

2 teaspoons minced garlic

10 pimento seeds

6 cups rice

Soak beans for several hours or overnight in enough water to cover. Drain and rinse. Place beans and 12 cups water in a large pot and bring to a boil. Cook at a medium boil for at least 1 hour or until beans are tender but still firm. Add remaining ingredients except rice. Return to boil. When coconut cream is dissolved, add rice and stir. Cook until water line is level or just below rice line. Cover and reduce heat. Cook about 25 minutes or until rice is still firm but cooked through.

Serves 6

Jamaican Jerk Hut

Known for: best Jamaican food in this hemisphere

Years in business: 6

Menu: traditional Jamaican with melting pot influences

Owner: Nicola Shirley

Chef's training: Johnson & Wales University

Chef's hobbies/ accomplishments: studying herbs and homeopathic medicine, badminton

Chef's favorite foods: anything sweet and sour

Chef's favorite cookbook: *Silver Palate*

lunch time

Cajun Blue Cheese Burger

Executive Chef Daniel Dogan
The Terrace at Greenhill, Wilmington, DE

1 pound ground beef
2 tablespoons Cajun spice
2 teaspoons A-1 Sauce
2 small shallots, minced
¼ teaspoon black pepper
¼ teaspoon salt
4 ounces blue cheese
2 large fluffy rolls, toasted
2 slices tomato
2 slices onion

Place ground beef in a mixing bowl. Add 1 tablespoon Cajun spice, A-1 Sauce, shallots, pepper, and salt. Mix well. Divide mixture in quarters and form into four ¼-inch-thick patties. Place blue cheese on top of 2 patties and cover with remaining patties. Seal edges. Season with remaining Cajun spice. Grill to your desired doneness. Place burgers on rolls and garnish with tomato and onion.

Serves 2

Wine Notes

Recommended Wine: St. Hallet's "Faith" Shiraz 1997 ($18.00)

Description: This big, bold, ripe, and rich mouthful of Shiraz will stand up to the strongest of flavors, and this dish is a powerhouse.

Sommelier: John McNulty, Triangle Liquors

Open--faced Portobello Mushroom Sandwiches

Executive Chef/Owner Jon Hallowell
Mixmaster Café, Malvern, PA

8 portobello mushrooms
½ cup extra virgin olive oil
1 bunch asparagus
1 pound crabmeat
4 slices white bread
2 cups Béarnaise Sauce (Recipe appears on page 290.)

Preheat oven to 450°. Remove stems from mushrooms. (Save them for soup or discard.) Brush both sides of mushrooms with olive oil. Place on a cookie sheet and reserve.

Trim off 1 inch from bottom of asparagus stalks and discard. Place stalks in boiling water and boil for 3 minutes. Remove and place in an ice bath for several minutes. Remove and shake off excess water. Brush stalks with olive oil. Place on cookie sheet with mushrooms. Season with salt and pepper. Bake for 9 minutes. Remove pan from oven and top mushrooms with crabmeat. Bake for 3 minutes more.

Toast bread. Top each slice with 2 crab-covered mushrooms. Stack asparagus tepee style with the points up. Ladle béarnaise over top. (Omit crabmeat for a lovely vegetarian lunch.)

Serves 4

Mixmaster Café

Known for:
great lunches; excellent service; small, intimate dining rooms

Years in business: 1

Most requested table:
by window in private room

Menu:
eclectic/Mediterranean

Chef: Jon C. Hallowell

Chef's training:
The Restaurant School and home training (Jon's grandfather, Juan Balaguer, was the chef for over 25 years at the "old" Ritz Carlton which closed in 1954.)

Chef's hobbies/ accomplishments:
creating unusual recipes, skiing, travel

Chef's favorite foods:
paella, filet mignon, pasta, mussels

Grilled Shrimp with Thai Peanut Butter Spread

Chef/Owner Michael McNally
London Grill, Philadelphia, PA

1 pound medium shrimp
3 tablespoons olive oil
Salt and pepper
4 tortillas (6-inch size)
Thai Peanut Spread (see recipe)
Apricot Marmalade Glaze (see recipe)

Toss shrimp with 2 tablespoons oil and salt and pepper. Grill for 2 to 3 minutes on each side. Lightly rub tortillas with remaining oil. Place on grill for 30 seconds on each side. Spread with Thai peanut spread. Lay 5 or 6 shrimp on each tortilla. Place 1 tablespoon glaze on shrimp. Roll up and serve.

Serves 4

Thai Peanut Spread

1-inch long piece fresh ginger, chopped
3 cloves garlic, chopped
1 teaspoon curry paste
1 cup chunky peanut butter
3 tablespoons sugar
3 teaspoons Thai fish sauce
¾ cup coconut milk

Combine all ingredients in a food processor and process until smooth.

Apricot Marmalade Glaze

1 cup apricot marmalade
1 cup cider vinegar
½ teaspoon black pepper
1 star anise
½ teaspoon ground coriander
2 teaspoons minced ginger
2 tablespoons chopped cilantro

Combine all ingredients in a saucepan; bring to a boil. Simmer until syrupy and strain.

Open-faced Salmon B.L.T

Executive Chef David Leo Banks
Harry's Savoy Grill, Wilmington, DE

4 small fresh plum tomatoes
1 teaspoon salt
1 teaspoon freshly ground black pepper
2 teaspoons balsamic vinegar
Fresh basil and oregano, chopped, optional
2 tablespoons capers, drained
1½ cups mayonnaise
Juice of 2 lemons
8 slices good quality smoked bacon
4 boneless salmon fillets (5 ounces each)
Butter, oil, or nonstick spray for grilling
4 slices sunflower honey wheat bread or Branola
4 pieces green leaf lettuce, washed and dried
Flat-leaf Italian parsley, washed and dried

Slice tomatoes into 4 slices per tomato. Sprinkle each slice with salt, pepper, and vinegar. Toss gently in a bowl with herbs. Allow to stand at room temperature.

Crush capers slightly and combine with mayonnaise. Stir in lemon juice to taste; set aside. Cook bacon in a single layer in a 350° oven. (Do not allow bacon to get too crisp.) Drain on paper towels and set aside. Leave oven on.

Skin salmon fillets. Use a charcoal grill or a raised-grill skillet on high heat. Coat fillets with butter, oil, or nonstick spray. Grill, skin side up, until deep brown grill marks appear on meat side of fish. Turn fish over and briefly grill other side. (Fish should not be cooked through or this will hinder the slicing.) Remove fish from heat or take out of pan.

Cut salmon fillets one time diagonally and put into hot oven to finish cooking. (The fish is best left slightly rare.)

Toast bread in oven: inside of each slice should be "spongy." Spread an even layer of lemon-caper mayonnaise on toast and place 1 piece lettuce on top. Place a piece of salmon on top of leaf lettuce. Place 2 slices bacon on salmon; top with another piece of salmon to hold bacon in place. Layer 4 slices marinated tomatoes in center of sandwich and spread a generous amount of lemon-caper mayonnaise on tomatoes. Garnish with parsley and serve.

Serves 4

Crab and Garlic Tart with Asparagus Coulis

Executive Chef David Grear
La Terrasse, Philadelphia, PA

1 pound butter, chilled and diced
4 cups all-purpose flour, sifted
¼ cup sugar
½ teaspoon salt
¼ cup ice water
6 eggs
1 teaspoon olive oil
10 cloves garlic, crushed
1 medium onion, diced
1 quart heavy cream
Pinch of grated nutmeg
1 pound asparagus tips
Asparagus Coulis (Recipe appears on page 298.)
Crab Sauté (see recipe)

Place butter, flour, sugar, and salt in a mixing bowl and blend with pastry cutter until mixture is coarse. (Do not overwork.) Mix in water and 2 eggs. Blend until smooth dough forms. Divide dough into 6 equal portions. Roll out one portion on a clean work surface and fit into a 4-ounce scalloped-edge baking mold. Repeat with remaining portions. Set aside.

Heat oil in a large sauté pan. Add garlic and sauté until slightly browned. Add onion and sauté for 5 minutes. Add heavy cream and nutmeg. Cook at a low simmer until liquid is reduced by half. Remove from heat.

Preheat oven to 350°. Transfer mixture to a blender and puree. Lightly beat remaining 4 eggs in a bowl and add to blender. Mix again until fully blended. Pour mixture into pastry shells, leaving ¼-inch head room for expansion. Bake until set: the consistency should be that of quiche. (Do not overcook or filling will rise too high, and the texture will become too soft.)

Steam asparagus tips until tender, about 3 to 5 minutes.

Spoon a 6-inch ring of asparagus coulis in the center of each plate. Place garlic tart in center of coulis. Top with warm sautéed crabmeat. Garnish with 3 to 5 asparagus tips.

Serves 6

Crab Sauté

½ cup dry white wine
6 ounces garlic butter
4 plum tomatoes, peeled
1 red bell pepper, finely diced
1 yellow bell pepper, finely diced
3 jalapeño peppers, finely diced
¼ bunch fresh chives, chopped
12 fresh basil leaves, chiffonade
1 pound jumbo lump crabmeat
Salt and pepper

Heat white wine and garlic butter in a sauté pan. When butter is melted, add all vegetables and herbs. Just before serving, stir in crabmeat and cook until heated through. Season to taste with salt and pepper. (Drain most liquid out before serving.)

Wine Notes

Recommended Wine: Dominique Roger, Sancerre "La Jouline" 1997 ($21.50)

Description: A minuscule quantity of this beautiful wine is produced each year. From the chalky-clay soil of the village of Bué, very old vines, and carefully selected fruit vinified without the support of wood, this Sauvignon Blanc goes beyond the varietal description: rich, multilayered, very smooth and silky on the palate, with very enticing scents and a long aftertaste. This cuvée is dedicated to great-grandfather Roger and his love of wine making.

Sommelier: Chris Kurlakovsky, Moore Brothers Wine Co.

Norwegian Strudel

Chef Marie Jarzenski
Warsaw Cafe, Philadelphia, PA

4 tablespoons butter
1 cup chopped onions
2 green peppers, finely chopped
1 cup chopped mushrooms
4 cloves garlic, minced
2 tablespoons Hungarian paprika
1 tablespoon black pepper
8 chicken breasts, cubed
4 cups shredded lettuce (Romaine works well.)
1 cup ground toasted almonds
¾ cup currants
¼ cup chopped parsley
4 tablespoons soy sauce
4 tablespoons sesame oil
Juice of 1 lemon
1 tablespoon grated lemon peel
Dough (see recipe)
2 egg yolks, lightly beaten
Sauce Mornay (see recipe)

Warsaw Cafe

Known for: only area restaurant serving Eastern European food

Years in business: 20

Most requested table: front window tables

Menu: Central and Eastern European cuisine

Chef: Marie Jarzenski

Chef's training: worked at various European and Philadelphia restaurants

Melt butter in a large braisier or stockpot. Add onions and sauté for 3 minutes. Add peppers, mushrooms, garlic, paprika, and black pepper and sauté for 3 minutes. Add chicken and sauté for 3 minutes. Add lettuce and sauté until lightly wilted. Remove pot from heat. Mix in almonds, currants, parsley, soy sauce, sesame oil, lemon juice, and lemon peel. Reserve and cool before adding to dough.

Preheat oven to 400°. Roll out dough to ⅛-inch thick on a well-floured work surface. Transfer to a baking sheet. Place cooled filling on half of dough. Fold other side over to cover filling. Seal ends. Brush with egg yolks. Bake for 40 to 50 minutes until golden brown. Slice into portions and top with sauce.

Serves 8 to 10

Dough

1½ cups flour
¼ teaspoon salt
¼ cup butter
2 tablespoons vinegar
½ cup tepid water

Combine flour and salt in a mixing bowl. Work butter into flour mixture using fingers and palms. Make a well in center of mixed dough and add vinegar and ¼ cup water. Mix with fingers in a spiral motion until dough gathers into a ball. (If dough seems too dry, add more water and continue to mix until a ball forms.) Refrigerate until ready to use.

Sauce Mornay

2 tablespoons butter
4½ teaspoons flour
1 cup milk
1 small onion, whole
¼ teaspoon nutmeg
2 bay leaves
3 tablespoons grated Gruyere cheese
2 tablespoons grated Parmesan cheese
Salt and pepper

Melt butter in a saucepan. Stir in flour and cook gently for 2 minutes. Whisk in milk. Add onion, nutmeg, and bay leaves and allow mixture to thicken over gentle heat. Add cheeses and stir until cheeses are melted and mixture is well blended. Season with salt and pepper. Remove onion and bay leaves before serving.

Chef's Note
This savory strudel takes some effort and coordination, but the results are a great reward.

Rembrandt's Celebrated Duck Strudel

Executive Chef Paul L. Henderson
Rembrandt's Restaurant and Bar, Philadelphia, PA

2 large skinless duck breasts
1 tablespoon olive oil
2 leeks, washed and diced
10 button mushrooms, cleaned and destemmed
½ cup chopped walnuts
6 ounces Philadelphia cream cheese
1 large egg, beaten
Salt and pepper
12 to 16 sheets phyllo dough
½ cup butter, melted

Preheat oven to 375°. Roast duck for 45 minutes. Allow to cool.

Heat olive oil in a skillet over medium heat. Add leeks, mushrooms, and walnuts and sauté until golden brown. Transfer mixture to a large mixing bowl. Add cream cheese, egg, and salt and pepper to taste. Shred cooled duck and add to mixture. Mix well.

Preheat oven to 350°. Spread 3 or 4 sheets phyllo dough on a flat work surface. Brush each sheet liberally with melted butter and stack. Place about 6 ounces duck mixture in center of pastry and fold into a rectangle. Brush all sides with melted butter. Repeat to form 4 strudels. Place on a baking sheet and bake for 20 minutes or until golden brown. Serve warm.

Serves 4

Wine Notes

Recommended Wine: Domaine St. Martin Marsannay "Les Finottes" 1996 ($15.00)

Description: A rich and supple mouthful of Pinot Noir with length and elegance and plenty of tasty raspberry and strawberry flavors and spice. A classic combination for anything with duck and mushrooms.

Sommelier: John McNulty, Triangle Liquors

Zucchini Crab Cake

Executive Chef William Fischer
Caffé Aldo Lamberti, Cherry Hill, NJ

½ cup mayonnaise
1 large egg
1½ ounces roasted peppers, chopped
½ teaspoon Old Bay Seasoning
1½ tablespoons chopped chives
1 pound jumbo lump crabmeat, shells removed
24 ounces packed spinach (young spinach preferable without veins)
16 ounces zucchini, cut to match-stick size (Use outer most portion without seeds.)
Salt and pepper
8 tablespoons breadcrumbs
Vegetable oil
Butter Sauce (Recipe appears on page 291.)

Combine mayonnaise, egg, roasted peppers, Old Bay, and chives in a bowl and mix with a spoon until just blended. (Don't overmix egg or it will break down and give you a denser crab cake.)

Carefully squeeze out any moisture from crabmeat, making sure not to break up lumps. Fold into mayonnaise mixture. Set aside.

Season zucchini with salt and pepper. Place a layer of zucchini into bottom of 6 six-ounce ring molds. (You can also use tuna cans with tops and bottoms removed.) Use only enough to completely cover bottom. Spoon crabmeat mixture equally into each mold or until level with top of mold. Top with remaining zucchini. (It's okay if it's above the rim of the mold, as it will cook down while in the oven). DO NOT PACK DOWN. Evenly cover with 4 tablespoons breadcrumbs.

Preheat oven to 400°. Heat a generous amount of vegetable oil in an ovenproof sauté pan over high heat. Place molds in pan and sauté until brown and crisp. While cooking, top crab cakes with remaining breadcrumbs. Carefully flip each crab cake over and place sauté pan in oven for about 10 minutes or until cakes are golden brown on top and bottom.

Steam spinach and season; then sauté until dry. Divide evenly between 6 plates. Place crab cake on top of spinach. Cut around edges and remove ring. Top with butter sauce. Serve at once.

Serves 6

Smoked Duck and Goat Cheese Quesadillas

Executive Chef Andrew Berks
Twelve Caesars Radisson Hotel, Philadelphia, PA

1 medium onion, sliced
1 medium bell pepper, sliced
8 soft flour tortillas
7 ounces smoked duck breast, cut into thin strips
4 ounces goat cheese, crumbled
3 ounces pepper Jack cheese, shredded
¼ cup chopped cilantro
Sour cream

Lightly sauté onions and pepper until onions are translucent. Lay 4 tortillas out on a clean work surface. Evenly divide vegetables, duck breast, and cheeses among the 4 tortillas. Cover with remaining tortillas.

Heat griddle pan or skillet over medium high heat. Gently place quesadillas on griddle and cook until crispy on both sides. Cut into pie-shape wedges. Serve garnished with cilantro and sour cream.

Serves 4 to 8

Twelve Caesars Radisson Hotel

Known for:
26-ounce Delmonico steak

Years in business:
brand new!

Most requested table:
rear corners

Menu:
'60s deco steakhouse

Chef: Andrew Berks

Chef's training:
The Restaurant School

Chef's hobbies/ accomplishments:
food and wine

Chef's favorite foods:
prime meats

Chef's favorite cookbook:
too many to mention

Crab Quesadillas

Teacher Kristin Albertson
Incredible Edibles, Wynnewood, PA

½ pound crabmeat or shrimp, diced
4 ounces Monterey Jack cheese, pepper Jack, or Cheddar cheese, grated
½ cup chopped fresh tomato
2 scallions, chopped
1 teaspoon chopped fresh garlic
4 flour tortillas (8-inch size)
Salsa
Coriander or parlsey leaves
Lime wedges

Preheat oven to 400°. Mix together crabmeat, cheese, tomato, scallions, and garlic. Lay 2 tortillas flat on baking sheets. Spoon equal amounts of crab mixture on each tortilla. Spread over tortilla, leaving a ½-inch border. Cover with remaining tortillas. Bake until cheese melts, about 3 to 5 minutes. Cut into wedges. Garnish with dollops of salsa, leaves, and lime wedges.

Serves 4 to 6

Wine Notes

Recommended Wine: Cantina del Castello, Soave Classico Monte Pressoni 1997 ($15.00)

Description: Very ripe, choice Garganega grapes from the hilly slopes of Monte Pressoni, a confined wine-producing area immediately north of the village of Soave, yield very fine wines with all the qualities of an elegant *crú di Soave Classico*. This is a wine of fruity scents, brilliant gold color, creamy texture, and long finish.

Sommelier: Jonathan Read, Moore Brothers Wine Co.

Hungarian "Goulash"

Chef/Owner Fritz Blank
Deux Cheminées, Philadelphia, PA

¾ cup (or more as required) lard, duck or goose fat, or bacon drippings
5 pounds beef chuck or pork shoulder, cut into ¾-inch cubes
2 tablespoons Chef's Salt (Recipe appears on page 301.) or Lowrey's Seasoned Salt®
1 cup (or as needed) all-purpose flour
8 cups chopped onions, ½-inch pieces
⅔ cup Hungarian or Spanish sweet paprika
6 to 8 cups beef stock
¼ cup tomato paste
1 tablespoon caraway seeds, bruised with a spoon
Salt and freshly ground black pepper
¼ cup sugar
½ teaspoon cayenne pepper, optional

Heat ¼ cup lard in a heavy cast-iron skillet over medium heat. Season meat cubes with chef's salt and dust with flour. (The meat must be fried immediately after dusting with flour so it is best to work in small batches.)

Place floured cubes into hot fat without crowding, allowing about 1 inch of space between each piece. Carefully brown the meat; then transfer to a large heavy braiser. Proceed until all meat is browned, adding additional lard as needed.

Add remaining ½ cup lard to the empty skillet and add sliced onions. Sweat over medium heat until onions are limp and translucent. Add onions to meat cubes. Sprinkle with paprika and stir for 2 to 3 minutes over low heat. Add beef stock, tomato paste, and caraway seeds. Stir just to mix ingredients together. Cover pot and simmer very gently over low heat for 1½ hours or until meat is tender. Check occasionally and add more stock or water as needed.

Taste and season with salt and black pepper, sugar, and/or additional paprika to taste. Serve in a soup tureen along with thick slices of crusty bread, sliced raw sweet Hungarian or bell peppers, and a sauce boat of sour cream (for those who wish "paprikas").

Serves 6 to 8

Hearty White Chili

Owner Ann-Michelle Albertson
Parties in the Kitchen, Wynnewood, PA

2 tablespoons canola oil
1 cup chopped onion
2 tablespoons minced garlic
1 tablespoon ground cumin
1 pound ground turkey, white meat without skin
2 pounds skinless, boneless turkey breast, cut into ¼-inch cubes
⅔ cup pearl barley
2 cans chickpeas (16 ounces each), rinsed and drained
1 minced jalapeño pepper
6 cups chicken broth
1 teaspoon dried marjoram
½ teaspoon crumbled dried savory
Salt and pepper
8 ounces Monterey Jack cheese, coarsely grated
½ cup thinly sliced scallions

Heat oil in a 6-quart pot over low heat. Add onion and garlic and sauté until limp. Stir in cumin. Cook for 5 minutes.

Raise heat to medium. Stir in ground and cubed turkey and cook until no longer pink. Add barley, chickpeas, jalapeño, broth, marjoram, and savory. Cover and cook for 45 minutes, stirring occasionally.

Uncover and simmer for 15 minutes, stirring every 5 minutes. Season with salt and pepper to taste. Ladle into heated bowls and garnish with grated cheese and scallions.

Serves 8 to 10

brunch

Joe Brown's Beignets

Chef/Owner Joe Brown
Melange Café, Cherry Hill, NJ

2 cups flour
1 teaspoon salt
1 tablespoon baking powder
1 teaspoon cinnamon
2 eggs
¾ cup milk
¼ cup sugar
½ teaspoon vanilla extract
Oil for deep frying (enough to cover beignets completely)
1 cup confectioners' sugar

Sift together flour, salt, baking powder, and cinnamon into a large mixing bowl. Cover and set aside. In a separate bowl, beat together eggs, milk, sugar, and vanilla extract. Pour wet ingredients into dry ingredients. Stir to form dough.

Turn dough out onto a lightly floured work surface. Knead until smooth and elastic, about 3 to 4 minutes. Roll dough out to a ¼-inch-thick circle. Slice diagonally to form diamonds that are approximately 3 inches tall.

Heat oil to 375° in a deep fryer. (If oil smokes, reduce to 350°.) Fry beignets in oil, a few at a time, turning once, until golden brown. Remove with a slotted spoon and drain well on paper towels.

Smother with confectioners' sugar and serve warm with a good cup of coffee.

Serves 4

Chef's Note

Beignets are the official doughnuts of Louisiana! Here's a Louisiana-inspired way to jazz them up . . . Heat honey and butter in a sauté pan. Add chopped pecans and stir to coat. Sauté until crispy. Roll beignets in glazed pecans.

Metropolitan Millet Muffins

Owners James Barrett and Wendy Smith Born
Metropolitan Bakery, Philadelphia, PA

6 ounces unsalted butter
1 cup brown sugar, firmly packed
3 eggs
¼ cup milk
1 tablespoon pure vanilla
2 cups all-purpose flour
1¼ teaspoons baking powder
½ teaspoon baking soda
¾ teaspoon kosher salt
1 cup millet, lightly toasted and cooled

Preheat oven to 375°. Prepare muffin pan. Using the paddle attachment of a mixer, cream butter and sugar well. In a small bowl, combine eggs, milk, and vanilla. In another bowl, sift together flour, baking powder, baking soda, and salt. Toss in toasted millet. Alternating between milk mixture and flour mixture, fold mixtures into creamed butter. Do not overmix.

Spoon batter into prepared muffin pan and bake for 20 to 25 minutes or until inserted skewer comes out clean.

Yields 12 muffins

Biscuits with Fresh Cream and Berries

Pastry Chef Kelly McGrath
City Tavern, Philadelphia, PA

2¼ cups all-purpose flour
½ cup sugar
1½ teaspoons baking powder
¾ teaspoon baking soda
½ teaspoon salt
6 tablespoons butter
½ cup buttermilk
1 egg yolk
Milk
2 cups heavy cream, whipped
Strawberries, blueberries, blackberries, raspberries

Preheat oven to 400°. Combine dry ingredients and butter in a food processor. Pulse until crumbly. Add buttermilk and yolk. Process until dough holds together. (Do not overwork dough.)

Roll dough out on a floured work surface. Use a biscuit or cookie cutter to cut out biscuits. Place biscuits on a baking sheet and brush tops with milk. Bake for 15 to 20 minutes or until golden. Cool.

Cut biscuits in half horizontally. Place whipped cream and berries on bottom halves and then cover with top halves.

Serves 8

Sour Cream Coffee Cake

Owner/Baker Roz Bratt
Homemade Goodies by Roz, Philadelphia, PA

1 stick margarine
½ cup vegetable shortening
2 cups sugar
3 large eggs
3 cups flour
3 teaspoons baking powder
½ teaspoon baking soda
1 cup sour cream
1½ teaspoons almond extract
1½ teaspoons vanilla extract
½ cup chopped nuts
2 teaspoons cinnamon

Preheat oven to 350°. Grease a 10-inch tube pan. Cream together margarine, shortening, and 1½ cup sugar. Add eggs and mix for 2 minutes. Combine flour, baking powder, and baking soda in a separate bowl. Add dry ingredients to wet, alternating with sour cream. Stir in almond and vanilla extracts.

In a separate bowl, mix together remaining sugar, nuts, and cinnamon.

Spoon one-third batter into pan. Sprinkle with one-third crumb mixture. Repeat two more times. Bake for 60 minutes or until inserted toothpick comes out clean.

Yields 12 to 14 slices

Cheddar Grits

General Manager Trish Morrissey
Jack's Firehouse/Down Home Diner, Philadelphia, PA

2 cups heavy cream or milk

2 cups water

2 tablespoons butter

½ teaspoon salt

1 cup grits

1 tablespoon vegetable oil

¼ cup sliced scallions

1 bell pepper, diced

½ to ¾ cup grated Cheddar cheese

Bring milk, water, and butter to a boil in a large pot. (Be sure liquid does not boil over.) Add salt. Slowly stir grits into boiling liquid. Reduce heat to low and cover. Cook, stirring occasionally, for 5 to 7 minutes or until thickened.

While grits are cooking, heat oil in a skillet over medium-high heat. Add scallions and bell pepper and sweat for 3 minutes. Stir vegetables and cheese into cooked grits and mix thoroughly. Serve hot.

Serves 4

Jack's Firehouse/ Down Home Diner

Years in business:
Firehouse - 10; Diner - 14;

Most requested table:
Firehouse - center table #14; Diner - booth;

Menu:
American cuisine

Chef: Trish Morrissey

Chef's training:
Drexel University and The Restaurant School

Chef's hobbies/ accomplishments:
teaching, shopping

Chef's favorite foods:
Honestly, my mom's, plus I have a weakness for French fries.

Chef's favorite cookbook:
Julia Child's Baking, The New York Cookbook

Savory Saffron French Toast

Executive Chef Pamela Horowitz
Museum Catering Company, Philadelphia, PA

3 eggs
¾ cup milk
½ teaspoon saffron threads
1 baguette
Butter for frying
¼ cup sour cream
Peach chutney or other type of choice

Beat together eggs and milk in a shallow bowl. Add saffron and let stand for 45 minutes.

Diagonally slice baguette into ½-inch rounds. Soak bread in egg mixture. (Allow excess liquid to drain off when bread is removed from mixture.)

Melt butter in a hot skillet or on a griddle. Fry bread, about 3 minutes per side. Top each slice with sour cream and chutney.

Serves 4

Museum Catering Company

Known for:
catering large events effortlessly!

Years in business: 10

Menu:
new American

Chef: Pamela Horowitz

Chef's hobbies/ accomplishments: ballet and jazz dance/ appearances on CNN, Fox, NBC, and Food Network

Chef's favorite foods:
chocolate bread pudding

Chef's favorite cookbook:
The Way to Cook by Julia Child

Cinnamon French Toast with Apple Sour Cream Filling

Chef/Owner Donna Leahy
Inn at Twin Linden, Churchtown, PA

8 ounces cream cheese, softened
¼ cup sour cream
2 tablespoons sugar
½ teaspoon cinnamon
¾ cup chopped apple (about 2 medium apples)
6 slices cinnamon bread (2 inches thick each)
3 eggs
¼ cup heavy cream
1½ tablespoon corn oil
1½ tablespoons butter
Cider Syrup (see recipe)

Use an electric mixer to combine cream cheese, sour cream, sugar, and cinnamon until smooth. Fold in chopped apple. Slice a 2-inch-wide opening in the center of the top of each piece of bread, cutting down almost to the bottom. Spoon approximately 2 table-spoons apple filling into each pocket. Wipe off any excess filling.

In a separate bowl, whisk together eggs and heavy cream. Dip stuffed bread into egg mixture, coating each side evenly. Place on a lightly greased baking sheet, cover, and refrigerate overnight or until ready to serve.

Preheat oven to 375°. Heat corn oil and butter in a large skillet over medium heat. When butter is melted and foamy, add as many slices of bread as will fit comfortable in pan. Sauté about 1 to 2 minutes per side until golden brown. Continue until all slices are browned. Transfer to a lightly greased baking sheet. Bake until filling is puffed and lightly browned, about 10 to 12 minutes. Serve with warm cider syrup.

Serves 6

Inn at Twin Linden

Known for:
romantic country inn setting for enjoying fresh seasonal cuisine

Years in business: 10+

Most requested table:
near fireplace

Menu:
four-course prix fixe with seasonal flair

Chef: Donna Leahy

Chef's training:
self taught/former video producer

Chef's hobbies/ accomplishments:
author of *Morning Glories* and *Wisdom of the Plain Folk*

Chef's favorite foods:
sweetbreads, caviar, chocolate souffle, great cheeses

Cider Syrup

1 cup apple cider
½ cup corn syrup
½ cup brown sugar
½ teaspoon cinnamon
¼ teaspoon ground cloves
2 tablespoons butter

Combine all ingredients, except butter, in a medium saucepan over medium high heat. Bring to a boil. Lower heat and simmer until slightly thickened, about 8 to 10 minutes. Add butter and stir until melted.

Chef's Note

Perfect for a brunch buffet, this delicious stuffed French toast may be prepared a day ahead and baked just before serving. Use firm, slightly tart baking apples like McIntosh or Rome for this tasty filling.

Oatmeal Sunflower Pancakes with Honey Butter

Executive Chef Andrew Berks
Twelve Caesars Radisson Hotel, Philadelphia, PA

½ cup shredded sweetened coconut
1 cup whole wheat flour
1 cup oatmeal
1 tablespoon baking powder
1 teaspoon salt
¾ cup sunflower seeds
1 tablespoon corn oil
2 cups milk
1 large egg
½ cup sweetened butter
½ cup honey

Preheat oven or toaster oven to 350°. Toast coconut on a baking sheet for 5 to 7 minutes. Cool.

Combine coconut and remaining dry ingredients in a mixing bowl. In a separate bowl, beat together oil, milk, and egg. Add wet ingredients to dry and stir to combine.

Whip together butter and honey and reserve.

Spoon batter onto hot greased griddle and cook until surface bubbles appear. Turn and cook until golden brown. Spoon honey butter on hot pancakes and serve.

Serves 4

Lobster and Shiitake Mushroom Crêpes with Kiwi Emulsion

Executive Chef Brandon Carter
David's Yellow Brick Toad, Lambertville, NJ

3 tablespoons butter
2 teaspoons minced fresh ginger
6 ounces lobster tail meat, diced
10 medium shiitake mushrooms, sliced with stems removed
2 tablespoons plum wine
Salt and pepper
Brandon's Crêpes (Recipe appears on page 247.)
Melted butter
Kiwi Emulsion (see recipe)

Melt butter in a saucepan over medium heat. Add ginger and let simmer for 1 minute. Add lobster and shiitake mushrooms and cook for 5 minutes. Add plum wine and salt and pepper to taste. Cook for 2 minutes. Remove from heat and let cool.

Preheat oven to 350°. Place approximately 1 tablespoon lobster mixture at one end of crêpe and roll into a tight cigar shape. Repeat with remaining filling and crêpes. (This should yield 16 crêpes.)

Brush a cookie sheet with melted butter. Place crêpes on sheet and brush with melted butter. Bake for 5 minutes. Serve immediately with kiwi emulsion.

Serves 8

Kiwi Emulsion

5 kiwi, peeled
5 tablespoons plum wine
2 tablespoons lemon juice
2 tablespoons sugar

Place all ingredients in a food processor and blend until emulsified.

Crêpes

Chef Marie Jarzenski
Warsaw Cafe, Philadelphia, PA

1 cup flour
6 eggs
½ cup milk
¼ cup water
¼ cup oil
Pinch of salt
Pinch of sugar
Pinch of nutmeg
Butter for frying

Combine ingredients, except butter, and blend until smooth. (Batter may be prepared 1 day ahead and refrigerated.)

Heat a 7-inch frying pan over medium heat. Coat pan with butter. Reduce heat to medium-low. Slowly pour in ¼ cup batter and roll around to evenly distribute batter over entire surface of pan. When edges are light brown, turn over briefly. Stack crêpes between wax paper and keep warm until all crêpes are prepared.

Serve alone, with butter, or filled with Russian Crêpe Filling (Recipe appears on page 41.).

Yields 12 crêpes

Brandon's Crêpes

Executive Chef Brandon Carter
David's Yellow Brick Toad, Lambertville, NJ

2 cups sifted cake flour
½ teaspoon salt
3 eggs
2 cups milk
7 tablespoons oil

Pour flour into a bowl and fashion a well in center of it. Place eggs and salt into well. Beat very hard with a wooden spoon. Add milk very gradually, beating constantly to eliminate lumps. Beat in oil. Let batter rest for at least 2 hours.

Heat a 5- to 6-inch crêpe skillet over medium heat. Stir batter and pour 1½ tablespoons into pan. Tilt pan in a circular motion to cover whole bottom of pan. Turn up heat for a few seconds and then lower it and cook crêpe for 1 minute. Flip with a wide spatula and cook for 1 minute. Remove from pan. Repeat with remaining batter.

Yields 16 crêpes

Philly Foodie Fact

Use the right tool for the job. Chef Carter recommends that you use a crêpe pan for this recipe: a 5- or 6-inch skillet that is only used for crêpes and never washed, just wiped clean. Specialty pans can be found at Fantes, Kitchen Kapers, and The China Outlet.

L'Osteria Crêpes

Chef/Owner Anthony Stella
L'Osteria Cucina Italiana, Wilmington, DE

3 eggs
¾ cup plus 2 tablespoons milk
¾ cup plus 2 tablespoon seltzer water
1 teaspoon salt
1 cup flour
1⅓ ounce butter, melted

Blend all ingredients, except butter, in a blender. Allow to rest in refrigerator for 1 hour or overnight. Bring back to room temperature and whisk in melted butter.

Heat a 7-inch frying pan over medium heat. Slowly pour in ¼ cup batter and roll around to evenly distribute batter over entire surface of pan. When edges are light brown, turn over briefly. Repeat with remaining batter.

Crêpes can be refrigerated for several days or frozen for 1 month as long as they are tightly wrapped.

Yields approximately 20 crepes

Smoked Salmon Scrambled Eggs in Puff Pastry

Executive Chef Eric Hall
La Campagne, Cherry Hill, NJ

2 sheets frozen puff pastry, thawed
4 tablespoons unsalted butter
8 eggs
Salt and pepper
¼ cup heavy cream, chilled
1 small onion, minced
1 bunch chives, finely cut
8 slices smoked salmon

Preheat oven to 425°. Roll out pastry onto a lightly floured work surface. Cut pastry into four 4 x 4-inch squares. Place pastry on a nonstick baking sheet and bake for 15 minutes.

Melt butter in a saucepan over medium heat. Beat eggs, season with salt and pepper, and pour into pan. Stir gently with a wooden spoon, scraping eggs from sides and bottom of pan until cooked to desired doneness. Remove from heat and stir in cream. Stir in onions and chives. Season to taste with salt and pepper.

Place puff pastry on 4 serving plates. Top with eggs and cover with smoked salmon.

Serves 4

La Campagne

Known for:
country French cuisine in 150-year-old farmhouse, elegant catering

Years in business: 12

Most requested table: near the fireplace

Menu: modern Provençal

Chef: Eric Hall

Chef's training: cooking — on the job; management — Widener University

Chef's hobbies/ accomplishments: enjoying life

Chef's favorite foods: just about anything, but essentially food prepared right

Chef's favorite cookbook: *From The Cooking School at La Campagne*

desserts

The White House Madeira Cake 252

Bourbon Spice Cake 253

My Mother's Favorite "Icebox" Strawberry Cake 254

Roz's Chocolate Zucchini Cake 255

Angel Food Cake with Framboise-scented Crème Anglaise 256

Jewish Apple Cake 258

Sour Cherry Almond Tart 259

Key Lime Pie 260

Chocolate Mousse Tofu Pie 261

Chocolate Mousse Log 262

Raspberry Chocolate Mousse Torte 263

Chocolate Torte Shell 263

White Chocolate Thin Mints Terrine 264

White Chocolate Mousse in Almond Tuile with Fresh Strawberry Puree 266

Tira Misu 268

Lemon Cheesecake with Roasted Strawberries 269

Chocolate Coeur à la Crème 270

Crème Caramel Grand Mère 271

White Chocolate Raspberry Crème Brûlée 272

Baked Chocolate Pudding 273

Rice Pudding 274

Dulce De Leche Ice Cream 275

Austrian Apple Strudel 276

Pears "Al Forno" 278   Almond Apple Ravioli 279

The White House Madeira Cake

Teacher Kristin Albertson
Incredible Edibles, Wynnewood, PA

1½ cups Madeira
1½ cups water
3 cups sugar
2 frozen pound cakes (10¾ ounces each), thawed
1½ cups pecan halves, toasted
6 egg yolks
2 teaspoons almond extract
½ teaspoon salt
3 cups unsweetened whipped cream
Candied violets

Combine Madeira, water, and sugar in a heavy-bottomed 3-quart saucepan. Bring to a boil. Reduce heat and simmer for 10 minutes. Remove from heat and cool. (Mixture will be syrupy.)

Cut cakes into 1-inch cubes. Gently toss with half of Madeira syrup.

Grind pecans in a food processor until powdery. Whisk together yolks, almond extract, and salt in a saucepan over medium heat. Stir in pecans. Stir in remaining syrup. Heat, stirring often, until mixture bubbles. Remove from heat.

Preheat oven to 350°. Spray a 9-inch springform pan with a nonstick spray. Layer one-third cake cubes in bottom of pan. Top with one-third whipped cream and one-third egg-pecan mixture. Repeat two more times. Bake for 1 hour. Cool for 30 minutes and unmold. Serve with extra dollops of whipped cream and candied violets.

Serves 16

Philly Foodie Fact

Candied fruits and flowers, such as the violets used in this recipe, can be found in most gourmet markets and specialty shops, including Fantes. Store them in an airtight container in a cool, dry place.

Bourbon Spice Cake

Executive Pastry Chef Robert Bennett
Le Bec-Fin, Philadelphia, PA

2 cups cake flour
1 tablespoon baking powder
1 teaspoon baking soda
1 teaspoon ground ginger
1 teaspoon ground cinnamon
½ teaspoon EACH ground cardamom, allspice, and cloves
¼ teaspoon salt
¾ cup buttermilk
½ cup good quality bourbon
½ pound unsalted butter, softened
1¼ cups sugar
2 eggs
Confectioners' sugar

Preheat oven to 350°. Generously butter and flour a 10-inch cake pan. Combine flour, baking powder, baking soda, spices, and salt. Reserve. Combine buttermilk and bourbon and reserve.

In a mixer, cream butter and sugar together with a paddle attachment until light and fluffy. Add eggs, 1 at a time, beating well between additions. Add about one-quarter dry ingredients to eggs, alternating with about one-third buttermilk-bourbon mixture. Keep alternating, beginning and ending with dry ingredients. Pour cake batter into prepared pan. Bake for 45 minutes or until a toothpick inserted in the middle comes out clean. Cool for 10 minutes; then invert onto a cooling rack. Cool. Dust with confectioners' sugar and serve.

Yields one 10-inch cake

Chef's Note

To experience the full savor and perfume of the spices, grind your own from whole seeds. Dedicate a small coffee grinder for this purpose. Grind 1 to 2 tablespoons whole seeds, at a time, and store in a tightly sealed glass jar. When measuring, don't be tempted to add a little extra. These spices are full of powerful volatile oils. Too much can make your cake taste unpleasant. Like most liquor-infused cakes, this one is best served with a pot of fresh brewed *café filtre*.

My Mother's Favorite "Icebox" Strawberry Cake

Owner/Director Charlotte-Ann Albertson
Charlotte-Ann Albertson's Cooking School, Wynnewood, PA

3 pints fresh strawberries, hulled
4 tablespoons sugar plus ⅓ cup sugar, optional
2 to 3 cups whipped cream
1 large tube-style angel food cake, homemade or from a boxed cake mix

Thinly slice 2 pints strawberries. Place strawberries in a colander set over a large bowl. Sprinkle with 4 tablespoons sugar. Let stand for 1 to 2 hours.

Use a portion of strawberry juice to tint whipped cream. Reserve remaining juice. Fold sugared strawberry slices into 1 cup whipped cream. Sweeten with additional sugar, if desired.

Cut cake horizontally one-quarter from top with a serrated knife. Carefully remove top and reserve. Cut out a tunnel in the remaining cake, leaving a ½-inch shell. Crumble cake removed from the tunnel and fold crumbles into strawberries and cream. Fill tunnel with this mixture. Replace top.

Ice entire cake with remaining tinted whipped cream. Halve remaining strawberries. Garnish top and sides with strawberry halves. Refrigerate for 8 to 12 hours. Use a serrated knife to slice cake. Serve with reserved strawberry juice, if desired.

Serves 12 to 16

Chef's Note

For a non-fat dessert, substitute a frozen non-fat whipped topping for whipped cream and do not add sugar.

Roz's Chocolate Zucchini Cake

Owner/Baker Roz Bratt
Homemade Goodies by Roz, Philadelphia, PA

2 cups sugar
3 large eggs
1 cup oil
2 teaspoons vanilla extract
2 cups grated zucchini
2 cups flour
2 teaspoons baking soda
1 teaspoon baking powder
1 teaspoon cinnamon
½ cup cocoa
½ teaspoon salt
Chocolate Glaze (see recipe)

Preheat oven to 350°. Grease a 12-inch Bundt pan. Mix sugar and eggs together. Stir in oil and vanilla. Mix in zucchini. Combine dry ingredients in a separate bowl. Add dry ingredients to wet and mix together.

Pour mixture into pan and bake for 55 to 60 minutes or until inserted toothpick comes out clean. Cool and glaze.

Yields 12 to 14 slices

Chocolate Glaze

2 cups confectioners' sugar
2 tablespoons cocoa
2 tablespoons butter, softened
½ teaspoon vanilla extract
2 to 4 tablespoons milk

Combine sugar, cocoa, and butter. Stir in vanilla. Add milk gradually until glaze is smooth.

Angel Food Cake
with Framboise-scented Crème Anglaise

Chef/Owner Tom Peters
Monk's Café, Philadelphia, PA

10 egg whites, room temperature (save 5 yolks for
　　Crème Anglaise)
1¼ teaspoon cream of tartar
¼ teaspoon salt
1 teaspoon vanilla extract
½ teaspoon almond extract
1¼ cups sugar
1 cup cake flour
1 cup fresh raspberries, optional
Crème Anglaise (see recipe)
Raspberries for garnish
Mint sprigs

Preheat oven to 350°.

Beat egg whites, cream of tartar, and salt with an electric
mixer until soft peaks form. Add vanilla and almond
extracts and blend. Add sugar and beat until egg whites
are stiff and shiny but not dry. Sift flour into mixture.
Sprinkle raspberries over mixture. Fold in carefully. Do
not break stiff egg whites.

Spoon mixture into an ungreased, nonstick tube pan.
Bake for 40 minutes or until an inserted toothpick
comes out clean.

Invert pan onto a cake rack and let cake cool in pan.
When cool, carefully run a knife around the outer and
inner edges of cake. Invert pan and gently shake until
cake slides out.

Cut into wedges and place on serving plates. Top each
wedge with 2 ounces crème anglaise. Sprinkle plates
with raspberries and garnish with mint sprigs.

Monk's Café

Known for:
over 200 world class
beers, great mussels, and
late night food

Years in business: 3

Most requested table:
the round table in the
back room

Menu: Belgian/American

Chef: Tom Peters

Chef's training:
worked in many
restaurants in Belgium
from 3-stars to corner
cafes

**Chef's hobbies/
accomplishments:**
travel and cooking

Chef's favorite foods:
lobster in truffle butter

**Chef's favorite
cookbook:**
Com Chez Soi
by Pierre Wynants

Crème Anglaise

1 cup milk
1 cup heavy cream
½ cup granulated sugar
1 vanilla bean, split
5 egg yolks
¼ cup Lindemans Framboise (Belgian beer)

Heat milk, cream, sugar, and vanilla bean in a heavy saucepan. Slowly bring mixture to a boil. Remove from heat.

Whip eggs yolks in a mixing bowl. Very slowly, add half of hot cream mixture to yolks, whisking continuously; then pour yolk mixture into pan containing cream mixture. Cook over very low heat until custard thickens enough to coat the back of a spoon. Remove vanilla bean and scrape seeds into custard. Transfer to a food processor or blender and mix until absolutely smooth.

Gently fold in Lindemans Framboise. Refrigerate until well chilled.

Chef's Note

Lindemans Framboise is a Belgian ale that is cellared in an oak barrel with fresh raspberries. It is very red and rather sweet. Lindemans Framboise is a great dessert beer. Try it with this dessert or with chocolate!

Jewish Apple Cake

Owner/Baker Roz Bratt
Homemade Goodies by Roz, Philadelphia, PA

3 cups flour
3 teaspoons baking powder
1½ cups sugar plus 5 tablespoons
4 large eggs
1 cup oil
2½ teaspoons vanilla extract
½ cup orange juice
5 apples, peeled, cored, and chopped
2 teaspoons cinnamon

Preheat oven to 350°. Grease a 10-inch tube pan. Combine flour, baking powder, and 1½ cups sugar in a mixing bowl. Add eggs and wet ingredients. Mix until batter is smooth and free of lumps. In a separate bowl, combine remaining sugar, apples, and cinnamon.

Pour half of batter in pan and then layer with half of apples. Repeat. Bake for 60 minutes or until an inserted toothpick comes out clean.

Yields 12 to 14 slices

Homemade Goodies by Roz

Known for:
coziest kitchen in Philly

Years in business: 2

Most requested table:
front table by window

Menu:
homemade goodies

Chef: Roz Bratt

Chef's training:
self taught

Chef's hobbies:
worked at home; then opened a retail store

Chef's favorite foods:
chocolate cake, pretzels, chocolate ice cream, M&M's

Chef's favorite cookbook:
Betty Crocker, Hershey's chocolate cookbooks

Sour Cherry Almond Tart

Executive Chef Eric Hall
La Campagne, Cherry Hill, NJ

8 tablespoons unsalted butter, melted and cooled
¾ cup sugar
Pinch of salt
2 teaspoons vanilla extract
½ cup finely ground blanched almonds
1½ cups all-purpose flour
5 tablespoons heavy cream
1 egg, lightly beaten
1 tablespoon kirsch, optional
1 pound sour cherries, pitted

Preheat oven to 350°. Butter a 9-inch tart pan.

Combine butter, ½ cup sugar, salt, 1 teaspoon vanilla, and 2 tablespoons almonds in a medium bowl. Add 1¼ cups flour and stir to form a smooth dough. Press dough firmly into bottom and up sides of pan. Prick bottom with a fork. Bake for 10 minutes or until pale brown.

Combine cream, egg, and remaining vanilla in a small bowl. Whisk in remaining flour and sugar, 2 tablespoons almonds, and kirsch. Sprinkle 2 tablespoons almonds on the bottom of baked crust. Top with cherries. Pour in filling and top with remaining almonds. Bake for 40 minutes or until firm and golden brown.

Serves 8

Key Lime Pie

Executive Chef Jeffrey Gutstein
Cresheim Cottage Cafe, Philadelphia, PA

1¼ cups cinnamon graham cracker crumbs

⅓ cup melted unsalted butter

3 egg yolks

1 can sweetened condensed milk (14 ounces)

½ cup plus 2 tablespoons fresh key lime juice or 5 tablespoons each fresh lime juice
   and fresh lemon juice

2½ teaspoons grated lime zest

1 cup heavy cream

3 tablespoons confectioners' sugar

½ teaspoon vanilla extract

Preheat oven to 350°. Combine graham cracker crumbs and butter in a mixing bowl. Mix to form a crumbly dough. Press into an 8-inch pie pan. Bake for 5 minutes. Remove crust but leave oven on.

Combine yolks and sweetened condensed milk in a mixing bowl. Beat with a mixer at high speed until light and fluffy, about 5 minutes. Gradually beat in key lime juice or lime-lemon combination and 2 teaspoons zest. Pour mixture into baked crust. Bake for 6 to 8 minutes or until an inserted skewer comes out clean and hot to the touch. Set pie on a baking rack and cool to room temperature.

Place cream in a well chilled bowl and beat until soft peaks form. Add sugar, vanilla, and remaining lime zest and beat until stiff. Spread or pipe over top of pie. Refrigerate uncovered until ready to serve. For best results, serve within 1 hour of adding whipped cream.

Serves 8

Chocolate Mousse Tofu Pie

Chef/Instructor Susan E. Roth
Dobbins Randolph AVTS, Philadelphia, PA

1 sleeve graham crackers, processed to fine crumbs (One 16-ounce box contains three sleeves.)
1 cup margarine, melted (soy preferred)
¾ cup sugar
10 ounces grain sweetened chocolate chips
1⅓ boxes Mori-nu Silken Tofu (12.3 ounces each), firm
½ cup maple syrup
1 teaspoon vanilla extract
Pinch of salt

Preheat oven to 375°. Mix together graham crackers, margarine, and sugar. Press with fingers into a 9-inch pie plate. Use another pie plate to help press down evenly. Bake for 8 minutes. Cool and reserve.

Slowly melt chocolate in a double boiler over low heat. Blend remaining ingredients in a food processor until smooth. Add melted chocolate and blend again until well combined.

Pour into prepared pie shell and chill thoroughly before serving.

This recipe is a great way to get the benefits of soy. No one will know it's tofu!

Serves 8

Randolph/Dobbins Vocational School "Flame & Steel"

Known for:
open to faculty, staff, and guests

Years in business: 21

Menu:
students and instructor prepare daily specials

Chef: Susan Roth

Chef's training:
N.O.C.C.I. certified

Chef's hobbies/ accomplishments:
organic gardener, herbalist

Chef's favorite foods:
Asian, Italian, French, vegetarian

Chef's favorite cookbook:
New Recipes from Moosewood, Fanny Farmer, Friendly Foods by brother Ron Pickarski

Chocolate Mousse Log

Pastry Chef/Owner Deborah Kaplan
Sud Fine Pastry and Café, Philadelphia, PA

8 large eggs, separated
1¾ cups sugar
9 ounces semi-sweet chocolate
4½ tablespoons espresso
3 cups heavy cream
Scant ¼ cup cocoa
1 tablespoon espresso powder

Preheat oven to 350°. Butter a jelly-roll pan. Line pan with wax paper and butter paper.

Beat together yolks and 1 cup sugar until thick and pale. Melt chocolate and espresso over low heat and stir until blended. Cool slightly and add to yolk mixture.

In a separate bowl, beat egg whites until stiff but not dry. Fold into chocolate mixture. Gently spread batter in pan. Bake for 15 minutes. Remove from oven and cover with a damp cloth for 30 minutes.

Whisk together remaining ¾ cup sugar, cream, cocoa, and espresso powder. Refrigerate for 15 minutes. Beat with mixer until stiff.

Loosen cake from pan and dust with additional cocoa. Turn over and place on wax paper. Spread with cocoa cream. Roll up like a jelly roll and place, seam side down, on serving plate. Dust with additional cocoa.

Serves 10

Sud Fine Pastry and Café

Known for:
custom wedding and occasion cakes

Years in business: 20

Menu:
custom, international pastries, espresso, cappuccino, teas

Chef: Deborah Kaplan

Chef's training:
Fine Arts degree; previous chef/owner of Café Sud

Chef's hobbies:
choral singing, Latin dancing

Chef's favorite foods:
avocados, oysters, and anything crunchy

Chef's favorite cookbook:
N.Y. Times, Craig Claiborne

Raspberry Chocolate Mousse Torte

Owner Lou Moore
The Pink Rose Pastry Shop, Philadelphia, PA

4½ ounces semi-sweet chocolate
3 tablespoons butter
3 egg yolks
2 tablespoons sugar
2 tablespoons chambord
Chocolate Torte Shell (see recipe)
Fresh raspberries
Whipped cream
Chocolate shavings

Melt chocolate in a double boiler over simmering water. Whisk in butter. Whisk in yolks. Whisk in sugar and chambord in a slow stream until thick. Remove from heat and whip with an electric beater until cool. Spread mousse evenly into baked shell.

Arrange fresh raspberries in the center of torte. Place whipped cream dollops around border. Sprinkle with chocolate shavings.

Yields one 9-inch torte

Chocolate Torte Shell

1½ cups flour
11 tablespoons cocoa
¼ cup sugar
½ teaspoon baking soda
¼ cup butter
1 egg

Preheat oven to 350°. Combine dry ingredients with butter and egg. Spread evenly into a 9-inch tart pan. Bake for 20 to 22 minutes.

White Chocolate Thin Mints Terrine

Executive Chef David Bennett
White Rose Café, Marlton, NJ

2 cups heavy cream
8 ounces white chocolate
1 envelope gelatin
8 egg yolks
3 egg whites
1 sleeve Girl Scout Thin Mints® cookies
1 cup sugar
1 cup shelled pistachios
Bailey's Bittersweet Chocolate Crème Anglaise (see
    recipe)
Fresh berries

Whip cream until soft peaks form. Refrigerate.

Melt chocolate over a double boiler. Dissolve gelatin in 2 tablespoons warm water. Beat egg yolks until pale and very thick. Add melted chocolate and gelatin and beat until thick.

Whip egg whites until firm peaks form. Stir in half of egg yolks until combined. Fold in remaining egg yolks. Crumble Thin Mints® into large chunks and add to egg mixture. Rewhip cream until soft peaks form. Fold cream into egg base. Pour batter into a loaf pan lined with plastic wrap. Refrigerate overnight.

Melt sugar in a heavy-bottomed saucepan over medium heat until golden brown. Stir in pistachios. Pour mixture (praline) onto a cookie sheet and allow to cool. Grind praline into a powder with a food processor or mortar and pestle.

Remove terrine from loaf pan and coat with most of ground praline. Cut terrine into ½-inch slices and serve with chocolate crème anglaise, fresh berries, and a sprinkle of praline powder.

Serves 8 to 10

White Rose Café

Known for:
private curtained booths

Years in business: 1

Most requested table:
#15 and #61

Menu:
global eclectic

Chef: David Bennett

Chef's training:
The Restaurant School in Philadelphia; Madeleine Kamman's School for American Chefs

Chef's hobbies/ accomplishments:
gardening

Chef's favorite foods:
Twizzlers, chicken cutlets, anything fried

Chef's favorite cookbook:
everything, especially Madeleine Kamman's and Jean Georges'

Bailey's Bittersweet Chocolate Crème Anglaise

2 cups milk
8 egg yolks
½ cup granulated sugar
Pinch of salt
1 teaspoon vanilla extract
¼ cup Bailey's Irish Cream

Scald milk in a small saucepan. In a separate pan, whisk egg yolks, sugar, and pinch of salt. Gradually add scalded milk to yolk mixture, stirring constantly. Cook over medium heat, stirring continuously, until custard reaches 165° and is thick enough to coat the back of a spoon. Strain mixture into a bowl. Stir in vanilla and Bailey's. Stir to reduce temperature and then refrigerate.

Chef's Note

"Ribbon" is a cooking term that describes the texture of an egg or egg and sugar mixture that has been beaten until pale and very thick. When the beater is raised, the batter falls slowly and forms a ribbonlike pattern on the surface of the mixture. When you beat the egg yolks for this recipe, you are "ribboning" them.

White Chocolate Mousse in Almond Tuile with Fresh Strawberry Puree

Chef/Owner Kathleen Mulhern
The Garden Restaurant, Philadelphia, PA

1 pint heavy cream
1 cup sugar
½ cup water
4 egg whites
1 pound white chocolate, chopped
Almond Tuile (see recipe)
Fresh Strawberry Puree (see recipe)
Raspberries

Whip cream to stiff peaks and reserve in refrigerator. Combine sugar and water in a saucepan. Boil until soft-ball stage (see Chef's Note). Whip egg whites until almost stiff. Combine sugar syrup with whipped whites, a little at a time, in a mixer at high speed. Whip for 1 minute more to cool mixture. Reduce speed to low and slowly add chopped chocolate, a little at a time. Turn off mixer when last bit of chocolate is added.

Gently fold chocolate mixture into whipped cream. Cover and refrigerate for 2 hours before serving.

Place tuiles on dessert plates. Spoon a generous amount of mousse into each tuile. Add fresh strawberry puree in a crescent shape inside rim of plate. Garnish with a few fresh raspberries.

Serves 6 to 8

The Garden

Known for:
5 private dining rooms and outside garden and covered deck

Years in business: 26

Most requested table:
#17

Menu:
Continental American, seafood, steaks

Chef: Kathleen Mulhern

Almond Tuile

4 eggs
1 cup sugar
⅓ cup flour
1 cup ground almonds

Preheat oven to 300°. Whisk together all ingredients. Place 1½ tablespoons of mixture on a nonstick baking sheet and swirl evenly to form a 6-inch circle. Bake in oven until golden brown but still soft, about 8 to 10 minutes. Remove from sheet while still hot but starting to cool down and press over an inverted 4-ounce ramekin or similar vessel to form a cup. Continue to repeat entire procedure until all batter has been used. Allow to completely harden; then carefully remove cups.

Fresh Strawberry Puree

1 pint fresh ripe strawberries
½ teaspoon powdered sugar

Remove tops and halve strawberries. Puree in a blender or food processor. Add sugar and process until frothy. Strain and sweeten with additional sugar, if desired.

Chef's Note

There are two ways to tell if a sugar syrup has reached the soft-ball stage. Use a candy thermometer. If it reads 234° to 240°, it's soft-ball. Or drop a bit of the syrup into cold water. If it forms a soft ball and flattens on its own, it's soft-ball.

Tira Misu

Executive Chef Nick Lo Bianco
Tuscan Twenty at Korman Suites Hotel, Philadelphia, PA

2 pounds mascarpone cheese
½ cup Marsala wine
1 quart heavy cream
¼ cup confectioners' sugar
1 teaspoon vanilla extract
12 ounces ladyfingers
2 cups strong brewed espresso coffee, cooled
4 ounces grated bittersweet chocolate
3 tablespoons unsweetened cocoa powder

Mix mascarpone cheese and Marsala wine in a large mixing bowl. Whip heavy cream, confectioners' sugar, and vanilla in a blender on high speed until thickened. Fold into mascarpone mixture.

Quickly soak ladyfingers in espresso.

Use half of ladyfingers to line bottom of a large 3- to 4-inch-deep serving dish. Cover with half of mascarpone mixture; then half of grated chocolate. Repeat procedure. Dust with cocoa powder. Refrigerate for 2 hours.

Serves 8

Lemon Cheesecake with Roasted Strawberries

Executive Pastry Chef Michael Vandergeest
Philippe on Locust, Philadelphia, PA

1½ pounds cream cheese
1½ cups sugar plus 4 tablespoons
4 ounces sour cream
4 to 5 eggs
2 ounces heavy cream
Juice and zest of 4 lemons
3 drops lemon oil
3 pints strawberries, washed and stems removed
4 sprigs mint, cut into very thin strips
Dash of white pepper

Preheat oven to 300°. Cream together cream cheese and 1½ cups sugar in a mixing bowl. Add sour cream. Scrape bowl down. Add eggs, 1 at a time, mixing after each addition. Stir in heavy cream, lemon juice and zest, and lemon oil. Pour into two 10-inch springform pans. Bake for 18 to 25 minutes until tops are tan colored. (Be sure cheesecakes don't rise too much or they will crack.)

Combine 2 pints strawberries with remaining sugar in a metal container. Cover tightly with plastic wrap. Place container in a large pot of boiling water and let steep for 30 minutes or until berries lose their color. Strain sauce. (This may be done in advance and chilled until ready to use.)

Preheat oven to 400°. Cut remaining strawberries in half. Place in an ovenproof dish with mint, sauce, and white pepper. Bake for 8 minutes. Serve cheesecake at room temperature with roasted strawberries and maybe a sprig of mint and thin crunchy cookies.

Yields 2 cakes

Chef's Note

Lemon oil, available at Assouline and Ting in Philadelphia, really gives this cake a kick. I recommend that you bake the cake the day before you plan on serving it. This allows the lemon flavor and taste to permeate the cake.

Chocolate Coeur à la Crème

Head Pastry Chef/Owner Diane Nussbaum
Diane's La Patisserie Française, Haddonfield, NJ

2 ounces semi-sweet chocolate
¼ teaspoon instant coffee, optional
½ pound cream cheese, room temperature
1¼ cups heavy cream
⅔ cup powdered sugar
1 teaspoon vanilla
Fresh raspberries, optional
Chocolate dipped strawberries, optional

Melt chocolate in a double boiler. Mix in instant coffee. Beat cream cheese until light and fluffy. Add ¼ cup heavy cream and beat until smooth. Add melted chocolate, sugar, and vanilla. In a separate bowl, whip remaining cream until soft peaks form. Gently fold cream into cheese mixture.

Line a 4-cup heart mold with damp cheesecloth. Fill mold with mixture and cover with another piece of damp cheesecloth. Refrigerate for 8 hours or overnight. Remove top cheesecloth, invert mold on a serving plate, and remove bottom cloth. Garnish with raspberries and chocolate dipped strawberries.

Serves 8

Diane's La Patisserie Française

Known for:
custom wedding cakes,
European styled pastries

Years in business: 14

Menu:
European and
continental pastries

Chef: Diane Nussbaum

Chef's training:
self taught

**Chef's hobbies/
accomplishments:**
modern dance, cycling

Chef's favorite foods:
homemade soups

**Chef's favorite
cookbook:**
books by Julia Child and
Jacques Pepin

Crème Caramel Grand Mère

Chef/Owner Michèle R. Haines
Spring Mill Café, Conshohocken, PA

1½ cups granulated sugar plus 1⅓ cups
½ cup water
7½ cups milk
1 teaspoon dark rum
10 eggs
8 egg yolks

Preheat oven to 375°. Combine 1½ cups sugar and water in a saucepan. Boil for 10 minutes without stirring until mixture is golden, not pale or dark. Pour equal amounts into 12 six-ounce ovenproof ramekins.

Combine milk and rum in a medium saucepan and heat to just below the boiling point. Remove from heat. Cool slightly and then remove skin from the top.

Put scalded milk, eggs, egg yolks, and remaining 1⅓ cups sugar in a mixing bowl. Beat until well mixed but not overbeaten. Pour equal amounts of mixture into ramekins over caramel layer.

Put ramekins into a deep ovenproof dish. Pour warm water into dish up to half the height of ramekins. Bake for 35 minutes or until a sharp knife inserted in the crème comes out clean. Do not overbake. Tops should be yellow but not brown. Cool completely; then refrigerate.

When ready to serve, run a sharp knife around edge of each ramekin to release crème. Put serving plate on top of ramekin, turn upside down, and shake until crème is released onto plate.

Serves 12

Spring Mill Café

Known for:
provincial French cuisine with Moroccan flavors

Years in business: 21

Most requested table: romantic corner F6

Menu:
French and Moroccan combinations

Chef:
Michèle R. Haines

Chef's training:
my grandmother

Chef's hobbies/ accomplishments:
photography/professor of cultural anthropology

Chef's favorite foods:
pâtés, fish

Chef's favorite cookbook:
anything by Julia Child and Jacques Pepin

White Chocolate Raspberry Crème Brûlée

Executive Chef Robert Cloud
The Oak Grill at the Marshalton Inn, West Chester, PA

3 cups heavy cream
2 tablespoons vanilla extract
6 egg yolks
4 tablespoons sugar
½ pound white chocolate chips
1 pint raspberries

Preheat oven to 325°. Combine heavy cream, vanilla, egg yolks, and sugar until well blended. Melt white chocolate chips over a double boiler or in a microwave and add to cream mixture. Divide raspberries among eight 6-ounce cups. Pour cream mixture over raspberries. Place cups in a water bath and bake for 60 minutes.

Serves 8

Baked Chocolate Pudding

Executive Pastry Chef Michael Vandergeest
Philippe on Locust, Philadelphia, PA

1 cup whole milk
1 cup heavy cream
14 ounces bittersweet chocolate, finely chopped
2 eggs

Preheat oven to 300°. Bring milk and cream to a boil in
a medium saucepan. Pour in chopped chocolate and mix
well. Add eggs, 1 at a time, mixing after each addition.
Pour into eight 4-ounce ovenproof molds or ramekins.
Bake for 12 to 15 minutes. Serve warm with cookies.

Serves 8

Philippe on Locust

Known for:
creative cuisine and
exquisite desserts

Years in business: 2

Menu:
French-Asian fusion

Executive Pastry Chef:
Michael Vandergeest

Chef's training:
Philadelphia's
Restaurant School and
many years experience
at hotels and restaurants

**Chef's hobbies/
accomplishments:**
gardening, home
improvements, fishing
with family at the shore

Chef's favorite foods:
PB&J on toasted English
muffin, bread, bread, &
more bread

**Chef's favorite
cookbook:**
Art Culinaire

Rice Pudding

Chef/Proprietor Walter Staib
City Tavern, Philadelphia, PA.

2 cups water
¾ cup uncooked long-grain white rice
2½ cups whole milk
½ cup sugar
3 large eggs
1½ tablespoons unsalted butter, softened
1½ teaspoons vanilla extract
1 teaspoon ground cinnamon

Preheat oven to 325°. Bring water to a boil in a 2-quart saucepan. Add rice. Cover and simmer for 15 to 20 minutes. Remove from heat and let stand for 5 minutes. Drain, if necessary.

In a separate saucepan, bring milk to a boil. Stir in drained rice and cook for 10 minutes more until grains are soft. In a large bowl, whisk together sugar, eggs, butter, vanilla, and cinnamon. Gradually stir hot rice mixture into egg mixture.

Transfer to a 2-quart ovenproof glass or ceramic dish. Cover and place dish into a larger high-sided roasting pan. Carefully pour boiling water into roasting pan to a depth of 1½ inches around dish. Bake for 20 to 30 minutes or until an inserted knife comes out clean. Garnish with additional cinnamon. Serve warm or cold.

Serves 6

City Tavern

Chef: Walter Staib

Chef's hobbies/ accomplishments: As founder and president of Concepts by Staib, Ltd., Chef Staib is the driving force behind six of the country's most unique dining establishments and is credited with having conceptualized and opened over 300 fine restaurants. Chef Staib is Ambassador to the Culinary Institute of America and Culinary Ambassador to the City of Philadelphia. He was the first inductee to the Caribbean Culinary Hall of Fame. In 1999 he received the Restaurateur of Distinction Ivy Award from *Restaurants and Institutions*.

Dulce De Leche Ice Cream

Chef/Owner Guillermo Pernot
¡Pasión!, Philadelphia, PA

1 teaspoon vanilla extract
2 cups milk
4 cups heavy cream
18 egg yolks
¾ cup sugar
56 ounces Dulce De Leche (see recipe)

Combine vanilla, milk, and heavy cream in a heavy-bottomed saucepan and bring to a boil. Meanwhile, whisk yolks and sugar to ribbon stage. Add a little hot milk mixture to yolk mixture to temper it. Reduce heat under milk mixture to low. Add yolks to milk mixture. Stir with a spatula until mixture coats spatula. Remove from heat and chill immediately.

Whisk in dulce de leche and fully incorporate. Place custard mixture into an ice cream maker and freeze according to manufacturer's directions.

Dulce De Leche

56 ounces condensed milk

Place milk in an enamel saucepan or double boiler. Cook until milk becomes light brown in color. Chill.

Austrian Apple Strudel

Executive Chef Harry Burns
Ludwig's Garten, Philadelphia, PA

½ cup raisins

¼ cup Meyers Dark Rum

2 sheets puff pastry (Pepperidge Farms is fine.)

3 to 4 Granny Smith apples, peeled, cored, and thinly
  sliced

1 cup brown sugar

1 cup breadcrumbs

1 teaspoon cinnamon

½ cup chopped walnuts

½ teaspoon nutmeg

1 cup sour cream

2 tablespoons vanilla extract

1 egg

Vanilla Bean Sauce (see recipe)

Soak raisins in rum and reserve. Place one sheet puff
pastry on top of the other. Using a rolling pin, flatten
and spread sheets to twice the original size.

Combine remaining ingredients, except egg and sauce,
in a mixing bowl. Stir in rum-soaked raisins. Add a little
water to loosen OR additional breadcrumbs to thicken
so that a paste-like consistency is achieved.

Preheat oven to 375°. Place mixture along the bottom
edge of pastry. Roll up to form a fat cigar-shaped log.
Place strudel on a greased cookie sheet. Beat egg with a
little water and brush over strudel. Use a knife to cut 2
or 3 slits on the top of the strudel dough. Bake for 45
to 60 minutes. Let stand for 20 minutes. Pour hot
vanilla bean sauce over strudel and serve.

Serves 4 to 6

Ludwig's Garten

Known for:
sourbrattan, strudel,
game menu, schnitzel,
beer selection

Years in business: 1¼

Most requested table:
"stomp dish" —
traditional corner table at
German restaurants

Menu:
contemporary German

Chef: Harry Burns

Chef's training:
on the job since 1975

**Chef's hobbies/
accomplishments:**
sports, music

Chef's favorite foods:
Italian, Indian

**Chef's favorite
cookbook:**
The *Moosewood* books,
Escoffier

Vanilla Bean Sauce

1 tablespoon cornstarch
⅛ cup water
1 pint heavy cream
3 tablespoons sugar
1 vanilla bean, split
½ cinnamon stick
2 egg yolks, beaten

Combine cornstarch and water and set aside.

Heat heavy cream, sugar, vanilla bean, and cinnamon stick in a heavy saucepan over medium heat. When very hot, whisk in egg yolks. Add cornstarch mixture and whisk until sauce thickens.

Pears "Al Forno"

Owner/Baker Gilda Doganiero
Gilda's Biscotti, Inc., Philadelphia, PA

4 red Bartlett pears, firm to touch
1 cup sugar
1 cup water
⅓ cup sweet Marsala wine or your favorite red wine
1 teaspoon vanilla extract
Zest of 1 lemon

Preheat oven to 375°. Wash pears. Remove a small portion from base of pear with a paring knife. (This will allow the fruit to stand upright in the pan and on the plate.)

Combine sugar, water, wine, vanilla extract, and lemon zest in a saucepan and bring to a boil. Reduce heat and simmer for 5 minutes. Stand pears upright in a deep oven-ready sauté pan. Carefully pour wine syrup over pears. Loosely cover pears with a piece of foil and place in oven. Bake for 15 minutes. Remove foil and baste pears with pan syrup. Recover and continue cooking for 1 hour, basting every 15 minutes. Skin should be golden and candied and fork should easily pierce flesh of pear.

Serve hot, warm, or cold with vanilla ice cream, crème fraîche, or toasted pound cake.

Leftover syrup is great for pancakes or waffles. Leftover pears make great spreads for morning toast and coffee.

Serves 4

Gilda's Biscotti

Known for:
really authentic Italian cookies

Years in business: 5

Most requested table:
my house

Chef: Gilda Doganiero

Chef's training:
Culinary Institute of America graduate; Le Bec-Fin; Four Seasons Hotel

Chef's hobbies/ accomplishments:
family, friends, wine, food, and dogs

Chef's favorite foods:
sushi, broccoli rabe, rare steak, frites

Chef's favorite cookbook:
books by Julia Child, Alain Ducasse, and Jaques Pepin

Almond Apple Ravioli

Chef/Instructor Garry Waldie CEC, AAC
The Restaurant School, Philadelphia, PA

2 tart apples, peeled and cored
Juice of 1 lemon
2 ounces toasted almonds, finely chopped
Pinch of sugar
2 sheets fresh pasta dough
Fresh mint leaves
2 eggs
2 egg yolks
¼ cup apple juice
⅛ teaspoon cinnamon
2 tablespoons butter

Using a grater with large holes, grate apples into a mixing bowl. Squeeze lemon juice over apples. Add almonds and pinch of sugar. Toss with a wooden spoon to combine.

Lay dough out on a clean working surface. Arrange mint leaves on half of the dough and fold over other half to cover. Flatten dough and roll thin with rolling pin. Cut dough into identical shapes using a round or square cookie cutter.

Place a small amount of filling in the centers of half of the cut dough. Moisten edges and cover with remaining cut dough. Press edges firmly to seal. Reserve.

Combine eggs, yolks, apple juice, and cinnamon in a saucepan and whisk to combine. Cook over a simmering double boiler until sauce thickens. Remove from heat and whisk in butter. (Sauce will keep for 30 minutes in a warm place.)

Cook ravioli in lightly oiled boiling water for 6 to 8 minutes until al dente. Drain well. Ladle sauce onto warm plates and place ravioli on sauce. Garnish with additional fresh mint.

Serves 2 to 4

sweet little somethings

Spicy Walnuts

Chef Paul Trowbridge
Vega Grill, Philadelphia, PA

2 egg whites
1 tablespoon cayenne pepper
1 tablespoon ground cumin
½ tablespoon ancho powder
½ teaspoon salt
½ teaspoon pepper
2 cups walnuts

Preheat oven to 350°. Combine egg whites and spices with a fork until frothy and well mixed. Add walnuts and stir until all walnuts are coated. Place walnuts on parchment-lined baking sheet. Toast for 10 minutes.

Almonds di Abruzzi

Owner/Baker Gilda Doganiero
Gilda's Biscotti, Inc., Philadelphia, PA

4 cups whole unblanched almonds
2 cups red wine (Never use cooking wine!)
2 cups granulated sugar

Preheat oven to 350°. Lightly toast almonds for about 10 minutes. Reserve.

Place wine and sugar in a heavy-bottomed saucepan and bring to a boil. Reduce heat and simmer until liquid is reduced by half.

Spread a piece of parchment paper over a sheet pan or cookie sheet. Pour almonds into wine syrup and stir well with a wooden spoon. Continue cooking until mixture becomes very thick. Carefully pour caramelized almonds and syrup onto sheet pan. Use a wooden spoon to spread almond mixture to a thin layer, being careful to NOT touch almonds with bare hands. Allow mixture to cool to room temperature. When cool, break almonds into bite-size pieces.

Caramel Nut Bars

Owner/Founder Eileen Talanian
An American Kitchen

Softened butter
¾ cup unsalted butter
1½ cups sugar
1½ teaspoons pure vanilla extract
3 large eggs
¾ cup unsweetened cocoa powder
1 cup all-purpose flour (preferably unbleached)
1 cup coarsely chopped pecans
30 vanilla caramels
⅓ cup plus 1 tablespoon heavy cream
3 ounces good quality white chocolate, coarsely chopped

Preheat oven to 350°. Line a 9 x 13-inch baking pan with foil and brush with softened butter. Beat together unsalted butter, sugar, vanilla, and eggs with an electric mixer on medium speed for 2 minutes. (The mixture will be light in color and fluffy.) Scrape bowl with a rubber spatula. Add cocoa and beat on low for 30 seconds. Scrape bowl again and add flour on low speed, mixing for about 20 seconds, just until evenly combined. Spread batter into prepared pan and smooth top. Sprinkle pecans over batter.

Melt caramels and ⅓ cup cream in a heavy saucepan over medium heat, stirring constantly until smooth. Pour over pecans. Bake for 25 minutes, reversing pan after 12 minutes.

Microwave remaining cream and chocolate in a covered microwave dish for 2 minutes or in a heavy pan over low heat until chocolate is almost melted. Remove from heat and whisk until smooth. Cool for 5 minutes; then drizzle over partially cooled bars. When completely cooled, cut into squares.

Yields 32 bars

From the book *Chewy Cookies* by Eileen Talanian

An American Kitchen

Known for:
exquisite cookies and brownie truffles

Years in business: 9

Chef: Eileen Talanian

Chef's training:
Purdue University for Communications

Chef's hobbies/ accomplishments:
collects antique cookbooks/on board of directors for Philadelphia Chapter of Les Dames d'Escoffier

Chef's favorite foods:
champagne, raspberries

Chef's favorite cookbook:
any by Marian Cunningham

Chocolate Truffle

Executive Pastry Chef Michael Vandergeest
Philippe on Locust, Philadelphia, PA

2 cups heavy cream
18 ounces bittersweet chocolate, finely chopped
2 tablespoons butter, softened
2 to 4 ounces dark rum
6 ounces chocolate, melted (approximate, depending on your taste)

Line a sheet pan with wax paper. Bring cream to a boil in a medium saucepan. Stir in chopped chocolate and mix well. Add butter and rum and mix well. Pour onto prepared sheet pan. Refrigerate until firm. Roll into small balls. Cover with melted chocolate and any additional desired coating. Best kept when stored at 50° to 55°.

Wine Notes

Recommended Wine: Domaine De La Pleiade, Maury 1994 ($18.50)

Description: A classic from the southwest of France, this important, fortified red dessert wine from the hamlet of Maury is an unusual encounter in the United States. Made with extra ripe Grenache grapes whose fermentation has been stopped with the addition of grape brandy, this wine is then exposed to the elements for six months to mature and develop port-like aromatics: a gem of a wine to savor with your favorite chocolate dessert.

Sommelier: Megan Shawver, Moore Brothers Wine Co.

Baklava Pastry

Chef/Manager Nina Kouchacji
Marrakesh, Philadelphia, PA

1 cup ground walnuts
½ cup sugar
1 tablespoon cinnamon
3 tablespoons rose water
20 sheets filo dough, cut into 3-inch strips
1 tablespoon oil
Rose Syrup (see recipe)

Preheat oven to 350°. Combine walnuts, sugar, and cinnamon in a bowl. Add rose water, 1 tablespoon at a time, until mixture sticks together. Knead mixture until it forms a ball.

Place filo strips on a clean work surface. Shape walnut mixture into finger-size rolls that are 3 inches long each. Place walnut roll horizontally on a strip end closest to you and roll strip away from you. Brush far tip of dough strip with water and seal. Repeat with remaining filo strips and filling.

Coat a baking sheet with oil. Place baklava, seam sides down, 1 inch apart on sheet. Bake for approximately 10 minutes. Turn logs over and bake for 10 minutes more.

Cool on baking rack. Drizzle with rose syrup or confectioners' sugar.

Yields 60 logs

Rose Syrup

1 cup sugar
½ cup water
1 tablespoon fresh lemon juice
1 tablespoon rose water

Bring sugar and water to a boil, stirring often. Add lemon juice and remove from heat. Stir well. Add rose water. Stir again.

Pine Nut Biscotti

Chef/Owner Patrick Given
Church Street Bistro, Lambertville, NJ

2 cups pine nuts
3 cups all-purpose flour
3 teaspoon baking powder
½ teaspoon salt
12 tablespoons butter
12 tablespoons sugar
2 large eggs
½ teaspoon vanilla

Preheat oven to 350°. Toast nuts for about 10 minutes. Cool and reserve. Leave oven on.

Sift together flour, baking powder, and salt. In a food processor, grind together flour mixture and half of toasted nuts.

Cream together butter, sugar, and eggs. Stir in remaining nuts and vanilla. Add to dry ingredients. Add a little water if dough is too dry.

Turn out dough onto a floured surface. Divide into quarters. Roll dough into 12-inch logs. Place on a parchment paper-lined baking sheet and bake for 30 minutes.

Remove logs from oven. Decrease oven temperature to 300°. When logs are cool enough to handle, cut each on a bias into ¼-inch-thick slices. Return slices to baking sheet and bake for 15 minutes. Store in an airtight jar.

Chocolate Crinkle Cookies

Chef/Owner Donna Leahy
Inn at Twin Linden, Churchtown, PA

½ cup butter
¾ cup sugar plus ¼ cup
¼ cup brown sugar
1 egg
1¼ cups flour
¼ cup Dutch process cocoa
½ teaspoon baking soda
½ teaspoon salt
2 tablespoons milk
3 ounces semi-sweet chocolate chips

Preheat oven to 350°. Combine butter, ¾ cup sugar, and brown sugar in a mixing bowl. Blend with electric beater until fluffy. Beat in egg.

In a separate bowl, sift together flour, cocoa, baking soda, and salt. Add dry ingredients to butter mixture and mix until just combined. Add milk and stir until just combined. Stir in chips.

Roll dough into approximately 16 walnut-size balls. (If dough is too sticky, add a little flour.) Roll each ball in remaining ¼ cup sugar. Bake on a lightly greased cookie sheet for 10 to 12 minutes until tops of cookies just begin to show cracks. Cool on a rack.

Yields 16 large cookies

sauces and such

Béarnaise Sauce

Executive Chef/Owner Jon Hallowell
Mixmaster Café, Malvern, PA

4 large shallots, minced
6 cloves garlic, minced
4 teaspoons chopped chervil or parsley
4 teaspoons chopped tarragon, fresh or dry
½ cup red wine vinegar
½ pound butter
6 egg yolks
4 tablespoons fresh lemon juice
Pinch of cayenne pepper
Salt and pepper

Combine shallots, garlic, chervil, and tarragon in a sauté pan. Add red wine vinegar and cook over low heat until liquid evaporates. Melt butter in a separate pan and cook until just under a boil.

Combine egg yolks, lemon juice, cayenne, and salt and pepper to taste in a blender. Blend for 15 seconds on medium speed. Slowly add butter, blending until light and fluffy. Add herb mixture. Serve warm.

Chef's Note
Béarnaise Sauce will separate if it is exposed to direct heat from the burner. Keep the sauce warm by putting it next to the stove or in a warm area of the kitchen.

Dijon Sauce

Executive Chef Chuck II
Friday Saturday Sunday, Philadelphia, PA

3 cups heavy cream
1 teaspoon salt
Pinch of pepper
1 teaspoon chopped fresh parsley
1 teaspoon chopped fresh thyme
¼ cup Dijon mustard

Combine all ingredients, except mustard, in a small saucepan. Bring to a boil, stirring often to keep sauce from burning. Reduce heat and simmer for about 15 minutes. Add mustard. Increase heat and bring back to a boil. Serve immediately.

Butter Sauce

Executive Chef William Fischer
Caffé Aldo Lamberti, Cherry Hill, NJ

½ cup wine vinegar
½ cup Chablis
1 shallot, chopped
Bouquet of thyme, bay leaf, peppercorns
1 pound unsalted butter
Juice of 1 lime
Salt and pepper

Combine vinegar, Chablis, shallot, and herbs in a saucepan. Cook until reduced by three-quarters. Add ½ pound butter. Cook on high until frothy. Add remaining butter and cook on high until frothy and expanding. Strain. Add lime juice and salt and pepper to taste. Reserve in a water bath until ready to serve.

Bechamel Sauce

Executive Chef Harry Burns
Ludwig's Garten, Philadelphia, PA

3 tablespoons butter
3 tablespoons flour
1 large onion, diced
1 quart milk
6 cloves
3 bay leaves
1 teaspoon nutmeg

Cook butter and flour in a small saucepan over medium heat until a smooth white roux forms.

Sauté onion in a skillet until translucent. Stir in seasonings. Stir in milk. Add roux and stir until sauce thickens. Strain and serve.

Beurre Blanc

Executive Chef Carolynn Angle
Fishmarket, Philadelphia, PA

1 cup white wine vinegar
3 cups white wine
2 cups minced shallots
1 tablespoon whole black peppercorns
3 bay leaves
2 cups heavy cream
1 pound sweet butter, diced

Combine all ingredients, except cream and butter, in a saucepan. Cook over medium heat until liquid is almost completely evaporated. Add cream and cook until liquid is reduced by more than half. Reduce heat to low and slowly whisk in butter. Make sure sauce does not get too hot. Strain and keep warm — but not hot — until ready to use.

Creamy Cheddar Sauce with White Wine

Chef/Owner Fritz Blank
Deux Cheminées, Philadelphia, PA

3 tablespoons butter or vegetable oil
3 tablespoons all-purpose flour
½ cup dry white wine
1½ cups milk or half-and-half or light cream or heavy cream (as your physician and conscience dictates)
1 cup shredded Cheddar cheese (as you like it — white or yellow, mild or strong.)
½ teaspoon salt
½ teaspoon freshly ground white pepper
Pinch of cayenne pepper or dash of Tabasco

Melt butter in a small saucepan over medium heat. Whisk in flour until a haze appears over the bottom. Immediately add wine and milk or cream. Continue whisking until a smooth sauce forms. Add cheese and continue to whisk until cheese has melted. Season with salt, pepper, and cayenne to taste. Keep warm until ready to use.

Sour Cream Dill Sauce

Chef Marie Jarzenski
Warsaw Cafe, Philadelphia, PA

5 tablespoons sour cream
½ teaspoon honey
1½ teaspoons cornstarch
1 teaspoon fresh lemon juice
Dash of salt and pepper
1 teaspoon chopped fresh dill

Combine all ingredients, except dill, in a saucepan over low heat. Cook for 3 to 5 minutes, stirring constantly. Add dill at last minute and blend.

Smoked Tomato Sauce

Executive Chef Andrew Maloney
Nodding Head Brewery & Restaurant, Philadelphia, PA

12 Roma tomatoes
1 tablespoon olive oil
2 cloves garlic, finely diced
1 tablespoon finely chopped fresh oregano
1 teaspoon finely chopped fresh thyme
1 teaspoon fresh sage

Slice stem ends off tomatoes (approximately ⅛ inch). Smoke for 30 minutes in a smoker. (See Chef's Note if you don't have a smoker.)

Remove skins from tomatoes. Dice tomatoes into ½-inch cubes.

Heat olive oil in a large sauté pan over high heat. Add garlic and sauté for 1 to 2 minutes. Add diced tomatoes and cook for 2 minutes. Lower heat to medium. Cook for 10 minutes. Add herbs and remove from heat. Let cool a bit. Puree in a blender or food processor. (Don't over blend: the sauce should be rustic with some tomato chunks.)

Chef's Note

This is a simple tomato sauce. We slowly smoke the tomatoes at the restaurant. If you don't have a smoker, you can improvise by using an inexpensive outdoor charcoal grill. Place a handful amount of warm charcoals on one side of your grill. Cover the grate on the other side of the grill with aluminum foil. Using a toothpick, poke three to four dozen holes in the foil. Place the tomatoes on the foil. Close the lid, leaving the air vents fully opened. Smoke the tomatoes. The smoking time will vary from grill to grill. (It takes about 15 to 20 minutes on my $25 grill.) If you don't want your sauce to have a smoky taste, simply blanch the tomatoes in boiling water for 2 to 3 minutes. This will allow you to easily remove the skins.

Broccolini and Plum Tomato Sauce

Executive Chef Alfonso Contrisciani
circa, Philadelphia, PA

1 tablespoon minced shallot
4 ounces white wine
Juice of 1 lemon
1 tablespoon capers
Pinch of crushed red pepper
2 cups chicken stock
2 cups chopped plum tomatoes
1 bunch broccolini, blanched
4 tablespoons butter
Salt and pepper

Sauté shallot in a sauté pan until translucent. Add wine, lemon juice, capers, and crushed red pepper and cook until liquid is reduced by half. Add chicken stock and cook until liquid is reduced by one-third. Add plum tomatoes, broccolini, and butter. Season to taste with salt and pepper. Serve with Herb Battered Soft-shell Crabs over Spinach Linguini (Recipe appears on page 96.), pasta, rice, chicken, or fish.

Marinara Sauce

Chef/Owner Anthony Stella
L'Osteria Cucina Italiana, Wilmington, DE

2 cans whole tomatoes (28 ounces each)
½ cup extra virgin olive oil
1 yellow onion, cut in half through root
1 teaspoon brown sugar
1 teaspoon black pepper
1 teaspoon kosher salt

Pass tomatoes through the fine screen on a food mill. Combine tomatoes, oil, and onion halves in a saucepan. Bring to a rapid boil and simmer vigorously until desired consistency is reached. Season with sugar, salt, and pepper.

Caramelized Shallot and Clementine Sauce

Executive Chef David Stoltzfus
The Ivy Grille at The Inn at Penn, Philadelphia, PA.

8 small shallots
2 tablespoons Madeira wine
Juice of 2 clementine oranges
¾ cup demi-glace
1 teaspoon chopped basil

Heat oven to 395°. Place shallots in a small pan and cover with aluminum foil. Roast for 25 minutes. Transfer pan to burner. Over medium heat, deglaze pan with Madeira. Add clementine juice, demi-glace, and basil. Heat until liquid is reduced by half.

Garlic Dipping Sauce

Chef/Owner Donna Leahy
Inn at Twin Linden, Churchtown, PA

1 egg
¾ cup corn oil
2 teaspoons white wine vinegar
1 teaspoon Dijon mustard
1 tablespoon minced fresh garlic
1 tablespoon chopped fresh parsley
½ teaspoon cayenne pepper

Place egg in a food processor or a blender and whip until light colored and smooth. Gradually add corn oil, whipping until oil is combined and mixture is creamy. Add remaining ingredients. Process until just combined. Refrigerate until ready to use or up to 24 hours.

Pickapeppa® Rémoulade

Chef/Proprietor Walter Staib
City Tavern, Philadelphia, PA

¼ cup chopped kosher dill pickles
¼ cup chopped yellow onion
1¾ cups mayonnaise
1 tablespoon Pickapeppa® sauce
1 teaspoon Dijon mustard
1 teaspoon finely chopped fresh dill
1 teaspoon fresh lemon juice

Puree pickles and onion in a food processor. Transfer puree to a medium mixing bowl. Add remaining ingredients. Mix well. Cover with plastic wrap and refrigerate until chilled, about 1 hour. Rémoulade will keep for up to 3 days.

Chef's Note

Pickapeppa ®, a West Indies condiment made from tropical fruits and spices, is available at most supermarkets and gourmet stores, such as Zagara's in Marlton, NJ, and the Spice Terminal in the Reading Terminal Market.

Charred Tomato Coulis

Executive Chef Daniel D. Bethard
Iron Hill Brewery and Restaurant, West Chester, PA

2 large ripe tomatoes
2 tablespoons olive oil
2 tablespoons aged sherry vinegar
Salt and pepper

Preheat broiler. Halve each tomato and squeeze out seeds. Arrange on a baking sheet, skin side up, and broil until skin is charred. Turn tomatoes over and roast until dark brown. Cool for 10 minutes. Place tomatoes in a blender and puree. While blender is running, slowly drizzle in olive oil and then vinegar. Season to taste with salt and pepper.

Asparagus Coulis

Executive Chef David Grear
La Terrasse, Philadelphia, PA

1 onion, diced
3 shallots, julienned
1 teaspoon chopped garlic
1 pound asparagus spears, sliced, tips removed (reserve for garnish)
1 quart clam juice
6 ounces crème fraîche
Salt and pepper

Sweat onion, shallots, and garlic in a hot pan. Add asparagus stems and sweat for 1 minute more. Add clam juice and cook until asparagus is tender, about 15 to 20 minutes. Transfer to a blender and puree. Strain through a fine sieve. Add crème fraîche and bend until smooth. Season to taste with salt and pepper.

Apple Cider Reduction

Chef/Owner Brian W. Duffy
Kristopher's, Philadelphia, PA

12 ounces apple cider
6 tablespoons butter

Cook apple cider in a saucepan over low flame until reduced by at least three-fourths. Increase heat and slowly whisk in butter until thick.

Green Apple Salsa

Chef/Instructor Philip G. Pinkney
The Restaurant School, Philadelphia, PA

⅜ cup minced cilantro
¼ cup minced mint
3 tart apples, diced
1 lime, zested and juiced
1 clove garlic, minced
½ jalapeño pepper, deseeded and minced
½ teaspoon confectioners' sugar
1½ tablespoons olive oil
Salt and pepper

Combine all ingredients. Prepare at least 1 hour before serving.

Clarified Butter

1 cup butter

Melt butter in a heavy saucepan over medium heat until butter bubbles. Remove from heat and let stand for 10 minutes. Skim off all foamy solids from the top. Spoon or pour the clear butterfat into a container. Discard residue that remains in the bottom of pan.

Red Onion Compote

Sous Chef Bruce Giardino
Marco's Restaurant, Philadelphia, PA

2 to 4 tablespoons vegetable oil
1 to 1½ pounds red onions, sliced
2 tablespoons rice wine vinegar
2 tablespoons apple cider vinegar
2 tablespoons white wine
¼ cup sugar
¼ cup golden raisins

Heat oil in a large skillet. Add onions and sweat for 2 to 4 minutes. Add remaining ingredients and simmer until syrupy, about 20 to 30 minutes. Let cool.

Yields 2 cups

Walnut Pesto

Sous Chef Bruce Giardino
Marco's Restaurant, Philadelphia, PA

1¾ cups toasted walnuts
2 tablespoons chopped fresh sage
2 tablespoons chopped fresh tarragon
1½ tablespoons chopped garlic
1 tablespoon lemon juice
2 tablespoons lime juice
½ cup blended oil
¼ cup olive oil
1 tablespoon Marsala wine
¼ cup fresh grated Romano cheese
Salt and freshly grated black pepper

Place walnuts, herbs, and garlic in a food processor and pulse chop until coarse. Add juices and puree. With motor running, slowly add oils. Season with Marsala, cheese, and salt and pepper.

Yields 1½ cups

Blackening Seasoning Mix

Chef/Owner Joseph Tucker
Pompeii Restaurant, Philadelphia, PA

2 tablespoons ground paprika
2 tablespoons chili powder
1 tablespoon freshly ground black or white pepper
1 tablespoon ground cayenne pepper
1 tablespoon onion powder
1 tablespoon garlic powder
1 tablespoon Old Bay Seasoning or seafood seasoning (any brand will do)

Mix all ingredients together. Store in an airtight container in spice cabinet.

Chef's Salt

Chef/Owner Fritz Blank
Deux Cheminées, Philadelphia, PA

6 pounds table salt
6 tablespoons Hungarian sweet paprika
1 tablespoon ground allspice
1 tablespoon finely ground white pepper
1 tablespoon finely ground black pepper
½ teaspoon garlic salt (Do NOT use powder.)

Combine all ingredients and mix well. Store in airtight containers until ready to use.

Chef's Note

Seasoned salt has been used by chefs and cooks throughout cooking history. Various formulations may be found in cookbooks and other sources, including the well-known commerical brand Lowrey's Seasoned Salt®. The recipe we use at Deux Cheminées is a variation of an original by Chef Louis Szathmáry.

Court Bouillon

Chef/Proprietor Walter Staib
City Tavern, Philadelphia, PA

16 cups (1 gallon) water
½ cup white wine
½ cup diced celery
1 large carrot, diced
½ large onion, cut into quarters
¼ cup sliced leeks, rinsed well
1 teaspoon salt
½ teaspoon whole black peppercorns
¼ teaspoon cayenne pepper
½ large bay leaf
½ lemon, halved

Place all ingredients in a 6-quart stockpot and bring to a boil. Reduce heat to medium and simmer, uncovered, for about 3 hours or until liquid is reduced by half.

Line a large colander or sieve with two layers of 100% cotton cheesecloth. Set colander in a large heat-proof bowl and carefully strain hot mixture through it. Let cool.

Bouillon will keep for 1 week in refrigerator; 1 month in freezer.

Yields 6 cups

Saffron Shellfish Stock

Executive Chef/Owner Marco Carrozza
Marco's Restaurant, Philadelphia, PA

1 pound shrimp shells
1 pound mussels, washed and debearded
1 tablespoon olive oil
1 small onion, cut into large pieces
12 ounces white wine
1 quart clam juice
2 bay leaves
5 parsley stems, no leaves
Large pinch of saffron

Place shrimp shells, mussels, oil, and onion in a small stockpot. Cook over high heat until mussels open. Add wine, clam juice, bay leaves, and parsley stems. Cover with cold water and bring to a boil. Lower heat and simmer for 5 minutes. Strain. Add saffron and steep for 5 minutes. Use in soups or sauces.

Marco's Restaurant

Known for:
eclectic tapas-style
international menu

Years in business:
30+

Menu:
It's all about the food!

Chef: Marco Carrozza

Chef's training:
former executive chef at
the original Café Nola
plus 30 years on-the-job
training

participating restaurants

333 Belrose
A Little Cafe
An American Kitchen
Arroyo Grille
Azafran
Blue Moon
Braddock's Tavern
Brasserie Perrier
Buckley's Tavern
Café Nola
Caffé Aldo Lamberti
Cater 2U
Chadds Ford Inn
Charlotte-Ann Albertson's School
Chez Amis Catering
Chin Chin
Church Street Bistro
Ciboulette
CinCin
circa
City Grill
City Tavern
Cock 'n Bull
Corned Beef Academy
Cresheim Cottage Cafe
Daggett's Catering
David's Yellow Brick Toad
Davio's
Deux Cheminées
Diane's La Patisserie Française

DiPalma Ristorante & Bar
Dobbins Randolph AVTS
Dock Street Brasserie
Down Home Diner
East of Amara
Euro Cafe
Fishmarket
Food for Thought
Fork
Fourchette 110
Four Seasons Hotel
Friday Saturday Sunday
G.G.'s Restaurant
Gilda's Biscotti
Harry's Savoy Grill
Homemade Goodies by Roz
Hotel Dupont
Incredible Edibles
Inn at Twin Linden
Iron Hill Brewery and Restaurant
Jack Kramer's Catering
Jack's Firehouse
Jamaican Jerk Hut
JeanneNatalia Bistro
Jenny's Bistro
Joe's Peking Duck House
Joseph Poon Asian Restaurant
Kansas City Prime
Kristopher's
La Campagne

participating restaurants

La Famiglia
La Terrasse
Le Bec-Fin
Le Colonial
London Grill
L'Osteria Cucina Italiana
Ludwig's Garten
Marco's Restaurant
Marrakesh
Melange Café
Metropolitian Bakery
MixMaster Café
Monk's Café
MontSerrat
Moshulu
Museum Catering Company
Nodding Head Brewery
Opus 251
Parties in the Kitchen
¡Pasión!
Peddler's Village
Philippe on Locust
Philippe's Bistro
Pirates Inn
Pompeii
Ram's Head Inn
Rembrandt's
Ristorante Panorama
Rococo
Rouge

Sansom Street Oyster House
Savona
Severino's
Solaris Grille
Sotto
Spring Mill Café
Sud Fine Pastry
The Art Institute of Philadelpha
The Black Walnut
The Garden
The Ivy Grille/The Inn at Penn
The Latest Dish
The Oak Grill at the Marshalton Inn
The Pink Rose Pastry Shop
The Red Hen Café
The Restaurant School
The Terrace at Greenhill
Thommy G's
Toto
Treetops/Rittenhouse Hotel
Tuscan Twenty
Twelve Caesars Radisson Hotel
Upstares at Varalli
Van M's Music Bar and Grille
Vega Grill
Viana's Italian Cuisine
Warsaw Cafe
White Rose Café
Yangming

wine people

Much thanks to the wine gurus who expertly matched our recipes with the perfect vintages.

Moore Brothers

7200 N. Park Drive · Pennsauken, NJ 08109 · 856-317-1177 · www.moorebros.com
1416 N. Dupont Street · Wilmington, DE 19806 · 302-498-0360 · www.moorebrosde.com

Greg Moore, owner, was the sommelier and general manager of Philadelphia's Le Bec-Fin for nearly twenty years. In 1996 he founded Moore Brothers Wine Company, a retail wine distribution company with stores specializing in small-production fine wines, which have been shipped and stored in the perfect conditions of temperature control. Greg regularly teaches wine classes at the College of General Studies at the University of Pennsylvania.

Frank Splan, general manager, has apprenticed as a winemaker in Fronton in Southwest France, and made wine in Vouvray, but his specialty is the wines of Italy, where he travels twice a year.

Luca Mazzotti, manager, grew up in Lombardia with his father, a novelist and wine lover, who frequently took him as a child to visit many of the best small producers in both Italy and France. In addition to his work with Frank Splan, Luca teaches Italian at the University of Pennsylvania.

Megan Shawver, sommelier and Moore Brothers "sister" by adoption, has a restaurant background.

Jonathan Read, sommelier, lived in Japan, is fluent in the Japanese language, and was the manager of a Philadelphia Japanese restaurant before joining Moore Brothers. He is a sake specialist.

Christian Lane, sommelier, is a Culinary Institute of American alumnus and a chef.

Dale Belville, sommelier, is a former teaching golf professional and an accomplished amateur chef.

Kevin McCann, sommelier, has a background in restaurants. He finds the time to travel in France and has worked with a producer in California during the "crush."

Chris Kurlakovsky, part-time sommelier, is a regional vice president of United Parcel Service. He considers it an "honor" to work at Moore Brothers on the weekends.

Triangle Liquors

1200 Broadway · Camden, NJ 08104 · 856-365-1800 · www.eatwelldrinkbetter.com

John McNulty is the wine consultant for Triangle Liquors, which publishes *Corkscrewed*, the area's most widely circulated wine publication. A popular wine educator, John also hosts "On the Town with John McNulty," a two hour radio program about wine, food, dining, and travel which is heard every Saturday on 96.5 FM WWDB in Philadelphia. A contributor to national publications, such as *The Wine News* and *The Wine Spectator*, John currently has a wine and food-related television program in development.

Index

books by small potatoes press

Please send the following:

_____ copies of **Philadelphia Flavor: Restaurant Recipes from the City and Suburbs** - $15.95

_____ copies of **Coastal Cuisine: Seaside Recipes from Maine to Maryland** - $11.95

_____ copies of **Local Flavor: Favorite Recipes of Philadelphia Area Chefs** - $15.95

_____ copies of **PB&J USA: Recipes for Kids and Adults by Kids and Adults** - $10.95

Sales Tax: **Philadelphia Flavor:** NJ addresses please add $.96 (6%)
Coastal Cuisine: NJ addresses please add $.71 (6%)
Local Flavor: NJ addresses please add $.96 (6%)
PB&J USA: NJ addresses please add $.65 (6%)

Shipping: $3.00 for the first book; $1.00 for each additional book

Payment: Please make your check or money order payable to:

Small Potatoes Press
1106 Stokes Avenue, Collingswood, NJ 08108

Questions?   Call us at 856-869-5207 or e-mail us at info@smallpotatoespress

Ship to:

Name _____

Address _____

City/State/Zip _____

Is this a gift?   If so, please include YOUR name, address, and phone number.

Name _____

Address _____

City/State/Zip _____

Phone number _____

Thank you!

about the authors

Connie Correia Fisher is the owner of Small Potatoes Press which provides publishing and public relations support for restaurants and food-related businesses. She is the founding publisher/editor of *Cuizine* magazine and the author of *PB&J USA*, America's only peanut butter and jelly cookbook.

Joanne Correia is Connie's mom and the former executive editor of *Cuizine*. She and Connie are the authors of *Local Flavor* and *Coastal Cuisine*.